OCT 1 7 1996

# How Do I Look?

# HOW DO I LOOK?

THE COMPLETE GUIDE
TO INNER AND OUTER BEAUTY:
FROM COSMETICS TO CONFIDENCE

## GALE HAYMAN

RANDOM HOUSE NEW YORK

*To all the women who have helped me understand*
*that the essence of beauty and style is grace*

ILLUSTRATIONS BY DURELL GODFREY

DESIGN BY JOEL AVIROM AND JASON SNYDER

Library of Congress Cataloging-in-Publication Data
Hayman, Gale.
How do I look?: The complete guide to inner and outer beauty:
from confidence to cosmetics/Gale Hayman.
p.   cm.
ISBN 0-679-44569-2
1. Beauty, Personal.   2. Self-esteem in women.
I. Title.
RA778.H39   1997
646.7'042—dc20      95-46181

Random House website address: http://www.randomhouse.com/
Printed in the United States of America on acid-free paper
98765432
First Edition

This book is for women of all ages, types, lifestyles. After years of working in the beauty business—in fashion, fragrance, skin care and makeup—I've learned that all women are basically the same. We all share the same desires to look our best, feel our best, achieve our best. We all want to be beautiful. I know this because I've worked with thousands of women for more than twenty years, seventeen of them in my own retail store, Giorgio Beverly Hills.

For all the beauty hype, information and misinformation out there, beauty remains, for too many women, an elusive goal. Not anymore. Because what I've learned from *inside* the beauty business is that we all *can* be beautiful. Beauty isn't something you're born with. It's something you *learn,* a skill you acquire, like learning how to play tennis. The lessons are all here, in this book. Take a look in the mirror, read and apply my beauty lessons, then take another look. This book will teach you to look in the mirror and like what you see.

*Learn* beauty. *Live* beauty. Enjoy being beautiful.

# ACKNOWLEDGMENTS

would like to thank all the many thousands of women who taught me what I know during my years at Giorgio. By observing, by listening and by helping them answer their questions "How do I look?" I came to understand the answers that I share with you.

Thank you, Allen Questrom, chairman of Federated Stores. Thank you, Marvin Traub and Robin Burns; Michael Gould and Jane Scott at Bloomingdale's, the store that launched Giorgio perfume and Gale Hayman Beverly Hills Cosmetics. Thank you, Doug Briggs, Darlene Daggett, Morgan Hare, Carollynn Chisena, and Jeanine Gendrachi at QVC television home shopping, who have become an important part of my growth and expansion.

I would like to thank my colleagues at Givaudan-Roure, Jean Amic and Geoffrey Webster, the philosopher and choreographer of fragrance for a truly "Delicious" perfume. And additional thanks to Barry Young and Beatrice Moser at Firmenich for their outstanding work on "Delicious Feelings."

Francesco Borghese, my new partner at La Parfumerie, who is a dream to work with plus Skip Borghese, Stephen Frieder and the entire staff.

Thank you, Walter Weintz at Random House and the wonderful bright energetic team, some of whom include: Joy de Menil, Miranda Brooks, Deborah Aiges, Amy Zenn, Bridget Marmion, Carol Schneider and Pam Cannon. Thank you, Bernie Klein, for expertly dealing with my color charts. Joel Avirom, thank you for your aesthetic guidance, Durell Godfrey for creative illustrations.

A big thank you to my assistant Jill Firestone and my publicists Sandi Mendelson and Barbara Kling. Thank you, Drs. Dan Baker, Robert Dewhirst, Frank Kamer, Harold McQuinn, Norman Orentreich, Maria Sauzier, and Dr. Stuart Orsher. Thank you, Kelly Lange, Russel Grandis, Yves Durif, Chris Hahan and Mike Abrams for enlightening me in your areas of specific expertise. Thank you, Ed Victor, my "Superman" agent. Susan Di Sesa, my extremely thoughtful and dedicated editor. To Cheryl Mercer, my collaborator, who melded and molded my words into shape, a thank you bigger than words can express. My good friend, Judy Miller, who "got it" first. A special thanks to Jason Epstein who provided original inspiration, believed in me and was always there with the right comment and perspective. He really made it happen. And finally to my husband, Bill, my partner in life, for his support.

# CONTENTS

## PART 1: HOW DO I LOOK?

## PART 2: HOW DO I DRESS?

## PART 3: HOW DO I LIVE?

## PART 4: HOW DO I FEEL?

# INTRODUCTION

I learned my first lessons about beauty as a dancer, and while I gave up ballet years ago, I've been studying—and teaching—beauty ever since. I began by studying retailing and fashion, and eventually became style consultant to many Hollywood stars. Then I studied fragrance, skin care and makeup. Today I have my own fragrance, called "Delicious," and my own makeup and skin-care lines.

I've spent my entire career behind the scenes—experimenting; trying every label, ingredient and product; subjecting myself to the oddest beauty rituals you can imagine. I learned everything. This book came about when I *unlearned* enough to know that I finally had it right—when I stopped learning beauty, and began *living* it.

When I first started out with the American School of Ballet, our lessons in how a dancer presents herself were just as rigorous as the practice sessions: We learned makeup application, how to carry ourselves in Karinska's beautiful costumes, how to eat to stay slim and fit and how to build up the physical stamina and forces of concentration that dancing requires.

Behind the scenes, however, on a tight student's budget, my life wasn't quite so glamorous. My offstage costumes were often thrift-shop finds, redraped here, retucked there, and accessorized with other thrift-shop finds; I can still scan a thrift shop better than anyone else I know. When it was time to take off the makeup, I used Crisco, and

Vaseline was my eye and lip cream. Awful as that may sound, they worked fine (certainly a thousand times better than most soaps and water).

After I left the ballet, I took the lessons I'd learned and applied them to fashion when my then-husband and I turned a tiny fashion boutique, which grew into Giorgio Beverly Hills, the fashion emporium at the intersection of Dayton Way and Rodeo Drive.

We furnished Giorgio like a club, with comfortable gold velvet couches and chairs (all reproductions, of course), a Marie-Thérèse crystal chandelier, a large pool table, magazine racks, a big copper espresso machine and a full-service bar. Customers would come in the first time because it was inviting, cozy and elegant—very European. They returned because the clothes were original in style, high fashion and flattering, made of quality fabrics and chosen with a point of view: *my* point of view.

Giorgio grew fast, but I had to grow even faster. Coming from the world of dance, I now had to learn everything there was to know about the business of fashion. At first, I spent mornings before we opened sweeping the sidewalk and cleaning the showcase windows. All day long I selected, shipped, received—and sold—our merchandise. At night, I stayed up late with every book on fashion and design I could borrow from the library, and pored over and clipped pictures from all the American and European fashion magazines. There wasn't even time to be intimidated; we had to pay the rent! My husband and I worked hard, six days a week; we were a great team. (Although I wasn't too happy when my feet grew a size and a half from being on them so much!)

Most of all, I listened. Our clientele eventually included some of the most glamorous women in the world—Barbra Streisand, Betsy Bloomingdale, Elizabeth Taylor, Princess Grace, Nancy Reagan, Jacqueline Bisset, Angie Dickinson—women who knew a lot, had styles of their own, traveled and were themselves experts in makeup, skin care and *living*. They taught me so well that soon *I* was giving the lessons, not only about clothes but also about skin care, cosmetics and creating a lifestyle (whatever the budget) that wraps a person up in elegance the way my store did.

I remember one time, for example, when Denise Hale, Liza Minnelli's stepmother, came in to try on clothes, and decided on a two-hundred-dollar dress, which looked lovely on her as it was, I thought. But no. Denise removed the belt, and asked us to slim down the sides two inches and take off the mandarin collar. When she was finished, that two-hundred-dollar dress looked like a ten-thousand-dollar Givenchy couture. The lesson for *me* was to look at every article of clothing not as a piece of finished goods but as a starting point.

I learned, too, that my most fashion-savvy clients never squeezed themselves into clothes, but always bought them one size bigger to make them look slimmer. Fashions may change, but the principle doesn't: If the size 8 fits like a glove, take the 10.

In time, I was discovering young, unheard-of designers such as Halston and Zandra Rhodes and giving them their first displays. I was also a stylist to various stars, including Barbara Walters, Joan Rivers and a young newcomer Merv Griffin once sent over: Vanna White. For a time, I styled the entire cast of *The Young and the Restless*. In the meantime, Giorgio became a one-stop shopping spot for everything fashionable—clothes for men and women, accessories, shoes, stockings, hats, gloves—all under one roof. Our prices ranged from $7.50 to $30,000, with something for every budget. We tried to make all our customers feel like royalty, whether they came in wearing diamonds or shorts and sandals. (Some of our biggest customers wore the sandals, as it turned out, and many of our bounced checks were from the ones in diamonds!)

We never sold makeup or skin care at Giorgio, but we were the first retail store to come out with our own fragrance—Giorgio Beverly Hills, which we launched in the early eighties. I wanted a fragrance that matched the sensibility of the times and the store—lavish, both—and I worked with the perfumers for more than two years just to get it right. It *was* right. We sold it to Avon in 1987, for the highest amount ever paid to a family-owned fragrance company. Sadly, my marriage was over by this time, but my career was entering a new phase. I enjoyed working with the perfumers and learning all the ways to use fragrance, and I was determined not only to launch another fragrance one day but also to convey what I'd learned to the world of cosmetics.

I started to spend more time in New York during this transition period, in which I also discovered that many of life's lessons—surviving a divorce, building a new life, imparting an "up" attitude (even when you don't feel it), controlling stress—are actually beauty lessons, too. Beauty works inside out as much as it does outside in, and how you feel will tell you a lot up front about how you look.

Thankful for my work, I started Gale Hayman Beverly Hills, Inc., back-to-back with the sale of Giorgio. I began at home, in my living room in Los Angeles, testing colors on women and developing my eye and skin-tone color palettes. I worked for two years with a French dermatologist on my skin-care line. I also worked personally with chemists to develop a separate formula for each makeup color (they thought I was crazy, since this is generally considered too expensive to do). I learned, from working with the chemists, what other companies—at least those that put more into packaging and advertising than they do into product development—aren't willing to do. For their part, the chemists learned what I *was* willing to do.

It took me a full two years to launch my "Youth-Lift" skin-care line, another two for my Treatment makeup line and another two for "Delicious," a more restrained scent than Giorgio (in keeping with our more restrained times), which is the fastest-growing new fragrance and is now sold in eighty countries. If you haven't seen them, my cosmetics—sold in Cosmetics Plus in New York City, Sears, Robinson's-May and elsewhere around the country, including on QVC television shopping and by calling 1-800-FOR-GALE—come in leopard packaging, a classic pattern that everyone loves. It's not a gimmick, though. I'm a woman who makes products for other women, and, with my name on them, my products have to *work*.

This book, however, is not a sales pitch for my cosmetics, and often you'll find the products you need to be beautiful and live beautifully as easily at your supermarket or corner drugstore as you will at the fancy makeup counters in department stores. For example, you can use Crisco in a pinch, although there are certainly more pleasant ways to remove makeup, such as by using Albolene cream, sold at drugstores in huge tubs for well under ten dollars. For another example, Lipton tea bags are still the best treatment there is (and I know, because I drove the chemists crazy trying to find a better one) for puffy eyes.

In developing my cosmetics, I learned more about ingredients than you can imagine, and sometimes all you need to know about a product is whether it has the key ingredients. Take sunblocks, for instance, the array of which used to be thoroughly confusing to me, particularly when I was living in Los Angeles, where the sun blazes all year long. My chemists taught me the simple truth about sunblocks and sunscreens: Forget about sunscreens, they said—they simply don't work; and sunblocks won't work either, unless they contain zinc oxide or titanium dioxide—that's all you have to remember, and that's all you have to look for.

No woman wants her beauty regimen to rule her life, and never has that been truer for me than it is today. I'm married now to a molecular biologist with a degree in chemistry (I focus on external beauty, he on the internal genetic makeup of the human being—quite a dynamic!) whose offices are outside Washington, D.C., while mine are not far from Cosmetics Plus in New York. It's an extremely interesting life, but it's also complicated. I shuttle between D.C. and New York every single week, in addition to a fair amount of traveling for my work, and thus have had to learn everything there is to know about traveling efficiently so that it won't wreak havoc on how I look and feel. I run two homes and have three offices, one in each home and the main office in New York. I just merged my company with La Parfumerie, founded by Francesco Borghese. We often travel on weekends to visit friends, and we entertain a lot in both cities. Health, family and beauty are my priorities and, by necessity, I keep my beauty regimen simple, as routine as brushing my teeth. I probably spend less time than most women do on beauty, but it's my business. I know what to do. I also know what *not* to do.

Throughout my career, I've been advising women on how to look and live their best. Today, along with creating and marketing my cosmetics, I also operate a mail-order phone service, 1-800-FOR-GALE, where women call to order our products and ask advice about *everything*. One twenty-five-year-old called the other day in a panic about the lines she's already noticing around her eyes. Lots of questions come in these days about hydroxy acids, the beauty "miracle" of the moment: Is there anything to them? I get calls about fashion, style, hair and skin care. One woman I met not long ago at a party called the next day, almost embarrassed, and asked how I managed to look so rested. Another woman once called in tears, believing that her husband was having an affair and wondering what to do and whether to confront him.

*All* these questions are beauty questions, because they all affect how we look and feel about ourselves.

And all these questions have answers.

"How do I look?" is so much more important a question than it seems on the surface. When we ask it, and we all do, we're asking for total affirmation of our very selves, inside and out—flaws, virtues, the clothes that "package" us for the world, the hair we've styled so carefully, the glow of our skin, the personal style that defines every aspect of our lives. And the answer we want to hear, of course, is, "You look beautiful."

Beauty is a subject that can be studied, learned and practiced like any other discipline. I know, because I've studied, learned and practiced it myself, and have built two successful businesses from my own vision of beauty, which is classic, ageless, timeless. When you have a sensible, thought-out regimen you follow every day, you become beautiful, flaws and all. You become yourself—your best self. When you learn quick-fix tricks for bad hair, beauty and fat days, it helps you get on with the day and off yourself. When you feel beautiful, it shows. And it matters, to how you're perceived by the world and, mostly, to how you perceive yourself.

How do *I* look? I look my best, and it's taken me my entire career to learn how. I hope the results of my study will help you look—and feel—your best, too.

I can't wait for you to get started, and *please, please* write me at P.O. Box 885, New York, N.Y. 10150, or call me at 1-800-FOR-GALE or fax me at 1-212-752-2541 with your questions and comments, because my next book is going to answer questions from *you*.

Have fun.

*Gale*

# PART 1

# HOW DO I LOOK?

**S**ome women collect jewelry. I've always collected makeup and skin creams. I've used placenta creams, caviar, seaweed, moldy French creams (the French don't use preservatives), estrogen creams (outlawed in America by the FDA), products from Japan and India and ones I bought after seeing promising ads in magazines. You name it, I've tried it. When you've tested as much as I have, you can tell right away what works and what doesn't. The ingredients I liked found their way onto my skin and, eventually, into my own line of products, but most of my experiments ended up moisturizing my hands and feet so that the money wouldn't be wasted. I do have good skin, but not from bouncing around from product to product, program to program. I have good skin because I always went back to my simple, sensible skin-care regimen that works, and because I've always followed my mother's advice to stay out of the sun.

Skin is the first place to show signs of age (hands, neck, face—there's nothing worse than a young face and old hands), and the first to show signs of neglect or abuse. It's also the first place to show signs of improvement and renewal the very first day you begin to take care of it. Skin care doesn't have to be expensive, time-consuming or complicated. What it has to be is *consistent*.

There is plenty of good news in the skin-care world today. Hype aside, good products actually *are* more advanced than they used to be because reputable manufacturers are taking a pharmaceutical approach to developing their products. Preventing damage and healing it are the standards—*protecting* the skin, not just covering it up cosmetically. How soon should consumers expect results from

# SKIN CARE

# READING SKIN-CARE LABELS

—

When I read a label, I first look to see if the product contains fragrance, alcohol or witch hazel, all of which are drying ingredients. If it does, I pass. In scented bath gels, for example, check to make sure there are conditioning ingredients to counteract the drying properties of fragrance. If you see one or more of the ingredients that follow, you're probably onto a good thing. These are among the ingredients you *want* to find in skin-care products, and it's a good idea to remember them like catchphrases somewhere in the back of your mind when you're shopping for such products:

VITAMIN B—protects against harsh environmental conditions

VITAMIN E—for skin, the healing vitamin

SQUALENE—extracted from avocados or shark oil. It's an oily substance that's very similar to natural skin sebum. It smooths.

COLLAGEN—protein in the connective tissue, one of the elements in our skin. Its use in products is to repair natural collagen. (A purer form is used in collagen injections.)

SHEA BUTTER—used for healing

skin-care products? Right away. Don't fall for products that have a six-month waiting period for results. Products that work, in every price range, start to work *immediately*.

It's also sinking in, finally, that sun damage, apart from being a direct cause of skin cancer, is absolutely the number-one cause of wrinkles, unnecessary aging and dry, leathery-looking skin. (For more information, write or call the Skin Cancer Foundation, Suite 2402, 245 Fifth Avenue, New York, N.Y., 10016, 1-212-725-5176.) Lifelong sun exposure first shows up as sun *damage* in one's mid- to late thirties. If you see a woman over forty with skin that's deeply bronzed, beautiful *and* unlined, you can be sure she's wearing a bronzer. (In response to demand, bronzing makeup is getting better—less orange—all the time. We sell a ton of it. See the Makeup chapter for how to use it.)

Sun protection is the most important beauty lesson you can teach your daughters. From day one, use sunblock, baby cream or lotion and baby soap on

CARBONER 934—a good stabilizing agent and thickener. It has a soothing consistency and leaves a protective film.

ELASTIN—protein in the connective tissue, another of the elements in our own skin. This one helps to firm and restore elasticity.

HYALURONIC ACID—a good firming agent

PLACENTA (available only in Europe)—repairs the skin

ESTROGEN (available only in Europe)—also repairs the skin

UREA—a water binder and emulsifier, which makes moisturizer adhere to the skin

GLYCERINE—a humectant. This absorbs and binds water, and also has conditioning properties. It makes the formula long-lasting, too.

LANOLIN—a by-product of sheep's wool, used for years because it's good. It's rich in emollients, and helps bind moisture to the skin.

MINERAL OIL—a synthetic blend. It also helps bind moisture, by forming an exclusive film.

LECITHIN—comes from plants or animals. It is a natural source of emulsifier and conditioner.

CHOLESTEROL—moisturizes and smooths the skin

ALMOND OIL—also moisturizes and smooths

LIPOSOMES—a breakthrough "delivery" system that encapsulates other ingredients and brings them more effectively into the skin

infants and young children, the way the French do. From age ten or at the onset of puberty, when hormones change, a toner, a light moisturizer, such as Pond's or Oil of Olay, for the young girl's face, body lotion after bathing or being on the beach and sunblock every time she goes out into the sun.

These essential moisturizing and protecting principles don't change as we age, but the *intensity* does. Baby lotion isn't protective or rich enough for drier skin that's been exposed to wear and tear from the elements twenty-four hours a day for years, for makeup application and removal or for hormones that change with each passing decade. That is why we must switch to a women's skin-care regimen upon reaching full womanhood.

What makes a skin-care product work is not always a "new" or "improved" ingredient. Some of the tried, true—and cheapest—ingredients are still the best. What does make the difference are the *quality* and *quantity* of the ingredients. Quantity is easy to figure out; the first ingredient listed is what the product contains the most of, and so on down the line. Quality is a little trickier. Collagen and elastin, for example, are sold by grade for different prices, like cars and shoes; the better the grade, the better the results, but you can't always tell the grade by the label. These ingredients are *expensive,* which is why products that list them prominently on the labels will cost a lot. If you buy a product with a good amount of either ingredient, you can expect look-good, feel-good results within a day. If not, return it.

With all the products (and too-good-to-believe promises!) out there, where do you start? By learning to read labels, so that you can read between the hype to choose the skin-care products that are right for you.

## SKIN CARE: START NOW TO REVERSE THE DAMAGE

I worry about Daryl Hannah every time I see her picture; the exposure she's had to the sun may show up in just a few years. Jodie Foster's skin will be fine. Melanie Griffith should be careful. Chris Evert should have been protecting her skin all along. Diana Ross, Raquel Welch, Barbra Streisand, Diane Sawyer, Kim Basinger, Connie Chung, Annette Bening, Demi Moore: They all protect themselves in the sun and practice great skin care—and it *shows.* Joan Collins, in her sixties, has fabulous skin, as do Angie Dickinson and Angela Lansbury. Despite her great body, Jane Fonda can't hide the sun damage. It's too soon to tell about Julia Roberts.

There are three causes of wrinkles: The first is sun damage, the big one; the second is abuse and neglect, which are strong seconds; and the third is biological aging, the least of our problems here. Good skin care addresses all three.

### SUN DAMAGE

Look around the beach the next time you go, and you'll begin to see a new look: Fewer oil-slicked, bikini-clad bodies stretched out in the blazing hot sun, more umbrellas, wide-brimmed hats, crisp shirts—à la Katharine Hepburn—with long sleeves, wide sunglasses. There's more on this in the Fashion chapters, but the way to reverse sun damage (you can't repair it entirely) is to protect yourself in the sun, beginning now.

Forget the SPF number on the sunscreen; you need a sunblock with either titanium dioxide or zinc oxide in it for real coverage. These ingredients act as a *barrier* between you and the sun. Either of these ingredients will provide the same protection as sitting in cool shade. A-FIL cream total block, a great product found at drugstores, provides very strong protection for the face and the backs of your hands, is tinted and not entirely natural looking, but it works (not for city use, but for boating, waterskiing, swimming, sitting on the beach: where it matters most, in other words). Reapply it at least every two hours and after swimming. Blend it in with a sponge. In addition to A-FIL sunblock, Clinique's Continuous Coverage and Physicians Formula Le Velvet Film makeup (available for about seven dollars at *the* Beverly Hills drugstore, Mickey Fine Pharmacy, 1-310-271-6123) are great sunscreening makeup products if you live in a sunny, hot climate.

The same sunblock will protect other exposed parts of your body at the beach as well, and is also good for stretches in the sun when you're out walking, gardening, skiing, whatever. I empty out little plastic bottles (the kind hotels leave for you in the bathroom) to decant any of the sunblocks listed below; when I'm outside—summer and winter—they're always handy.

Bain de Soleil's All Day waterproof sunblock

Hawaiian Tropic's SPF 45 plus

---

## SUNLESS TANNING

Still missing the *look* of a tan? A bronzer is my favorite way to give myself a glow, but many women also like the self-tanners now widely available. The number-one self-tanning products in Beverly Hills are Physicians Formula Sun Shield (sunless tanning cream for the face) and Neutrogena Glow sunless tanning spray for the body. These products cause you to look tan without the sun when the chemical dihydroxyacetone (DHA) reacts with the natural protein in your skin. Possible side effects with repeated use may include splotchiness (because of oil and instability in your skin), a tendency to yellow, or a slight odor.

Johnson & Johnson's Sundown

Ti Screen's SPF 16

"Block Out" Moisturizing Sun Block 40+ by Vaseline Intensive Care

Banana Boat's maximum sunblock

## ABUSE AND NEGLECT

The causes of abuse and neglect of the skin probably won't come as much of a surprise. Smoking abuses the skin, making it muddy and gray and causing wrinkles around the mouth. Excessive alcohol causes broken capillaries on the face and puffiness. Abusing drugs is the worst insult. It will cause you to age faster—to look both drawn and haggard. Squeezing pimples is obviously not in the same health-threat category, but it abuses the skin and can leave scars. So does treating facial skin roughly—pulling at it, removing makeup with a vengeance, using harsh eye pencils that you can actually see tugging at the skin. (Eye-shadow powders are the solution.) Using facial tissues on your skin in any way is abusive—they are made of wood pulp, which is very abrasive to the skin; that's why you get a chafed, red nose when you have a cold. Instead, buy a stack of inexpensive washcloths to remove makeup: *Used dry, washcloths provide exactly the right exfoliation to treat facial skin day after day.* Just throw them in the washing machine afterward and reuse.

Neglect means what you fail to do to your skin. If you neglect a moisturizer summer and winter, your skin will dry out—dehydrate—and wrinkle prematurely. Neglecting to use a sunblock will make your face look like a catcher's mitt. Neglecting to remove your makeup at night will cause clogged pores, skin eruptions, unhealthy-looking skin, loss of eyelashes and damage to the skin around the eyes.

The only way to reverse the damage from abuse and neglect completely is to change the habits that caused it in the first place. All the pallor disappears from a woman's face within a few days after she stops smoking, for example; I've seen it happen. Daily moisturizing, if you haven't been, will make you look (and feel) better at once. Keep reading for *positive* skin-care habits to begin to turn the damage around. Your magnifying mirror will be your encouragement.

## BIOLOGICAL AGING

Taking good care of your skin will minimize and *prevent* the inevitable effects of age, such as biological wrinkling, discoloration, age spots and the rest of it. With age, the skin loses some of its elasticity—its ability to "bounce back" into perfect form—and you may have to train yourself to keep it in perfect form in the first place.

Sleeping on your face definitely causes wrinkles, for instance. (I know: I used to sleep on my right eye, and you could tell by looking at it!) Use a soft pillow tucked under your ear to anchor your neck and prevent your face from grinding into the bedclothes. Oversized pillowcases will themselves wrinkle, and pass *their* wrinkles along to you. Hard, unmoldable spongy pillows—the kind many hotels provide—are the worst. If confronted with one, just use one end of it under your ear. (It takes only a week to adjust your sleeping habits.)

Habitual frowning and squinting also cause lines to set. Sooner or later we're all going to have lines; we might as well make them laugh lines. A conscious effort will help you to stop frowning and squinting; keep your expression relaxed deliberately. *Sunglasses in bright sun are a necessity.*

For a while, magazines were telling us that we could keep our faces younger-looking with facial exercises. Forget it. Unless you can continue every day for the rest of your life (I know *I* can't), the muscles will stretch and then drop. Deliberately keeping your face relaxed with a tranquil expression helps much more.

When it comes time to buy skin-care products, don't be sold an entire regime. Try one product, and if you see results, add products one at a time. With better cosmetic lines, ask for samples, definitely try the testers, even bring your own little empty bottles to take home a day's worth of samples. With drugstore brands, the price difference won't accommodate sampling. Read the

# DAILY FACIAL CARE

Facial skin should be treated like a cashmere sweater—protected, groomed and never stretched or abused; treated well, both will last a lifetime.

Most women have bathrooms full of skin-care creams; use the rejects to moisturize your hands, feet and elbows, and pare down to the skin-care essentials. These are:

**MAGNIFYING MIRROR** And the honesty to face it. This mirror will become your friend, and will tell you when products are working and when they're not. Looking at it daily will help you monitor the condition of your skin.

**MAKEUP REMOVAL** Never use soap on your face. To remove makeup, use Pond's cold cream, Albolene, baby oil or Crisco, all of which will remove both makeup and mascara, then wipe gently with a dry face cloth. I make a cleanser that removes mascara and every trace of makeup and rinses off. Liquid facial-formula Neutrogena and Johnson's Clean & Clear are excellent and inexpensive, but they don't do a good job of removing mascara. For that, first use Andrea eye-makeup remover pads, from any drugstore; they're terrific.

**TONER** Makeup removers such as Pond's, Albolene, baby oil and Crisco leave a greasy residue; even if you don't like the oily feel, you'll like the way your skin looks the next day. Gently wipe away the

label, take a chance, and if the product doesn't feel nourishing on your face, it will on your hands, feet or elbows. Or experiment with friends. If you don't like a product, they may. If they have products they like, scrape a little sample with a knife and try them yourself.

Using just these essential skin-care products, everyday skin care takes five to seven minutes.

### EVERY MORNING

There's no need to cleanse your face upon awakening; you did nothing to dirty it while sleeping. Stimulate circulation when you wake up by placing over your face a washcloth soaked with cold water from the tap. Pat dry with a towel, apply daytime moisturizer and that's it—on to makeup, if you're wearing it. If your skin is very oily—adolescents especially—you might want to use a cotton residue with a toner and cotton pads. Even with the cleansers that aren't greasy, you still need the toning step. If you're not wearing makeup, a toner will be enough to clean your face. Toners are not unlike astringents, but they're not as harsh, so they're less drying to the skin. They also close pores, stimulate circulation and firm the skin. There are many on the market; try any you like—Lancôme makes a good one, for example—but avoid those with fragrance, witch hazel or alcohol. How to tell if it's working? The right toner will make your skin feel good—clean, tingly, refreshed, but *never* dry. It will also make it look good: shiny and vibrant.

DAY MOISTURIZER/NIGHT CREAM This is one of the questions women ask me most: Yes, you need both. Day creams are light, protective, hydrating. If you're wearing makeup, they're the base for it. If not, they're a layer of protection against the elements. More concentrated night creams are treatments necessary to replace the nourishment we need, which is lost during the day. Good ones can be a little bit greasy (not too greasy), the trade-off for beautiful skin. (You don't need a special eye cream, by the way. A good night cream patted under the eye will do the trick, with occasional special attention to lines and wrinkles—see page 12.) How to tell if it's working? The right moisturizer will leave your face feeling moist *all day,* until makeup is removed. The right night cream still *feels moist in the morning;* you awake looking improved. You can test a moisturizer in a day, and a night cream in a night, by checking the mirror. They're like shoes: If they're not comfortable the first time out, they'll never be.

ball to apply toner to the T-zone *only* (forehead, nose, chin): That's where the oil glands are. For pimples, apply Maximum-Strength Clearasil with a Q-Tip onto the eruption. (Salicylic acid is the ingredient that fights acne best.)

## DURING THE DAY

No special care, except sunblock, if you're spending the day outdoors, or touch-ups, if you're wearing makeup.

Skin-care products to keep in the office include a moisturizer and Q-Tips (to clean up makeup smudges), hand cream and a lip balm. Keep a toner in the office, too, if your skin is oily; you might want to do a T-zone application during the day. Also, office telephones get dirty—makeup, oils from hair and hands; a little toner on a cotton ball rubbed over the receiver is the best way I know to clean them.

Cleansing, toning and nourishing are the three steps:

**To CLEANSE** If you aren't wearing makeup, skip this step and go on to toning. If you are, remove mascara and eye makeup first with eye-makeup remover pads. Then gently massage in your face-makeup remover. Just as gently, *wipe face clean with a dry terry washcloth*—under eyes, in crevices, over eyelids, in upward motions over the neck: The gentle washcloth massage is terrific for your skin and acts as a daily exfoliator.

**To TONE** Apply toner with cotton pads, wiping gently over face and under eyes. Wipe *upward* on the neck—always wipe *against* gravity—with the cotton pads until you feel clean. (You *are* clean: Don't use soap or water.) Don't worry about toning even if your skin is very dry; a good toner (no alcohol, witch hazel or fragrance, remember) acts as a finishing rinse, skin firmer and pore closer. Good toners aren't drying.

**To NOURISH** Pat on your night cream with your fingers, gently under the eyes, a dab on the eyelids, upward strokes of it on the neck (massaging upward helps circulation and keeps neck firmer—necks, like hands, show age *early* if not tended to), and down to the cleavage, which also gets dry and wrinkled. Extra night cream goes onto the backs of hands. I also recommend a dab of Vaseline on the lips for sleeping: It lubricates beautifully.

Spending a lot of money on skin care is not necessary. I'm opposed to facials,

for example. They often do more harm than good by overmanipulating and tugging at your skin, which enlarges your pores and, believe it or not, can create lines and scars. Pore-cleansing and exfoliating masks, on the other hand, are great; use once a week, if you have time. Many of the more expensive ones (Janet Sartin, Georgette Klinger, Aida Thibiant in Beverly Hills) are very good (and certainly cheaper than a facial); St. Ives Swiss Formula Apricot Scrub with elderflower is an inexpensive one—not as good but okay.

If you have deeply clogged pores, little bumps or spots, go to a dermatologist—much better than a facial, even for facial cleansings. Call the American Board of Dermatologists, at 1-313-874-1088, for referrals in your area, but don't accept their referrals at face value. Some dermatologists deal primarily with serious skin diseases and aren't cosmetically sensitive. Ask the nurse something like, "I have some blemishes and little bumps on my face. I want to have an overall skin cleaning [often called acne cleaning] but prevent scarring. Does the doctor do this kind of thing, or is he [or she] more a cancer and disease specialist?" If they don't know what you're talking about, you have the wrong doctor.

Nearly all routine facial pick-me-ups, however, can be accomplished right in your kitchen or bathroom.

**FOR HEALING SCARS, "IRONING" WRINKLES AND GOOD LUBRICATION**
Use vitamin E capsules. This works great for under-the-eye wrinkles. Puncture with a safety pin, apply under your eyes or on scars in a circular motion using your ring finger—ten times clockwise, ten times counterclockwise. Put a little on your lashes as well, and you'll see them grow. Leave it on to sink in. Do this daily for results. After a pregnancy, apply on stretch marks every night (here you have to be consistent). You'll see a difference. For use on large areas, buy pure vitamin E oil at the health-food store.

---

Don't skip this one; it's great. Once a season only—for Christmas, in the doldrums of early March, for Memorial Day and after Labor Day—pat equal parts of vinegar and water generously all over your face and neck for a couple of minutes, then rinse with cold water. This will adjust the skin's pH factor (acid-to-alkaline balance), and brighten and improve skin texture.

**QUICK-TIP WRINKLE SOFTENER** Take a little almond oil or sesame oil on your fingertip and apply it to your laugh lines (or frown lines, if you haven't been paying attention) in the morning before you've put on your moisturizer and makeup. Have breakfast, exercise, read the paper, whatever. Pat the excess oil off before applying moisturizer and makeup. Do this as often as you can. It softens lines and makes a quick visual difference.

**A NATURAL WRINKLE TIGHTENER** Slide an egg white, right out of the shell, all over your face, under eyes, on eyelids and over neck. Go about your business for twenty minutes, speechless with your face expressionless, while it dries. Remove with lots of cool water. If you have time, do this once a week. Works great!

**A NATURAL WAY TO EXFOLIATE** Sea salt will remove dry, flaky, dead skin. Wet face (or anywhere on the body—good for elbows), apply a couple of tablespoons of sea salt, then *gently* massage with a wet washcloth or fingers. Focus on T-zone and cheeks, avoiding the eye area. After one or two minutes, rinse with tingling cold water to tighten pores. You can do this up to once a week. This is important to do regularly, or else face-cream formulas will not penetrate.

**A NATURAL, EXFOLIATING FACE PEEL** Rub half a grapefruit or lemon, with most of the pulp removed, gently over your face and neck for a minute or two. Rinse. About 50 percent of women love this treatment; the other 50 percent find that it stings too much. If it stings, it won't kill you, and it's a good enough pick-me-up to try once. If it does sting, try rubbing cucumber slices—a milder version—over your face the next time. Do this up to once a week, time permitting.

**A HOMEMADE MASK AND PORE CLEANSER** This treatment is like oatmeal cookies for your face, without the calories. Mix into a paste a little honey, oatmeal and finely chopped almonds. Wet your fingers and apply gently, in circular motions, onto the T-zone and (only if your skin is oily) cheeks. Leave it on for twenty minutes. Remove with wet fingers and tepid water, again using circular motions. Finally, rinse in cold water with a washcloth containing six ice cubes (or as many as will fit) to reclose pores and stimulate circulation.

**THE CLASSIC TEA-STEEP** For decades, women have steamed their faces over a pot of steeping tea (chamomile is best) for five or ten minutes with a big towel over their heads to open pores naturally. It works. Use your pore cleanser and then cold-water splashes and a toner afterward to close them back up. Do this once every month or two.

I always cringe when I hear women say they're going home for a long, hot bath. A short bath (soak no

**DAILY BODY CARE**

longer than five minutes) in warm water (not hot) is the way to keep your skin from drying out. If it's dry already, add a capful of Sardo bath oil, almond oil or Neutrogena's sesame oil to the bath; they're all very nourishing. Rub dry afterward with a big towel, and you'll leave just enough oil on your skin to seep in throughout the night. It won't rub off onto the bedclothes. If you're achy, skip the oil and throw in half a cup of epsom salts instead.

To start the day, a quick shower will do the trick, and only when necessary. (We Americans tend to overwash.) In winter, for example, when the air is cold and drying and heating systems, which can also be drying, are on full blast, a shower every other day (with a vigorous sponge bath in between) is enough. Shave only when necessary. I prefer Nair or an electric razor to a bladed one— less chance of nicks and scarring. For soap, Dove or Ivory—as promised, they're mild, nondrying, and they clean well.

Many women ask me about Buf-Pufs and loofahs—too harsh? Not at all (but *never* use them on your face), although I prefer the natural sensation of a loofah, scrubbed vigorously all over, from the shoulders down. Don't forget the feet and ankles, which are too often neglected.

For a dry massage, use a horsehair glove, which is available at fine drugstores, such as Pasteur, Boyd's and Zitomer in New York City. They cost twice as much but last forever; loofahs have to be replaced about twice a year (and Buf-Pufs once a month, so that they won't spread bacteria). The difference is that the horsehair glove feels like your grandmother's scratchy old sofa—tougher, more friction, more exfoliation. *Great for applying cellulite creams.* But remember: The skin from the neck down can take it; facial skin can't.

Since moving back to the East Coast, I've noticed that women have a tendency to take better care of their faces than they do their bodies, chest and hands; perhaps sun-drenched West Coast women are more aware that these other areas, when exposed, receive as much scrutiny as those above the neck. After showering or bathing, the finishing touch—*always*—is to moisturize. Arms, elbows, shoulders, chest, neck, legs, ankles, feet. You'll notice softer, prettier skin all over within just a few days. (To keep the derriere smooth, wash your underclothes in fabric softener.) Good drugstore products for after the bath include Neutrogena skin oil (for dry skin), Lubriderm, Alpha Keri and Orlane B21 body cream, which is available in department stores.

### SPECIAL CARE FOR THE HANDS

I wash my hands a lot, to prevent picking up colds, flu and viruses and spreading oils and dirt to my face. For this, Neutrogena transparent soap—milder than Dove or Ivory, and therefore not strong enough for overall use—is great. The consequence, even so, is dry hands (which most women have anyway). Hands really do take a beating, and they need special care.

In addition to hand creams, use oils for a quick treatment, especially during winter or in dry climates. I keep oil by every sink in my house and office—vegetable, almond, sesame or sunflower—decanted into squeeze bottles. Pour a little on your hands after washing, and rub it in gently and well. Rinse and pat dry. You will have given your hands a luxurious treatment in five seconds; the results, if you continue every time you wash your hands, will be noticeable in a week. (You could also use Erno Laszlo's Active Phelityl Oil, which costs at least thirty-five dollars, but why bother?) The same oil goes on your hands as a healing treatment every time you wear rubber gloves—or any gloves. Jackie Onassis used to jog in Central Park wearing gloves, with face cream on her hands underneath. At night, a night cream to sink into the backs of the hands will also make a difference. Consistency is key.

To bleach your hands, after gardening, say, rub half a lemon over them, rinse, oil, rinse again and dry.

## SPECIAL CARE FOR THE KNEES AND ELBOWS

Elbows and knees get a beating, too. Treat them the same way as your hands—rub with oil and dry, and bleach with lemons as needed.

## SPECIAL CARE FOR THE FEET

Poor toes and feet are walked on all day long. Lavish a good moisturizer all over the feet and in between the toes every night before bed; they'll look and feel better—*much* better come summer. When your feet are achy and tired, rub with Dr. Scholl's Foot Balm, the way athletes and dancers do. I always travel with it. Concentrate your fingers on the arches and balls of the feet. (It's like having a reflexology massage; see page 171.)

Don't try to operate yourself on a deep corn or callus; you'll very likely make it worse. See a podiatrist for that. You probably won't need to, though, if you take preventive care of your feet. Use a pumice stone over the rough spots once a week for a good at-home treatment. Blackstone pumice stones (available at better drugstores, or order through Williams Lab, P.O. Box 101, Oradell, New Jersey 07490) are amazing, well worth ordering if you can't find them in the stores. Then use a pedifile (a huge nail file, like an emery board for your

18

feet, sold at drugstores), followed by a moisturizer. And treat yourself to a home or professional pedicure monthly.

TROUBLESHOOTINGTROUBLESHOOTING

**WRINKLES** Alpha hydroxy acids are the current miracle trend to get rid of wrinkles—half marketing gimmick, half real. Hydroxy acids come from citrus fruits, grapes and milk, and are the basis for numerous new creams—Avon's Anew and Clinique's Turnaround, to name just two. When they work, they tingle and exfoliate the face slowly and continually over time; results take about two weeks to begin to show. As with the lemon and grapefruit treatment described on page 14, about 50 percent of women love the tingling, and the other 50 percent don't. I can't use them, as I find them irritating (I am *not* particularly sensitive). They are worth trying. Experiment first with the grapefruit or lemon exfoliating peel; if that stings like crazy, they're probably not right for you. If it doesn't, before splurging on an expensive hydroxy system, try a generic brand from the drugstore, simply labeled Alpha Hydroxy or some such. You should feel a tingling; otherwise the product doesn't contain enough acid to do any good. The highest concentration you're likely to find is 12 percent. Dermatologists use the acids sometimes for mild peels, in concentrations of 20 to 70 percent—so the percentage in cosmetic creams is fairly low. Some hydroxy-acid products are mixed with moisturizers as well; if not, use them *under* your own moisturizer.

**MORE WRINKLING** For severe wrinkling, Retin A still has a big following, even if you don't hear about it so much anymore; the press has moved on. Prescribed by doctors only, it sheds the top layer of skin and can show great results on sun-damaged or acne-scarred faces and fine lines. The best application is a formula mixed with a moisturizer. You can't go out into the sun *at all* while using it, as this can damage your skin even more severely. If you and your doctor agree, and you're willing to stay sun-free, Retin A can work dramatically.

**PUFFY EYES** One of the most constant complaints from women is puffy eyes. To get rid of bags and puffiness, brew two bags of tea (Lipton works best) until

HOW DO I LOOK?HOW DO I LOOK?

strong. Recline on a flat surface to allow fluid in the spongy areas of your eyes to disappear. When the tea bags are cool enough not to burn, wring them out slightly and apply one to each eye, pressing lightly. Leave on for fifteen to twenty minutes, resaturating once. The tannic acid in the tea really does shrink the area. A quicker method, though not quite as effective, is to wrap a few ice cubes in a washcloth (never put ice directly onto skin; it can break capillaries), and hold the compress under each eye for a few seconds at a time. Avoiding salt, alcohol and caffeine will also help, as will eating fresh pineapple and papaya, which help to reduce fluid retention. If after all this you still have puffy eyes, which sometimes is genetic, consider removal by a plastic surgeon. It's a simple procedure, sometimes done with a local anaesthetic. Recovery time is usually from ten to fourteen days, and the results—including no scarring—are well worth it.

**ACNE** Use Maximum Strength Clearasil, applied on eruptions with a Q-Tip when skin is clean. Witch hazel and alcohol can be very drying, and generally I advise against using them. For severely oily adolescent skin, however, an astringent containing one or both ingredients can be helpful, applied with cotton pads on the T-zone area *only* whenever it gets really oily. If breakouts are massive, they call for a dermatologist.

**CRACKED HEELS AND ELBOWS** Use vitamin E capsules, A and D ointment from the drugstore or Crisco daily until the cracks have healed, then moisturize every day and use a pumice (preferably a Blackstone) every time you bathe to prevent them from happening again. Also, don't walk barefoot around the house and pool, as I did in Los Angeles for seventeen years. Even though I moisturized daily, I still had cracked heels.

**DRY LIPS** Dip a soft baby's toothbrush into Vaseline or Elizabeth Arden's eight-hour cream and gently brush away dry, flaky skin. Vaseline, by the way, can also be used as an eye cream, as a lip gloss, to tame eyebrows, to treat eyelashes at night, as a cuticle cream, and even to remove a tight ring!

**LARGE PORES** Shrink them with one part boric-acid powder to twelve parts witch hazel. Shake the mixture and apply morning and night.

**FACIAL HAIR** Nair is still the best product around. Every woman has a bit of fuzz over the top lip. It shows more when it's dark. Even if it's light, though, you'll still look better if you remove it. Another method for removing facial hair is electrolysis, a procedure I talk about in depth on page 68.

**CELLULITE** Some women never get it; to my horror, I had some at age fourteen. It's hereditary. In general, large-breasted women usually have thin hips and no cellulite, while hourglass figures usually inherit a proclivity for it. A low-fat, low-salt diet (see Diet chapter) helps. Exercise tones the area but won't get rid of cellulite. To reduce the appearance of it, first massage the area with a horsehair loofah glove in a circular motion to stimulate circulation. Then twice a day knead in, as if you were kneading dough, Biotherm's Contour Plus, available in some department stores. (If you can't find it, call Burdines department store in Miami—1-305-835-5151—and they'll send it to you.) Use deep pressure, in *S* shapes, to break down and dissolve the fat and water nodes that have accumulated. Massage as hard as you can (thighs can take it!), then go over the area again with the loofah. This really does help. If you do it consistently, you will see results within four to six weeks. If you happen to be in Paris, there's a terrific cellulite treatment called Cellu M6, after the machine that's used, which acts as a hand-held roller-style "vacuum." It increases circulation and lifts skin off cellulite pockets, smoothing them out. This treatment costs about seventy-five dollars, and two or three the first week can help a lot. (I wish someone would bring this to the United States.) This treatment is available at Espace Bleu Esthetique (31 rue Bayen, Paris 17ᵉ, tel. 44 09 7474) or at Kineform (2 ave Paul Daumier, Paris 16ᵉ, tel. 47 04 5836.)

**AGE SPOTS** Brown spots are pigment marks caused by the sun that form on the backs of our hands and sometimes elsewhere as we age. There are two good products that help, and they are available at most drugstores. Esoterica is one, and it comes with or without sunscreen. Even better (more expensive, though) is Neostrata, which contains more hydroquinone, the ingredient that lightens.

**VARICOSE VEINS** Again, these are hereditary; they often show up after a pregnancy, though they can appear anytime. If you have them, the dermatologist can treat them with saline shots. (Do this in the winter, before exposing them in summer.) To conceal them, Covermark's Leg Magic (waterproof, available in seven shades), Dermablend or Clinique's Continuous Coverage (available in department stores) are your best bets.

**BRUISING AND SWELLING** This is the occasional result of a treatment at the dermatologist. First apply an ice compress all over, for fifteen or twenty minutes. To conceal and reduce swelling, try B-X drying lotion; order it (in advance of treatment) from Vera's Retreat, 1-310-470-6362. A concealer or heavy makeup, such as Clinique's Continuous Coverage or Physicians Formula, with a light powder over it camouflages bruising. To minimize bruising after any cosmetic procedure, doctors also recommend taking Arnica Montana 30X, a homeopathic medicine, two tablets four times a day, beginning one week before through one week after the procedure. Bromezyme tablets, an extract from pineapple, two tablets four time a day, will also reduce swelling. Both can be ordered from Schreiner Pharmacy (9730 Wilshire Boulevard, Beverly Hills, California 90212, 1-310-276-1057).

## EMERGENCY— BAD FACE DAY

Instant "face lifts" in a jar are a quick fix; they'll boost your confidence and tighten your skin long enough to see you through an important afternoon or evening. *Vogue* recommends several, my Youth-Lift among them.

**COLLAGEN SHOTS** The shots are injected into facial folds, lines, wrinkles and pock marks and do a good job of filling them in—as long as you know they don't last and don't take the place of skin care itself. They're expensive, they last three to six months, then they dissolve and disappear. Start by calling the Academy of Facial Plastic and Reconstructive Surgery (1-800-332-3223) or the American Academy of Dermatologists (1-708-330-0230) for referrals. The doctor will give you an allergy test first. Afterward, you'll want to hide, as there will be swelling and, sometimes, bruising. (See above for how to treat swelling and bruising.) You can start and stop taking the shots with no problem. For more information about collagen injections, call 1-800-423-4900.

**CHEMICAL PEELS/DERMABRASION** "Should I have a professional face peel?" is another question I'm often asked. Only if you have badly acne- or sun-damaged skin. Trichloroacetic acid, which is much stronger than any ingredient found in creams, is what leading dermatologists use; the cost can be as low as fifty dollars, depending on the condition of your skin. Call the numbers listed above for referrals, and ask lots of questions: How many peels has the doctor done? Were there any complications? What will I look like after day one, two, three and so on? What changes can I expect in the look of my skin and the feel of my skin? Will it hurt? How much does it cost? Will the peel include the area around my eyes? Are there restrictions I must follow afterward? How long will the peel last? Ask, too, to see someone else he or she has done; usually someone in the office will have had one. And request a light peel: When it comes to your face, less can be more.

**BOTULINUM TOXIN** A recent trend is the use of botulinum toxin, the poison that causes botulism, injected into frown lines and furrows to erase wrinkles. The treatment is said to last three to six months. It works by paralyzing the underlying frown muscles. Even though doctors (and some women I know!) are doing this, I would not be comfortable injecting poison into my body. Also, it totally eliminates a woman's ability to frown: unnatural!

**LASER SKIN SURFACING** is the newest method used to remove fine lines and smooth out deep wrinkles and sun-damaged skin. It also removes birthmarks, stretch marks, acne scars and tattoos. I know a movie star who has had laser treatments on her cleavage, elbows and knees as well. The powerful light of the ultra pulse laser resurfaces skin irregularities and stimulates new skin formation. It also has a "shrink wrap" effect on skin resulting from collagen fibers shrinking. Laser is not a replacement for a "lift" because it doesn't tighten sagging muscles or work on neck tissue. Some complications that can occur are scarring and pigment changes. If done only around the eyes a raccoon effect is possible, especially on darker skin. Be sure to go to doctors with lots of experience *only* and ask the same questions as you would about a chemical peel/dermabrasion. For a referral to a board-certified laser surgeon write: American Society for Laser Medicine And Surgery, 2404 Stewart Square, Wausau, Wisconsin 54401 or call the American Society for Dermatologic Surgery at 1-800-441-2737. In New York City you could investigate Dr. Roy Geronemus at the Laser and Skin Surgery Center at 1-212-686-7306. In California, you could try Dr. Richard E. Fitzpatrick in La Jolla (1-619-455-7714) or Dr. Mark Rubin in Beverly Hills (1-310-556-0119).

**TATTOOING** A friend of mine had her lips (which had no color) tattooed, and now they are "naturally" rosy all the time. She had eyeliner tattooed as well, and eyebrow tattooing is also available. It sounds too permanent to me, and who knows when you might want the doe-eyed sleepy look? But if you decide to go ahead, as always use only a well-researched dermatologist.

**FAT INJECTIONS** Fat is taken from the hips and thighs and injected into the face, lasting three or four months.

**SUBCISION** This office procedure, developed by renowned dermatologist Dr. Norman Orentreich, eliminates deep wrinkles by plumping them up from underneath the skin. Nothing is injected. It is especially good for nasal-fold, forehead and brow furrows, with permanent results!

## SOME PLASTIC-SURGERY PROCEDURES:

———

❏ *Upper-eyelid surgery:* Very delicate surgery, but also very effective. Many stars and politicians—of both sexes—opt for this and nothing else. Consider it if you start to get droopy, tired-looking eyes when you're not tired. It's usually done only once.

❏ *Lower-eyelid surgery:* Some people get folds of skin, dark circles or pockets of fat that create puffiness under the eyes at any age no matter what they do (it's usually genetic). Surgery under the eyes

can also be hugely successful. Sometimes it can be done twice over the years for continued effect.

❏ *Raising the eyebrows:* This is done to eliminate forehead lines and drooping brows. The newest method is endoscopic surgery, which is also now used for gallbladder and appendix removals, among other procedures. The procedure is performed with a fiber-optic light, which runs through a telescope—no incisions! This reduces scarring and recovery time enormously. It's very new, so make sure the doctor is experienced.

❏ *A "rooster's neck" or a double chin out of nowhere:* This is sometimes genetic, sometimes caused by a

**PLASMAGEL INJECTIONS** This procedure was also developed by Dr. Norman Orentreich. Plasma taken from your own blood is separated and injected into lines and wrinkles to fill them in. This lasts from three to six months, depending on the person.

**FACE-LIFTS AND OTHER PLASTIC SURGERY** *The* last resort. Before investing your money in—and turning over your own individual looks to—a surgeon, thoroughly acquaint yourself with the procedures available and the questions to ask by reading *A Face Lift Is a Bargain,* by Nola Rocco (published by Hidden Garden Press, available by calling 1-310-550-6855), the best book I know about plastic surgery, which will tell you about the techniques available. Remember, too, that a lift does not fill in or remove crow's-feet or lines around the lips. If ever there's a time to be an informed, even defensive, consumer, this is it. Plastic surgery is irreversible. The Academy of Facial Plastic and Reconstructive Surgery (1-800-332-3223) will refer you to experts nearby.

If there's one single thing you *really* hate about your looks—a nose you despise, badly protruding ears, a birthmark that could be eradicated with laser treatments, breast size—go for it. It's not necessary to spend the rest of your life too-relaxed muscle that droops, causing neck creases and lines. The surgery lifts the area from chin to collarbone; it is very effective, relatively simple and usually needed only once. On a younger neck, sometimes liposuction is all you need.

❑ *Thigh and buttock lifts:* I think the scarring, which can be dreadful, makes the procedure not worth it. Your decision should be made based on how bad the problem is and how much it bothers you.

❑ *Tummy tuck:* Not for weight loss per se, but the procedure will help to eliminate excess skin from weight loss or childbirth. There's scarring, but to me it *is* worth it, as it's hidden in the bikini line.

❑ *Bee-stung lips:* Collagen injections into the lips give this new, trendy look, which you can spot a mile away—it always looks fake. To say nothing of the fact that it's painful and doesn't last.

❑ *Liposuction:* I've seen it work well, and I've seen it fail, with the fat coming back into newly (and oddly) shaped thighs, and elsewhere. Ask lots of questions. However, liposuction techniques and instruments are improving rapidly. For lots of good information, read *The Slim Book of Liposuction* by Alan M. Engler, M.D., Vantage Press, 1-800-882-3273.

feeling self-conscious. However, living in New York, Washington, Boston and especially Los Angeles, I've seen the results of a *lot* of surgery, successful and not. But surgery won't cure depression, turn you into a happy person, build self-confidence, bring you a husband or transform you from Jane Smith into Cindy Crawford. Surgery won't heal the problems *inside* you. I've seen successful surgery fail for just those reasons.

In general, less is more, and run as fast as you can from anyone who promises you more than you asked for or a rose-garden overhaul. Remember, a big reconstructive job looks better in photos than real life. A celebrity friend of mine, for example, felt ready for a lift, but studied the subject for more than a year before going under the knife, which is exactly what surgery *is*. In the end, she opted for an entire face-lift *without* touching her eyes. In other words, choose "spot lifting," and choose a doctor who shares that point of view. One such doctor ("to the stars") of plastic surgery for the body is Dr. John Grossman in Beverly Hills (1-310-557-2307). For the face: Dr. Frank Kamer (1-310-556-8155) and Dr. Steven Hoefflin (1-310-451-4733). Or call American Society for Plastic and Reconstructive Surgery (1-800-635-0635).

The questions about makeup that women ask me most often are these:

- ❑ How can I apply makeup without *looking* made up?
- ❑ How can I conceal dark circles and puffy eyes?
- ❑ How do I apply eyeliner?
- ❑ Where do I apply my blush?
- ❑ Color confuses me. How should I choose eye and lip color without making mistakes—and wasting money?
- ❑ What should I do with my eyebrows?
- ❑ How can I apply my makeup in five minutes or less?
- ❑ How can I make my eyes look bigger?
- ❑ How do I choose the right foundation color *for me*?
- ❑ How can I prevent my lipstick from "bleeding" into those little lines around my lips?

I've asked these questions; every woman has. My clients at Giorgio, even the really glamorous ones, would come in frustrated, holding a new expensive lipstick or eye shadow, wondering why it looked so good in the promotion and in the store, but terrible when they got it home. They'd feel frustrated, too, after they'd just splurged on an expensive makeover, only to be told by the men in their lives: "Wash it off!" Since I was helping them choose their clothes, they also began to ask me about "dressing"

# MAKEUP

their faces: Makeup is, after all, fashion for the face. I kept a list of their problems (and mine!), then set out to solve each one. Pretty soon I knew brand names and shades by heart, and could recommend specific products, down to the right colors for each woman.

I learned much more, of course, later on, working with the chemists and cosmotologists who helped me develop just what I wanted in my own makeup line, and now I've got this art down to a science. It never takes me more than five minutes to apply my makeup. I now know what we can—and can't—expect from makeup. Makeup can't *transform*, for example, and turn you into Cindy Crawford or Lauren Hutton. What makeup *can* do absolutely is to bring out your best self— enhance your good features and compensate for those you aren't so happy with. Makeup can make you *feel* better, every day. Products, baffling as the wide array of choices and colors can seem, aren't really the problem. There are plenty of perfectly good products out there—I know: I've tried them all. Artful makeup comes from understanding color, harmony—and method of application.

## INSIDE THE MAKEUP BUSINESS

Are makeup brands and products basically all the same? Sometimes yes, sometimes no. Prices vary, depending on quality of ingredients, pigment colors and formula design; cost of research, development and packaging; and advertising and marketing costs. As to distribution, a mass-distributed line sold self-service on a shelf or on hanging cards costs the manufacturer less than maintaining and staffing a counter in a department store. The disadvantage to buying self-service is that you can't always test the products. If you feel confident about color, then you'll be pretty safe buying self-service foundation, blush, powder and nail enamel; Revlon, L'Oréal, Maybelline and Max Factor are all worthy drugstore brands, with accurate color charts to choose from.

Lip color is different. Purchasing lip color when you can't test is a gamble with a 99 percent failure rate. There's no way to know in advance how a color is going to look on your skin, because each formula and what we call the lay down of color are different. Also, the color your lips are in the first place—darker, lighter, pinker—will affect the appearance of the lipstick once it's applied. That's why all your impulse-buy lipsticks are sitting, unused, in a drawer. (Pass them on to a friend, and maybe you'll get one back that you *can* use.)

*Efficacy* is the buzzword used to describe the feel of a product on the skin: The more emollient the product, the more efficacious. You can tell if your makeup is kind to your skin, or "treating" it, by the way you look in a triple magnifying mirror. If your skin looks soft and supple, your products are working for you. If your skin (eyelids, too) looks creased, dry or flaky, they're working against you. Foundation that treats the skin is not essential, particularly if you take good care of your skin, but if it works to your benefit, why not? My entire philosophy is about taking every beauty opportunity wherever and whenever you can, making it routine, building beauty right into your life. Foundation, lipstick and concealer that condition the skin all day long will fill in little lines and crevices, moisturizing as well as tinting the skin. This will cost more, but it will be better makeup, less abusive to the skin—and you can always skimp on eye shadow.

When I first decided to learn about makeup, I thought it would be smart to go to professional makeup artists and see how *they* did it, then use their products and techniques myself. Big mistake. Most pros are trained to apply makeup for the camera, not for real-life women in real-life light, and, while their contouring powder and glittering blush look very dramatic in their studios and sensational in photographs, outside the studios they look artificial and pretty silly. The way to learn makeup instead is to study your face, your coloring, your features. Test makeup product-by-product, sampling whenever possible by applying the makeup in the store, then going outdoors to see how it looks in natural light. Follow your face, not the trends you see in fashion layouts. Case in point: those dark brown lip colors that turn up in so many ads. Dark colors on light-colored skin are strange-looking and make lips look half their size—*not* attractive in real life.

By the time I was ready to start my own line, I knew more and did the testing myself, on real women—friends of friends, employees of friends, teenagers (they loved it!)—right in my living room. When I opened my offices in Beverly Hills, I added women from local law, accounting and dentists' offices; I was forever dragging in women, practically off the street, and putting makeup on them. (I definitely stick to not asking friends for their opinions on makeup, though.) Based on what women asked me, told me and complained about, and based on how the dozens of formulas I actually experimented with worked or didn't work on dozens of women, I finally understood the ground rules for recognizing and buying good makeup:

❑ Good foundations and concealers start with an oil or moisturizer base (as opposed to water, which is best for teens with oily skin) to which the color is added. For years I wore Revlon's Touch & Glow foundation, and also liked Countess Isserlyn, by Charles of the Ritz, for dress-up. Max Factor's International Pan-Stik ultra-creamy makeup provides excellent coverage (for slightly less coverage, apply with a damp sponge). Lancôme and Cover Girl make good concealers. One or more of these ingredients suggest that you've found a good product:

 *Castor oil*—has a conditioning effect

 *Mineral oil*—binds moisture to skin

 *Hydroxylated lanolin*—also binds moisture to skin

 *Jojoba oil*—lubricates and conditions skin

 *Tocopherol acetate*—synthetic vitamin E, the healing vitamin for skin

 *Isopropyl lanolate*—a conditioning emollient

 *Allantoin*—a soothing agent

 *Dimethicone*—a moisturizing agent

 *Hyaluronic acid*—holds moisture; a firming agent

 *Wheat germ glycerides*—for softening and conditioning

 *Titanium dioxide*—sunblock (optional in makeup)

 *Zinc oxide*—sunblock (optional in makeup)

30

❑ Avoid frost in powder and blush; it looks fake. Women don't *glint* in real life; we *glow*. A little moisturizer in powder and blush (see ingredients above) will help it bind, so you won't leave a powder-blush trail behind you or have it end up on your clothes. Coty makes a famously good drugstore-brand face powder, and Cover Girl and Lancôme both make good blush.

❑ Unless you're a whiz at sharpening makeup pencils (I never could get it right, even when I kept them in the refrigerator, which *does* make them work easier), choose retractable pencils, which won't ever need to be sharpened—no waste. Origins, Maybelline and Max Factor make good brow pencils. For lip pencils, I'd vote for mine first because of its tapered point, but Clinique, Origins and M-A-C also make good ones.

❑ Frosted eye shadows light up your eyes at night, but look awful for day wear; matte looks best for day. I like eye shadow that can be applied wet—as eyeliner, for a well-defined effect—or dry, either as over-the-eyelid shadow or with an eyeliner pencil, as eyeliner, for a soft, smudged effect. Wet/dry shadows are still a new concept. I make them, and so does the Make-Up Center in New York, 150 West 55th Street, 1-212-977-9494.

❑ An eyelash curler is not, technically speaking, makeup, but it might as well be. I've seen this result on every woman I've tried it on: Nothing widens and opens the eye like curling the lashes, even if you do only the tips. Kurlash, Revlon and Max Factor make good eyelash curlers. I do it every day, before applying mascara. On weekends, I curl my lashes and skip mascara; lashes are delicate and this gives them a break. Panthenol, a conditioner with vitamin B, is one good ingredient to look for in a mascara or any hair product. Protein, collagen and hyaluronic acid are others. Maybelline's Great Lash is still the best drugstore brand, and Lancôme also makes good mascaras.

❑ As with foundation and concealer, lip color with emollients added (see ingredients above) will condition throughout the day—better for your lips. Other than that, you can't tell much from reading lipstick labels. Each color has a different level of pigment, which determines how deep the color will be, how the formula will lay down on the lips and how long it will last. In general, lip stains and sheers last the least amount of time, while creme and matte formulas last longer. Lips not only lined but also filled in with lip pencil first will hold any lip color longer. Test for color and texture before buying. Both Revlon and Clinique make good lipsticks.

❑ Good makeup comes in small packages. Shelf life is generally a year, by which time liquid foundations tend to separate and lose their spreadability. Mascara, which dries up, is very perishable, followed by matte lipstick; sooner or later you'll have to scrape it on. When I insisted to my chemists that my makeup be packaged small (to fit in purses as well as to get used up *fast*), they told me, "Women will think you're cheating them." Instead, women like the portability. Buy only what you need for now.

## THE LAYERED LOOK

The worst makeup mistake there is is to wear no makeup. A naked face is not the same as the natural look we're always striving for. I've talked to men about this, too. All men like to see the women they care about looking their best—but also looking like themselves, the women they know. They dislike artifice—too much makeup, or makeup that looks unnatural. To men (to women, too!), that's not feminine or pretty, but vulgar and unattractive. If anyone tells you—or you feel like telling yourself—to "wash it off," all it means is that you're wearing the wrong makeup.

I've had the best teachers and role models, and still it has taken me years to figure out how to simplify makeup and get it right. "Less is more" may seem like odd advice for someone who's in the business of selling cosmetics, but it's the best makeup advice I know. Keep it simple. Five minutes *maximum*—and that's for a full-dress party look— is all it takes. For complete makeup instruction see pages 37–44.

Layering makeup means, simply, that you add, or layer, makeup as the day goes on and your makeup needs evolve. There are four looks, based on the way we live:

## 1 NATURAL/A.M./SPORT MAKEUP
### 2 MINUTES

- Curl eyelashes
- Pat concealer into eye socket (see page 38)
- Apply a slightly deeper "nude" color eye shadow
- Apply a lip color in a soft pink, nude, rose or coral shade, or substitute a lip-pencil outline and fill in or a colored lip gloss

## 2 CAREER/DAY MAKEUP
### 3 MINUTES

- Follow steps in Look #1
- Add foundation
- Touch up eye shadow
- Add a light application of eyeliner for definition
- Touch up lip color with lip pencil or lip brush
- Powder T-zone—center of forehead, nose, chin
- Add blush
- Add mascara

## 3 DINNER/EVENING MAKEUP
### 4 MINUTES

- Remove old lip color with a tissue
- Clean up any under-eye smudges with a Q-Tip dipped in moisturizer
- Reapply concealer
- Add more foundation (as the lights go down, makeup colors can intensify)
- Repowder T-zone, if needed
- Reapply blush
- Add fresh application of eye shadow
- Reapply eyeliner (go heavier, for more definition at night)
- Reapply mascara
- Apply fresh lip color with lip pencil or lip brush

## 4 PARTY MAKEUP
### 5 MINUTES

- Do *all* the above steps
- Stronger eye colors, if desired
- Deeper lip colors, if desired
- False eyelashes, if desired

Before applying anything to your face, study your features closely in a mirror. American women tend to copy celebrities and models, thereby giving themselves a "mismatched" look, like a composite sketch that doesn't quite work—scary Joan Crawford eyebrows, for example, with a lush Sharon Stone mouth. The best way—and this works for every woman—to give your face instant strength, recognition and style is to *design your eyebrows, eyes, and lip line to match the shape of your eyes. Your mouth, eyes and brows should all have the same essential shape. Reconsider your lip line at the same time. Is your lower lip fuller than your upper lip? If you're like most women, it is, and a few quick strokes of a lip pencil or lip brush will give you an instant expression lift.*

This subtle shaping technique is the way to get your face to look as if it "fits together," and there's nothing difficult, artificial or complicated about it. It's a gentle shaping to accentuate the symmetry you were born with, a way to "align" your face to emphasize and flatter your individual features.

## HOW TO DESIGN YOUR EYEBROWS, EYES AND LIP LINE TO MATCH THE SHAPE OF YOUR EYES

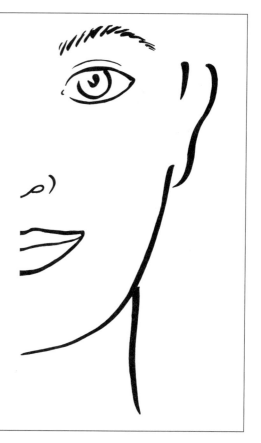

**Start with your eyes, which, along with the lips, are the most expressive features on the face. *Follow* the shape of the eyes. If your eyes are round, for example, lightly shape your brows round to match, then round your lips. If your eyes are almond-shaped, lightly shape brows, then lips, to follow. Eyeliner, eye shadow and eyebrow pencil are the tools you'll need for your eyes and brows and the subtle shaping will become automatic after the first or second time you try it.**

As for lips, most of us have fuller lower lips and upper lips that are narrower. If you follow these lip lines just as they are, the more angular upper lip will bring the whole mouth down, and the result will be a hard, downtrodden expression. That's where lip pencils and lip brushes—the greatest (and most often underused) beauty tools—come in. For large lips, use the pencil or brush just *inside* the natural lip line, still rounding the top line the same way. If you feel you're going over (or under) your lip line, you are, but ever so slightly; your lips will still look like your lips, just slightly fuller or less prominent, and softer and more upbeat either way, whether you're smiling or having a thoroughly dreadful day. It is a real expression booster.

## THE PALETTES: CHOOSING YOUR COLORS

If I were a chef, I would analyze other chefs' cuisines to see what I could learn. As it is, I analyze makeup everywhere I go. New Yorkers, I've noticed, tend to wear makeup colors too dark, too beige on their faces; they also succumb to brown cheeks—"contouring" will never put cheekbones where nature didn't—and lip colors too brown or blue-hued. In the Midwest I see heavy blue eye shadow on blue eyes—no, it doesn't make them bluer; coral shadow does. No makeup at all—which I see in Cambridge, Massachusetts, especially—makes women look washed out. In Washington, D.C., the overall look is a bit dated—blue eye shadow on blue eyes again, odd lip colors, brows badly made up. In Los Angeles, too often I see Day-Glo lips, often too "California coral" or a look that's too suntanned overall—face, cheeks, lips. Occasionally, everywhere, I see makeup way too thick and unnatural, but generally the mistakes have more to do with *color* than with application.

When I started my makeup line, I set out to create color-selection palettes to solve the problem of color confusion. Having tried preselecting colors every which way, I finally found the one way that *works*, every time, for every woman: *Key lip color, eye-makeup color and blush to the color of your eyes and skin tone, and you'll never go wrong again.*

It's as simple and mistake-proof as that, and French women—who *do* always get it right—have always started with their eyes when they dress and make up. Blue/gray eyes need a blue-toned lip color and gray-toned eye shadow, for example, while brown eyes clash with blue tones. Brown eyes come to life, however, with yellow- or orange-toned lip and eye color. And so it goes. Start with the color of your eyes, and use as many or as few of the colors in your individual palette as you want: see the color section for my custom makeup charts for each eye color—blue/gray, brown, hazel/green, women of color/dark eyes, and Asian eyes—including how to match eye shadows, lipsticks and blushes.

## LIP COLORS TO GO WITH EYE-COLOR AND SKIN-TONE PALETTE

❑ **Blue/gray eyes:** These eyes look good in colors with blue or mauve undertones, neutrals with rose and mauve undertones, light pink to fuchsia, peach, reds (light to dark, with blue undertones) and mauves.

❑ **Brown eyes:** These eyes look good in colors with yellow, orange or brown undertones, orange to terra-cotta, coral, reds (medium to dark reds, with yellow or brown undertones) and warm neutrals with brown or orange undertones; no mauve or blue undertones.

❑ **Hazel/green eyes:** These eyes look good with rose and burgundy or brown undertones, naturals with brown or rose undertones, medium pinks with rose undertones, reds with rose, burgundy or brown undertones and rose to fuchsia.

❑ **Women of color:** These eyes look good with both orange and blue undertones, deep reds with blue, wine or brown undertones, mocha and cinnamon to brown, roses to fuchsia, coral and orange to terra-cotta and neutrals with brown, rose or wine undertones.

❑ **Asian eyes:** These eyes look good with rose and wine undertones (no yellow or peach), neutrals with rose and wine undertones, reds with blue or wine undertones, deep mauves and blue-pink to rose.

## "COLOR CORRECT": CHOOSING YOUR FOUNDATION

*Choose foundation and concealer not to match but to compensate for your natural skin tone.*

Conventional wisdom always has us struggling to *match* skin tone and foundation, and for years I followed this advice—and was never very happy with the results. My skin is olive, so I was always applying olive foundation to my olive skin. And the resulting double-olive was drab. One day, however, I can't remember why, I tried a peach-toned foundation, which brought some *glow* to my skin. It *compensated* for the olive, rather than reinforcing and doubling the effect of it. I've used peach-toned foundation ever since. *Color correct,* I call it.

Other examples: I have a friend with porcelain-white skin, who loves the look and chooses a pale foundation and very red lips: It's her look, her choice, and she carries it off perfectly, confident with the dramatic effect. Another friend, with the same porcelain skin, color-corrects her skin a shade or two darker, to a medium beige—a look she prefers. Someone else I know complained to me that her skin looked too ruddy; to tone down her flushed look, I gave her a true beige foundation, and she applies two light layers of it. Too yellow? Compensate with a pink-toned foundation.

You can easily tell whether a foundation is peach-toned, pink-toned or whatever by trying it on the back of your hand in the store, then taking it outdoors to examine it in the natural light. You'll be amazed by how clearly the tones come through. If it works on the back of your hand, it will also work on your face.

If you'd like to correct the nuance of your skin tone, experiment with the color that looks best, *not* the color that comes closest to matching the color you didn't want to emphasize in the first place: color correct.

---

### TYPES OF FOUNDATION

❏ *Liquid:* **Comes in a bottle and offers light coverage and a natural finish. An application of powder afterward is optional.**

❏ *Liquid cream:* **Heavier than liquid, comes in a tube or jar and offers medium coverage. This gives a moist, dewy finish and makes powder optional.**

❏ *Cream/powder:* **Comes packaged solidly in a compact with a sponge, offers medium coverage and a matte finish. With this, you can skip powder altogether.**

Concealers come in stick form, like lipsticks, and in a creamy form that looks like mascara—you pull out a wand coated with coverage. Avoid the sticks; they're drying, they cake and they tug at the delicate skin around the eyes. The liquids in tubes are terrific. Apply with a pinkie, or whatever finger feels comfortable, in gentle patting motions; this works much better than using the wand. The heat from the finger *places* the concealer and blends it.

In general, most of us need only one concealer, one shade lighter than our skin tone, regardless of what shade of foundation we're using. There are camouflaging tricks, however, that call for a *darker* concealer as well. See Troubleshooting (page 47) for these.

**APPLICATION**

My stepdaughter started to wear a little blush and pink lipstick to school when she was thirteen; for parties she added mascara. Teaching her how to use makeup was an important "rite of passage" ritual—for both of us. I wanted her to learn to do it right. I took her shopping for classic "starter" brands, such as Almay, Bonne Belle, Maybelline and Max Factor. We spent time in the bathroom going over application and use and, to my surprise, she liked to watch me do the whole nine yards as often as she could, planning for her future. She hated curling her lashes, but *loved* fruit-flavored lip gloss. After endless (sometimes messy) experimenting with my colors in the big mirror, she began to realize why they didn't work for her (her eyes are hazel, mine are brown), until eventually she understood her face and what to look for. It takes that kind of scrutiny, for all of us, before making up becomes second nature—and never takes more than five minutes a day.

Natural light is the most unforgiving, and therefore the best light for applying makeup. If you look good in natural light, you'll look good in any light. Bad planning has seen to it that most of us have to spend time in fluorescent lighting, which is absolutely the worst. Never apply makeup in fluorescent lighting—you'll look overly made up the minute you step into any other light.

Failing natural light, use bulbs of at least 100 watts (250 watts is better) either above your face or on each side of it.

**To CURL EYELASHES** For a wide-eyed, upbeat expression in a matter of seconds, curl your lashes. Keep the eye open while setting the curler in place, about halfway out from the base of the lashes. The most important thing is to keep the curler clamp straight up and down (not at an angle); otherwise the lashes will come out slanted. Don't worry about curling every lash, especially the ones in the corners; even curling just the tips looks great. If you can reach all the lashes, fine, but the main thing is to get the center lashes up. Look down while gently squeezing the clamp for two or three seconds only. Release—and that's it.

**To APPLY CONCEALER** Concealer, one shade lighter than your skin tone, goes on first, either by itself or with foundation going on afterward. Apply three or four dots from the inner corner of your eye to just beyond the center; too far out will give a raccoon effect. Apply as well to nose-to-mouth lines and over blemishes as needed, blending with your pinkie (or the finger of your choice); the heat from your finger will "set" the concealer.

Now take a look at the inside corner of your eyes, where the socket meets the top of the nose. If you're like most of us, you'll see that it's dark in there, and shadowy—and dark definitely makes the impact of the eyes recede. A couple of drops of concealer patted gently over the inside of the socket with your pinkie will take years off, open up the eyes and lighten the whole area. It's a great trick. It gives a subtly different wide-eyed look, and it will work anytime, with or without foundation, even when you're wearing the barest trace of makeup.

**To APPLY FOUNDATION** Whether you're using a liquid, liquid/cream or cream/powder foundation, it *always* goes on smoothest if you apply it with a makeup sponge. The same way concealer sets where you want it from the heat of your pinkie, foundation should seem to *glide* smoothly over the skin, filling in and covering as it goes, and the finely porous sponge holds and delivers foundation perfectly. (You can use the sponges for a long time if you wash them regularly with a liquid soap.) With the sponge, blend foundation throughly into hairline, onto earlobes, under the chin and over the jawline, trailing off where jaw meets neck.

For a perfectly even look—and to keep eye colors in place and lip colors from bleeding—apply as well a light application of foundation all over the eyelid and lip line. (Powder applied over the foundation will also keep colors from moving. Color comes *last.*) Many makeup artists apply eye makeup before the foundation, which allows easier cleanup under the eyes. After experimenting both ways, however, I find it *much* smoother to apply foundation first, everywhere. Then, when I get to my eyes, any stray eye-shadow powder is easy enough to flick away with the pointed side of the makeup sponge.

**TO APPLY FACE POWDER** Apply to the T-zone only—forehead, nose and chin. The old adage that powder applied under the eyes accentuates fine lines is absolutely true; keep it well away from the eye area. Even if you're skipping powder altogether, *a light dusting over the eyelids and lip line will set the color and prevent it from moving.* This is important—it really works.

**TO APPLY BLUSH** Choose powder blushes; liquids leave spots and streaks, tug at the skin and never blend right. Apply blush one inch below the outer corner of your eye, and blend with the brush in an upward oval motion, fading color into the hairline as you blend. If you smile as you brush the blush in, you'll see the "apples" of your cheeks—the bull's-eye of the blush zone.

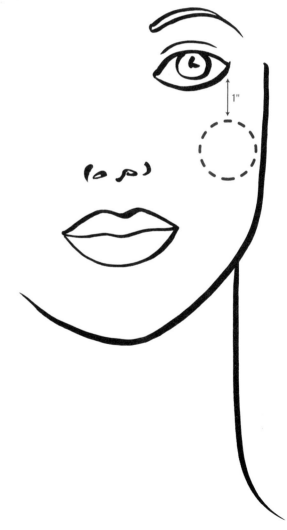

**TO APPLY EYE SHADOW** I will probably disagree with everything you've ever heard about eye shadow, but I'm very sure of myself on this subject; please try it once my way and see for yourself: *Never use dark shadows in the creases of your lids.* Dark colors sink in and recess the eye, and no one needs dark definition there because when we open our eyes, we have a natural crease. *Light shades in the crease, on the other hand, will open up the eye.*

— BROWBONE

— CREASE
— UPPER LID
— LASH LINE

— LOWER LID

Before applying any shadow, make sure your eyelids are completely dry (otherwise the color will not go on smoothly); foundation and/or powder pressed over the lids will also make the shadow adhere and give a smooth look. Tap off surplus color from the brush, and if you make a mistake, simply erase it with a Q-Tip dipped in foundation or moisturizer. Choose any of the neutral or lighter colors from your palette and apply them *on* the lid as a base, *in* the crease and up to and blended into the brow bone. Use the brush or sponge applicator that comes with the shadow or, if you don't like it (some don't apply the shadow evenly or well), treat yourself to a special shadow brush (see page 45 for a list of accessories).

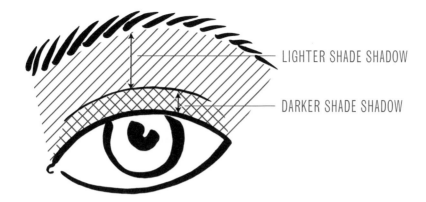

LIGHTER SHADE SHADOW

DARKER SHADE SHADOW

The darker shades from your palette go *next to* the lash line—as close as possible—over the eyelid and up to the crease. I have found that a short, tapered, bristled brush gives more control over the application and also creates a soft pencil effect without tugging at the eyes the way pencil application can.

**TO APPLY EYELINER** I'm as sure of myself with eyeliner as I am with eye shadow: *Never line your eyes all the way around the lash line. Instead, use your pupil as a guide, tapering the line from the inside of the pupil, top and bottom, to the outer corner of the eye. This will make your eyes look bigger, rounder.*

All eyes are enhanced by lining them, and using your pupil as a guide in this way, your eyes will be fully defined, with upper and lower lines meeting at the outside corner of the eye to create a V-shape.

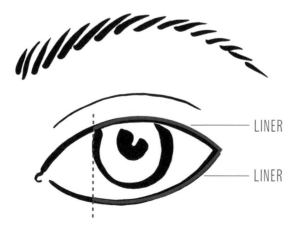

LINER

LINER

Here's how to do it: Choose the darkest colors from your eye-shadow palette to line the eyes. Slightly moisten a short, bristled, tapered eyeliner brush (use the same one you use to apply eye shadow, if you like) and use it with the dark eye shadow or a cake eyeliner. (Moisten only *slightly:* A brush too wet dilutes the color.) Keep your eyes open, look at the mirror as you apply gently in a back-and-forth motion, and create the V-shape by applying the liner close to the lash line, from the inside of the pupil, top and bottom.

**TO APPLY EYEBROW PENCIL** Eye color determines the color of eye shadow, lip color, etc., but *hair* color determines brow color. Your brow color needn't match your hair color exactly, and after a certain age it probably won't, but they should *blend* together well and harmonize. If you begin to color your hair, it's a signal that you may also need to reconsider your brows—brows too dark, much darker than hair color, for example, look unnatural and aging. (See page 65 for how to lighten, pluck and trim brows.)

Brows should always look soft and natural, pencil lines never apparent. Use a pencil only to fill in very lightly. A taupe color works for blondes, brunettes and redheads. A dark brown works for very dark or black hair. Black never works—it always looks like a pencil, never an eyebrow. Apply the pencil lightly, with backward feathering motions, for the most natural look. Then brush brows into place. An alternative to brow pencil is to dip a brow brush into brown eye shadow and brush into your shape.

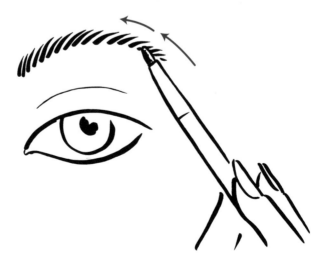

**TO APPLY MASCARA** First look down and apply mascara to the top of the lashes in a downward motion. Then look up, to reapply mascara from underneath. When applying mascara to lower lashes, gently brush the *tip* of the applicator across them. If the lashes clump together, separate carefully with a lash comb or toothpick, or brush again with an old mascara wand, well cleaned of old mascara.

**TO APPLY FALSE EYELASHES** A fun flourish for special evenings, false eyelashes may take a little practice, so don't try it five minutes before leaving for the biggest party of the year. Andrea lashes, available inexpensively at the drugstore, are great. False lashes come in straight lines, whereas our eyes are round, so the lashes have to be cut, both for a natural look and for easy application. Using a cuticle scissor, cut eash lash into small clusters of three or four lashes each. Keep a piece of paper handy to hold the lashes, and a magnifying mirror, which makes the job a whole lot easier. Using a tweezer, dip the base end of the lashes into Duo, the specially formulated lash glue available at the drugstore. With the tweezer, place the lashes as close to the baseline of your own as you can, filling in wherever you want the greatest impact; generally, the mid to outer lashes look fabulous in false lashes. Press gently but firmly with something blunt—the blunt end of an orange stick works well. Repeat with each cluster. Apply mascara either before or after you apply the lashes. To remove, gently pull them off with tweezers.

**TO APPLY LIP COLOR** Lips too glossy look sticky; lips too matte recede. Moist, soft and dewy is the look that's freshest and most natural: surprisingly easy to get wrong, but just as easy to get right.

Stick to the colors in your individual palette, and vary them as much or as little as you like. When in doubt, stay with the naturals in your palette—the neutral lip colors, pinks and roses. Choose the colors you look good in and forget about what you're doing or where you're going; the neutrals can look terrific at night, even for dressy occasions, and bright red can look fine in the daytime. If your blouse or scarf color (the color closest to your lips) is in the pink, red or or-

## HOW TO APPLY LIP COLOR

1. Foundation first, top and bottom. This keeps the color from moving, or bleeding, and also helps the color stay on longer.

2. Gently powder over, top and bottom. This also holds the color and keeps it from bleeding.

3. With a nude-colored lip pencil or lip brush outline the lips, rounding the lip line as you go (see Shaping Your Face, page 33) and paying special attention to the corners.

4. Apply lip balm before applying lip color. (I find the ones without camphor less drying. Elizabeth Arden's eight-hour cream is great, and so is plain old Vaseline decanted into a little purse-sized pot. *Don't apply a balm near the lip line, or the color will bleed.* Apply only in the center of the lips.

5. Fill in with lip color of your choice, and top, if you like, with a little gloss. And that's it.

ange family, check your lip color against it carefully; these are the colors that can clash. Rub a little lipstick on the back of your hand and hold it next to the blouse. If it clashes, you'll see it right away. Choose a neutral in that case instead.

Half the time for simple day wear, I line my lips with a nude-color lip pencil, color them in with the pencil as well (this makes the color *last*), then top with a lip gloss or glaze—a great going-about-your-day look. The point here is that *lining* the lips is just as important or more as coloring them. Lip pencil will give the lips definition and showcase the smile; trapped on a desert island, I'd rather have a lip pencil than a lipstick any day.

The one makeup accessory I find indispensable is a great makeup mirror, with a regular side and a magnifying side. The Chambers catalog (1-800-334-9790) features vanity mirrors in chrome or brass, which help to make application mistake-proof. If you like the sponges and brushes your own makeup comes with, that's all you need. If not, you might want to invest in brushes of your own; the good ones are made of sable or goat, and they last a lifetime.

For good brushes, try better makeup departments in beauty salons, department stores or good drugstores. (I've also found great brushes at artist-supply shops, along with terrific little paint boxes to decant lip colors, foundation and concealer for traveling.) Among my favorite brush outlets: M-A-C at Bendel's; Pigments sold at Ménage à Trois in Beverly Hills, Shu Uemura at Barney's New York City; Il Makiage and The Make Up Center in New York City; Vincent Longo at MCM Salon in New York.

## MAKEUP BRUSHES

❑ *Eyeliner brush:* **The best ones are short, skinny and pointed, and will make a fine line (or a great smudge!) with no trouble at all. If your eyeliner brush isn't making application easy for you, a new one will be a good investment.**

❑ *Flat sponge-tipped shadow applicator:* **Not imperative but a good tool, especially for light colors and when you want to lay down a lot of color—on lid, on brow bone—at once. Such colors as peach, beige, coral and rose take up a lot of space on the eyelid and need to go on** *smoothly.* **A flat sponge tip will help with this.**

❑ *Fluff brush:* **This is a soft, longer-haired flexible brush that "finishes" the eye-shadow appli-**cation by pulling or fluffing all the colors together: a super blending tool. Or, if you're in a hurry, fluff on a neutral nude to medium brown color for a quick bit of definition on the lids; the softness of the bristles lays down a bare trace of color. Add mascara and your eyes are no longer naked.

❑ *Smudge brush:* **A fatter version of the liner brush and much firmer than the fluff, this one is used to smudge and blend darker colors so that you don't end up with owl eyes. I find this very useful.**

*(continued)*

❏ *Concealer brush:* A luxury, definitely not a necessity. I like to use it to blend concealer into my eye socket when I'm too lazy to tap it on with my finger. It's also a great "eraser" for smudges under the eye. The pointed wide brush also substitutes for your finger or a Q-Tip when you dab it into foundation for touching up.

❏ *Powder-blending brush:* This fat, tapered brush is used for dusting on loose powder all over the face after foundation and before you apply eye shadow, blush and lip color. I use mine only when applying makeup for evening. For day, a quick pat of powder with a powder puff (Shiseido makes a good one) over the T-zone (plus lips and eyelids) is all it takes. Wash the powder puff from time to time in liquid soap and a little fabric softener.

❏ *Blush brush:* A smaller version of the powder-blending brush, and totally unnecessary unless you hate the one that comes with your own blush.

❏ *Lip brush:* For applying lipstick like a pro. Flat at the tip, short-haired and firm, this brush transports lip color to the lips much better than a direct swipe from the tube, and also gives you better control of the lip line you want to make. Really great. This can also take the place of a lip pencil if you're in a hurry.

Articles depicting makeup strategies for when we're in our twenties, thirties and forties used to

confuse me a lot, until I grew more confident with makeup—and more comfortable with myself. Should you stop wearing brown eye shadow at forty-five, or red lipstick at fifty? Of course not. Choosing and using makeup is an ongoing process of evaluation and reevaluation. There are some famous actresses out there who still wear heavy blue and green eye shadow, black eyeliner, "reddish" foundation (for the healthy look, do you believe it?) and overly drawn shiny red lips. They're afraid to change the look that made them famous. That look wears *badly.* A woman's makeup should never be the first thing you think of when you think of her. Take Diane Sawyer, Lauren Hutton, Julia Roberts, the Princess of Wales, Diana Ross, to name a few women who look fabulous. Their makeup's great—and it's also the last thing you think of when you picture how they look.

If anything, women who look great go lighter and softer over the years; it's the way we live now. Use makeup to enhance and compensate, not to cover up and obscure. It's a fun subject—makeup—and when you get tired of applying it and seeing your best self emerge, that's perhaps one clue that it's time for a change. Barbara Walters is an example of someone who updates her makeup regularly and always looks great.

Some makeup techniques never change, however, and with a stroke of a brush or a dab of color, you can often work magic on less-than-perfect features or improve those that are great to begin with. These are all concerns that women have asked me about over and over:

**TO MAKE SMALL LIPS LOOK LARGER** Apply a little Vaseline or lip gloss to the middle of the bottom lip, which brings the lips *out,* making them look larger.

**TO MAKE LARGE LIPS LOOK SMALLER** Use the deeper colors in your palette (deep color makes the lips *recede*), and stick to a matte formula; keep away from shiny glosses.

**48**

**TO CREATE THE EFFECT OF MATTE LIPS WITHOUT USING MATTE LIPSTICK, WHICH CAN BE DRYING** Apply regular lipstick and blot with a tissue. While the tissue is still stuck to the lips, sprinkle loose powder over the tissue, then gently pull off. The powder will sift onto lips and adhere when the tissue is removed.

**TO TONE DOWN A TOO DARK, ALREADY PURCHASED BLUSH** Apply blush as usual, then top with face powder; blend together with the blush brush.

**FOR EYES TOO CLOSE TOGETHER** Open up your eyebrows by plucking a few hairs out of the inside corners.

**FOR EYES TOO FAR APART** Bring your brows "in" with a brow pencil to "close" the area just a bit.

**FOR WAYWARD EYEBROWS** Hair spray on a brow brush or an old toothbrush will keep them in place.

**FOR PUFFINESS UNDER THE EYES** Use a concealer one shade darker than your skin tone right on and directly under the swollen or puffy area. Apply your usual concealer (one shade lighter than skin tone) in the corner directly under the eye. The dark shade will make the puffy area recede, and the light/dark contrast will definitely give an optical illusion of less puffiness.

**TO REDUCE THE APPEARANCE OF A LARGE NOSE** Lightly blend a concealer one shade darker than your skin tone onto nostrils only.

**IF YOUR MAKEUP LOOKS WASHED OUT IN THE SUMMER** Bronzing makeup to the rescue. Apply as you do any foundation, blending especially carefully as the bronze will be a different color than your skin. You can also perk up your summer look by turning again to your lip color palette: Pinks, corals, browns, terra-cottas, brown-pinks, brown-reds and brown-corals are great looks for summer.

**IF YOU WEAR GLASSES** Glasses do magnify the eye colors you're wearing. For day, stick to the more natural colors in your palette, and for evening, go all out with color: Your eyes will look *huge*.

**SPECIAL CONCERNS FOR WOMEN OF COLOR** No special concerns, really, if you stick to your palette. Some companies do a better job than others with makeup for women of color. Revlon and Clinique offer good colors. Iman's line is also great—available at Sears and through QVC. Fashion Fair also offers a good selection of foundations, as well as a skin-bleaching product called Vantex, which evens out dark spots and discolorations.

**FOR SMALL LIDS OR ASIAN EYELIDS** Blend dark taupe shadow just *above* and into the natural crease, which will give the illusion of wonderfully deep-set eyes.

**FOR VERY PALE LASHES** If it's too difficult to get the mascara wand into the lash base, fill in lashes with eyeliner. This works especially well for lower lashes.

**FOR SUPER EVENING COVERAGE** To extend coverage, apply foundation once and let dry. Apply a second layer, then brush on loose powder. Let it set while you do your eyes, then brush off excess powder with the brush.

**IF YOUR EYELINER LINE LOOKS TOO HARSH** Apply a light touch of nude, bronze or taupe eye shadow over the liner for a soft, smoky effect rather than harsh, sixties-type definition.

*Dear reader:* Photocopy this page and use it for your personal notes. Experiment with the makeup tips you've learned in this book. Apply color right onto the page. Get aquainted and have fun.

**T**richology is the scientific study of hair, as I quickly learned when I moved back to New York from Los Angeles. After years of exposing my hair to sun, chlorine and blow-drying, I had a serious case of "Los Angeles hair"—damaged and all dried out. I wasn't willing to cut off all the damaged parts, which would have helped, so when someone told me about Philip Kingsley, a hair specialist with clinics in London and New York, I went right away. A bad hair day is one thing, but I was looking at a couple of bad hair *years.*

The questions Kingsley asked were based on my health habits and lifestyle, which brought home to me the fact that how we take care of ourselves shows in our hair, as well as everywhere else. (See page 199 for a nutritional supplement you can take for your hair.) Then he did a hair analysis under a magnifying glass, and from that formulated a custom-made shampoo and weekly and monthly conditioners, which made a big difference immediately. I went for scalp massage and heat-lamp treatments every month or so in the beginning, then every two or three months, until totally healthy hair grew in. I've been taking good care of my hair ever since. There has been so much written about hair care, but what I've included here is information on how to cut through the confusion—how to keep it *simple.*

What I learned from Kingsley, finally, is that hair care is not unlike skin care (think of trichology as an extension of dermatology)—it's basic, and in order to work, it has to become routine and be consistent. With hair, it's a matter of cleaning and nourishing; special care for special needs (coloring, perms, conditioning); a *great cut;* and a style you can learn to handle.

We all know how important hair is. It frames the face. It's our most noticeable feminine feature. If a woman's hair looks great, she *feels* great; on the other hand, very little ever goes right on a bad hair day.

Luckily, this is a great era for hair. Ease in hair care is what we're all looking for, and it's available—great shampoos and conditioners; easy-on-the-hair products for color, control and shine; sophisticated stylists well trained to cut styles that *move*. It's your hair, your choice and your individual look—but the principles that will help you find the look are the same for everyone.

### CHOOSING THE STYLE

Conventional wisdom has the shape of the face dictating hairstyle. An oval face can supposedly wear any style; a triangular one requires volume around the chin to "fill in" the triangle; an angular face, square or rectangular, will have its angles softened with curls; a long face will look fuller with layers around the face; and a round face can give the illusion of angles with short hair with or without bangs. But the overall look is more important than the shape of the face. A high forehead doesn't necessarily require bangs; a round face *can* wear hair pulled back; women past "a certain age" won't always look better with their hair cut short. Over the years I've read and observed all the so-called "hair rules" and then watched some of the most stunning women I know break them all and look fabulous.

How? By "restyling" the rules for the way we want to look now. Things to remember:

❑ *It's not the shape of the face that counts, but the size of the face. Proportion is the key.* This one's simple. Too much hair surrounding a small face can be overwhelming. You can wear long hair, but keep it close to the head and neat. Fill out a very narrow face by choosing a style with fullness on the sides. A larger face can carry "bigger" hair, but downplay volume on the sides to reduce the fullness of a very round or very square face.

❑ *Your neck and shoulders support the style: Consider the contours.* Don't rely on your makeup mirror to assess your style; for this you need a full-length, two-way mirror, to see whether the look "fits" the rest of you—your neck, your shoulders. In general, if your shoulders are wide, shoulder-length or longer hair balances and melds into the width. Huge curly hair can overpower narrow shoulders. A long neck is great, and can take any type of hairstyle. A shorter neck usually looks better with short hair or longer hair pulled back. This is not to say you can never have long hair; just be sensitive to the mirror—front and back—when deciding.

❑ *Work with your texture, not against it.* The choice of style also depends on texture; you'll have a much easier time if you choose a style that lets hair do what it wants to *naturally.*

As a rule, *fine hair* has an overall appearance of softness, which can be very feminine and appealing. It should be layered slightly, even if the final look is to be blunt; this will give an appearance of thicker hair, whether it's long or short. A soft body wave adds fullness, and hair coloring also gives fine hair more body and makes it look thicker. Try thickening shampoos from your favorite brand. Aveda's Volumizing Tonic or Rene Furterer RF80 hair treatment is good, too.

*Coarse hair,* where each strand is thick, is usually thick itself and has an overall heavy look: hair that makes a statement. It can have a mind of its own, and even stick out in spots. Here, cut is everything, and a cut that shapes the face will also help to control the hair. Even if you're after the look of a blunt cut, a very subtle layering will encourage the hair to "lie down" where it's supposed to. Coloring will soften the texture by filling in and smoothing out the cuticle.

*Straight hair* can be thick or thin, and when in perfect, shiny condition, gives the impression of a shimmering *sheet* of hair. A straight, blunt cut to the length you decide is best. For movement, look into a body wave. Curlers will help to add height, and you can also get soft curls—more body—with pin-curl clips, bobby pins or by sleeping on sponge rollers.

*Curly hair* is perhaps the most versatile. You can blow-dry it straight, use rollers of various sizes to adjust the natural curl—or let it go soft and curly on its own. As for the cut, blunt or soft layers work equally well.

❑ *Lifestyle affects hairstyle.* Such movie stars as Goldie Hawn, Sharon Stone and Julia Roberts go for a sexy just-out-of-bed look, a look, by the way, that takes hours and many visits to the hairdresser to keep up. They're actresses, and the look is a dramatic expression of what they do. But would Diana Ross's beautiful long tresses work for her if she were a banker? Probably not. Would Jackie Kennedy have been such a graceful First Lady with a Farah Fawcett haircut? Definitely not. Would Diane Sawyer choose a pixie for national TV? No. When choosing a style, the questions to ask yourself are: Who am I? Where will I be "wearing" my hair? Who's going to see it? Common sense will probably tell you to stick with a simple, easy-to-maintain style whatever length you choose, and save the flourishes for evening.

❑ *The long and short of it.* Contrary to what many people believe—and what some women who cut their hair short without thinking it through come to know all too well—very short hair is not always the easiest solution, and is often not the most flattering. Just cutting it all off into a no-style cut does nothing to flatter anyone. Hair needs *styling*, not just cutting, and short hair requires spiking on top for height, or bangs for softness, and careful maintenance; it also has to be cut every four to six weeks to keep the style intact. Very short hair also shows facial lines and wrinkles more. On the other hand, hair below shoulder length generally has a tendency to drag a woman's face down as she gets older. For most of us, in between—a little shorter here, a little longer there—works best. How to tell *before* making a fateful mistake?

## CHOOSING THE STYLIST

One way to find a great stylist is to ask a woman whose hair texture is similar to yours and whose cut is terrific whom she goes to to have her hair done: the ultimate compliment, and women do it all the time. Having been the victim of several terrible cuts (the last one, a "stepladder" disaster, took nine months to grow out), now I know to interview three stylists when choosing a new one. There's no charge for a consultation visit, and no reason to be intimidated: You're the client. If you feel intimidated, try someone else.

When interviewing the stylist, go dressed and made up so that he or she can see the image you project—the image you want your hair to enhance, not detract from. During the consultation, ask questions (How would he or she style my hair, given its texture? How will I maintain the style between cuts?) and also listen to what the stylist has to say. Good stylists will usually ask *you* questions, too, about your lifestyle and maintenance needs.

At your appointment, tell the stylist, "Please, *no* surprises." Agree beforehand on *exactly* the length you want (hold your finger to the spot) and watch carefully, at least the first time or two, while it's being cut.

If the stylist makes you wait at your first visit (some tend to overbook), call first the next time; if he or she is running behind, you can save time by going later.

❑ *Test before going longer or shorter.* Try wigs before taking any big step— cutting short, growing long, coloring—and use a full-length mirror to analyze the prospective new look from every angle. This is the only way to judge the proper proportion of your hair to your individual shape. Another way to "test" a style is to visit one of the Styles on Video salons nationwide (1-800-995-0352). Their video-image system allows you to superimpose your face on six hundred different hair styles for about forty dollars. Also, you might want to go shorter—or longer—a few inches at a time. If the new look works, go for it—but only with absolutely the best stylist you can find.

## CHOOSING THE COLOR

A woman can color her hair anytime, of course, but when you begin to go gray is the time to *really* decide. Some women confidently choose to go gray, and that's fine (see page 66 for tips on caring for gray hair), but too many women, confused, perhaps, by so many color options, simply do nothing, let the gray take its inevitable course and then feel it's too late. One woman I know, for example, just "didn't get around" to doing anything about her gray, and then hated the way she looked when she was "suddenly" gray all over (it actually took several years). When she and her husband decided to move to Santa Fe, she saw her opportunity, went light brown on moving day and has felt better—and looked younger—ever since.

Coloring does take off years, and also can add volume and shine as well as improve the texture of the hair. (Shafts of hair gone gray grow in coarser.) In general, the lighter your skin tone, the lighter you can go; even one or two shades lighter as you get older will give you a big lift. *Eye color goes with any hair color, so it's skin tone you want to pay attention to.* In fact, the contrasts of blue eyes against black hair or brown eyes against blond hair are very attractive. Consider, too, your natural color. Medium-brown hair always "converts" well to ash brown, which itself can take blond highlights. Dark brown beginning to fade or go gray will look great "translated" to auburn or medium brown. If you go blond, it should never be one solid color blond, because natural blond hair never is. If you're over the age of twenty-five, it's best, too, to keep away from white-blond shades; they can look lovely, but they often "read" more gray-white than the white-blond you had in mind. Highlights, which last about two months, are attractive and give a natural look with both blond and brown shades. Thin highlighting streaks are sometimes known as weaving. The best way to start changing your hair color is gradually: lighter, darker or redder by stages—by increments.

*When you change your hair color, be sure to adjust the color of your eyebrows as well. This is very important and often overlooked.* (See page 42.)

Sometimes hairstylists also do a good job with color; colorists specialize in color alone. If you're going to have your color done professionally, ask your stylist and discuss at length what you want—less is always more, at least at first: a few highlights to start, a shade or two lighter or darker. Once you've colored, always be sure to ask for a copy of your formula, in case you need it while traveling or if the colorist isn't available the next time your roots need attention.

If you decide to color your own hair at home, spend some time at the hair-color aisle in the drugstore. Among the better drugstore brands are L'Oréal, Clairol and Revlon—they have great instructions and toll-free phone numbers to call if you have a question. The color charts are excellent, and they'll show you the shades that will revitalize your own color: Dark brown goes with dark red or light brown, for instance; medium brown goes with medium red or a very dark blond. Stick close to your natural shade, in other words.

There are many *kinds* of products to choose from as well:

- ❑ If the label reads *temporary,* the product is more of an enhancing shampoo to enrich your own color. Results will last a single washing only.

- ❑ *Semipermanent,* which lasts about a month, is a color lift to enrich your own color and add body; it won't cover all the gray and it won't lighten—but it will give drab hair a vitality boost.

## HAIRCOLORING TIPS

- ❑ When *covering gray* is the goal, try Miss Clairol's shampoo-in formula, L'Oréal's Excellence Creme Colorant or Colorsilk by Revlon. For touch-ups, apply *only* to the roots. Otherwise, your hair will get too dark with what's called color buildup.

- ❑ Permed or straightened hair has already been chemically treated, and so should be treated only with a *single-process hair color;* temporary color or highlighting is the safest bet, or try one of the new perm solutions that offer semipermanent color with the neutralizing step.

- ❑ If your hair is very long or very thick, buy *two coloring kits at a time,* in case you need a backup.

- ❑ *Start with the roots,* working down to the ends of the hair. The ends are porous, and need only about two minutes to absorb color before washing when doing a touch-up. For the first application, leave on for the minimum amount of time suggested on the box.

❑ A subcategory of semipermanent is *demipermanent,* which lasts a couple of weeks longer and fades gradually, without leaving a clear root demarcation. These products (Revlon Shadings is a good one) can lighten a bit better than semipermanent, but they won't cover all the gray.

❑ *Permanent* colors are just that: They last until the roots grow out. They'll lighten, darken, cover gray and change the color *entirely,* and they work by removing your own color and replacing it with the shade you've chosen. This can be hard on the hair, so never use permanent color yourself if your hair is permed or straightened.

When applying color at home, just follow the directions. Highlighting, which requires that you wrap foil around *skinny* strands of hair on top of your head and around your face, is tough to do yourself, so practice separating and wrapping the strands before you actually use the color.

## ROUTINE HAIR CARE

In the same way that natural light is best for applying makeup, it's also the best light in which to scrutinize your hair, front and back, every day—to check its condition or to see if you have split ends, faded color or roots showing (disaster!). Other than that, daily hair care consists of very little: touch-up styling every morning as needed, and brushing morning and night to stimulate follicles, encourage growth and remove dry skin—basically an exfoliating treatment. The one hundred daily strokes of legend aren't obligatory; just brush enough so that you feel the stimulation.

Washing your hair every day is unnecessary and time-consuming unless you have very oily hair; you be the judge. Bangs can be done daily. Blow-drying your hair every day can be very drying. Most of us need to wash our hair only every three to five days—diesel fuel in big cities notwithstanding—and only when it begins to stop looking and feeling fresh. Brush your hair before washing it; any tangles are easier to remove when dry. Apply shampoo once if the hair is not too dirty, twice if it's dirty, then rinse a *lot* for the final rinse, making sure that there's no shampoo left at all. One tip is to concentrate the shampoo onto the scalp and roots, not the tips of the hair, which can dry out. (Enough will wash down to the tips to reach them when you rinse.)

For years I've heard about shampoo buildup and how you should switch shampoos from time to time to strip the residual shampoo from the hair shafts, and I don't find this true *at all*. I find instead that the more I use products I like, the better my hair is. My own theory is that the shampoo residue may be protective, to keep hair in good condition. Stripping the residue may, in fact, also strip essential oils—like overcleaning the skin. The only time to switch is when you're ready to try something new. (And if that new shampoo doesn't work, use it to wash lingerie.)

*Alcohol-free* is an important criterion for choosing hair products, because alcohol dries. As with skin care, rich emollient formulas will show instant results; panthenol, a vitamin E extract, is great in any hair product. Look, too, for botanical ingredients—plant extracts and pectin (found in roots and stems). Rene Furterer's line of hair products, available in some department stores and better drugstores, are fabulous and offer a good breakdown of state-of-the-hair options: dry hair and scalp; oily scalp; flaking scalp; permed hair. Nexus, Paul Mitchell, Klorane, Aveda and Sebastian are also good drugstore brands. For children, Johnson & Johnson makes a great baby shampoo.

If shampoo should be concentrated *on* the roots, creme rinse and conditioner, which "soften" and smooth the hair (and thereby reduce body), should be concentrated *away* from the roots—on the shafts and ends of the hair. One or the other should be used to protect the hair after every shampoo. Creme rinses detangle and provide a light conditioner, adding suppleness and shine. Conditioners are more concentrated and penetrating; they relax the hair, restoring health and adding nourishment and shine. Then do a final rinse in cold water to close the hair cuticle and stimulate scalp circulation.

## A TIP FOR SHINY HAIR

If you happen to have any leftover champagne lying around, a champagne rinse will add shine and sparkle. So will a white-vinegar rinse—one quarter of a cup of vinegar mixed with three quarters of a cup of water: Pour it on, then rinse off. This is also good for dandruff. If tangling is a problem, Rene Furterer and Clairol both make good detanglers.

Combs are for styling, detangling and maneuvers requiring control—making parts, inserting rollers, folding curls, teasing. To detangle when wet, use a very wide-tooth hard-rubber comb (never metal, which breaks the hair). Brushing revives, fluffs, adds volume. Mason & Pearson makes a wonderful natural-bristle flat brush set on a rubber bed—works great and lasts for years. (For brushes for blow-drying, see below.) Clean brushes and combs regularly with liquid soap, or take them into the shower with you and wash with shampoo.

### ROUTINE STYLING

Mousses, hair sprays and styling gels, which come in light or strong hold, are applied after styling to give body and hold the curl or line; which ones you use is a matter of preference, but look for *alcohol-free* on the label. Setting lotions are applied before styling. Products called volumizers, applied before styling, add *fullness* and are great for thin hair. I love a full, coated feel when my hair is styled. Some women don't mind a little stickiness. Whatever works. Your styling cues come from the cut and the stylist; watch carefully and ask questions to learn what the stylist does to create the style.

**TO BLOW DRY** A 1,400- to 1,600-watt handheld blow dryer with hot and cool settings—Conair makes good ones—is practically essential. If you use rollers or pin curls, a hood attachment, which also frees your hands while the dryer dries,

is a helpful extra, as is a diffuser (you've seen your stylist use one), which is used to maintain curls and, because it spreads the air with a lot less force, is not as harsh and drying to chemically treated hair. The cords on blow dryers are always maddeningly short, so I attach an extension cord to every one, including my travel dryer.

Start by bending your head over and, brushing with a huge, flat wide-tooth brush, blow-dry until hair is 80 percent dry. From there, use a big, fat round brush (the longer the hair, the fatter the brush and the bigger the curl) with natural or nylon bristles to dry fully and style. An alternate way is to get the hair 80 percent dry, put in Velcro rollers, then either run the blow-dryer over to dry or let it dry naturally.

**VELCRO ROLLERS** One of the great recent inventions! Roll dry or damp hair spritzed lightly with hair spray or volumizer onto rollers. Make sure ends of hair are smoothly and evenly pressed onto each roller—otherwise they will be frizzy. A hair-dryer bonnet (available at better drugstores) will dry it the fastest, or you can run the blow dryer over it or let it dry naturally. Use a blast of cool air from the blow dryer before removing rollers to set the curl.

**HOT ROLLERS** Another classic that endures. The newest ones are steam rollers, and heat up with water. They're excellent for straight hair, kinder to permed or chemically treated hair, but terrible for wavy or curly hair because they take the "blow-dry set" out of wavy hair. Again, a blast of cool air before removing the rollers will help set the curl. Ask your stylist which kind is best for your hair. If you have split ends, use end papers, available at drugstores, before rolling.

**CURLING IRONS** Available in small or larger sizes that determine ultimate curl size, they are good for spot curling, but pay attention—they can burn.

## 62

**WRAPPING** For long, curly hair only, this was very popular years ago, and still works well to straighten without taking away body. When the hair is completely wet, comb through a good setting lotion, put two big Velcro rollers on top of your head and anchor with clips. Comb the rest of the hair smoothly around the head, right to left, with a medium comb. Keep combing and smoothing until hair is completely wrapped and flat around the head. Hair must be completely smooth for this to work. Anchor the ends with flat clips (these won't leave a mark). Sit under a salon-type dryer to dry it, or use a hood attachment.

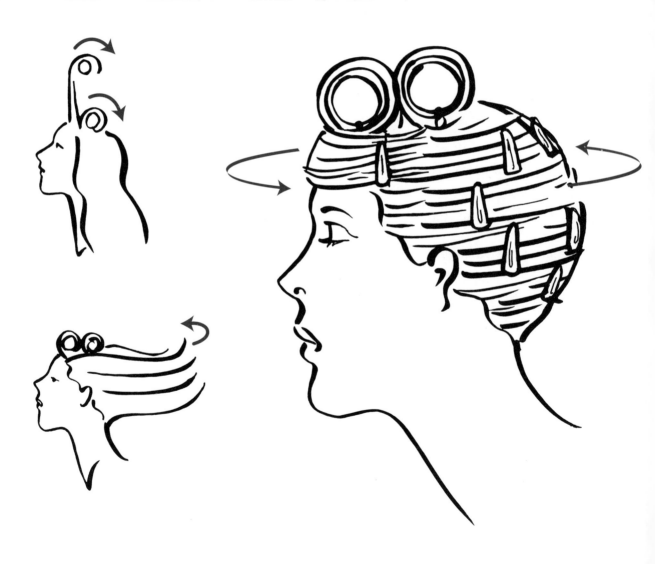

As we all know, sleeping can do some very odd things to your hair, all of which need to be undone come morning. To prevent them, or to style your hair as you sleep, consider these options on nights when you can. You'll get a good night's sleep—none of these is uncomfortable—and wake up with your style all ready to go.

**TO STRAIGHTEN AND SMOOTH OUT WAVY HAIR** Wrap your hair as described above, cover with a triangular hair net and "sleep" it dry overnight.

**TO GIVE STRAIGHT HAIR BODY** Draw your hair up into a loose ponytail on the top of your head. By morning, the hair will have "lifted" on the front and sides; to hold the lift, apply a little gel.

**FOR SOFT CURLS** The Cybill Shepherd or Cindy Crawford look. Using bobby pins or, even better, pin-curl clips, which are flat and don't mark the hair, shape even-sized clumps of wet or dry hair (sides and bottom only, not hair on top) into pin-curl shapes, clip into place and go to sleep. For extra staying power, comb a gel or setting lotion through the hair, wet or dry, before making the pin curls.

**FOR A CRIMPED EFFECT** Divide the hair into six to eight even-sized clumps, braid each (tighter or looser braids for tighter or looser crimps) and go to sleep. Or you can crimp with pin curls, by twirling the strands of hair before making the pin curls.

**FOR HEIGHT** Sleep with two or three Velcro rollers on top of your head.

**FOR TIGHT CURLS** Several good new products enable curling and sleeping at the same time. Benders are like pipe cleaners, but come in fabric with a wire inside for twisting—you roll dry hair around them (more or less hair for looser or tighter curls), then pull the ends together. Ray's Beauty Supply (721 Eighth Avenue, New York, New York 10036, 1-212-757-0175) carries them, and there's a red-rubber version increasingly available in better drugstores. Another new product, called Soft Hair Curlers, works the same way.

**FOR DEEP CONDITIONING TREATMENT OVERNIGHT** Slather on a penetrating conditioner, cover with a shower cap—and go to sleep. Hair feels terrific by morning. If your hair is long, pile it on top of your head with a big barrette. The shower cap won't fall off (I did this for years in Los Angeles when my hair was sizzled), but for security, wrap your pillow in a bath towel.

## SPECIAL HAIR CARE

It's when you don't know what works for your hair and what doesn't that taking care of your hair feels like constant work. By simplifying basic hair-care rituals to those described above—and paying attention to the special hair-care strategies described below—the process is one, two, three, and your hair will look better than ever before.

**CONDITIONING** All important! The best cut and most beautiful color will look terrible if your hair isn't in good condition. Hot olive-oil treatments benefit any kind of hair, particularly hair that's dry, damaged or chemically treated. Warm the oil, apply to your head and massage into your hair. Cover with a shower cap, then wrap around with a hot, wet, wrung-out towel. Or wear a Ladyworks deep-heat conditioning cap (1-800-428-8977), which heats with microwaves. Leave conditioner on for at least twenty minutes, then wash well twice. Alberto VO5 conditioning hair dressing is also good when used as a treatment with a hot towel. Hi-Pro-Pac is another good beauty-supply brand. As a general rule, coarse hair needs more conditioning; limp hair, less. But everyone benefits from this treatment—once a week, if possible, or as often as you can.

**HENNA** Extracted from natural vegetable dyes such as walnut oil, henna adds life and reddish tones to dark hair, although it doesn't show on blond hair and doesn't conceal gray. Lots of women use it as a "bridge" when their hair starts to fade and before they begin to use color. It's kind to the hair—no chemicals—and also acts as a conditioner. (Don't use it if you color your hair.) Following package directions, you wash it in with your shampoo. It's great for teenagers.

**PERMS** Half the confusion over perms is in the language: What's a perm? What's a body wave? A body wave is softer than yesterday's kinky perm, and is available in herbal formulas, formulas that add semipermanent color as well and "reverse perms," which relax the hair, making it look straighter. Perms can give a great lift to limp hair, but the procedure is still harsh, and permed (or straightened) hair always needs extra conditioning. Always try a test curl before doing the whole head. If you're trying it at home, remember that bigger rods give the softest curls. Lilt, Toni and Ogilvie make reputable at-home kits; have a friend help you if you can. Personally, I'd feel safest going to a professional.

**EYEBROWS** Brows are very independent and don't always grow back the way they were, so overplucking can result in a permanent mistake. Groom them first. Using a brow brush or a toothbrush, comb them straight up and down, snipping irregular points with a cuticle scissor. Then brush into place. If they're unruly, Max Factor's brow tamer (or a little hair spray sprayed onto a toothbrush) will set them. If they still need plucking, first apply concealer or foundation over the hairs you're planning to pluck, to see if you'll miss them.

*Whether or not you color your hair, lightening your eyebrows two or three shades lighter than your hair color softens the face, making it look younger and prettier.* If you've gone blond, this is not to say that you want blond brows, too—just lighter brows, to soften the contrast. *Even if your hair is black, brows should be a couple of shades lighter.* To do this at home, apply Jolen cream bleach for a few seconds only. Or have your hair colorist "lift" your brows (or color them, if they've gone gray) as well. Stylists don't necessarily do this routinely; sometimes you have to ask for it.

## SUN CARE

Like skin, hair needs protection in the sun, which dries and fades the color. Wearing a hat is always a good idea, and sun oils and mousses, which offer good SPF protection, are terrific. The oils give a slick, wet look, and the mousses can be blown dry. One great sun look is simply slicking the hair back with sun oil into a ponytail, and then making a braid. Rene Furterer makes a good oil and mousse, and Phyto oil and jelly are also excellent. Always rinse hair right away after swimming.

GOING GRAY "NATURALLY" If you decide to go gray—or stay gray—a lovely mane of silver can be beautiful, but a coarse mop of gray is *not*. Gray or graying hair has to be treated thoughtfully. To prevent yellowing (a big problem with going gray) use a violet-toned shampoo; Clairol's Shimmer Lights is a good one. A good antiyellow rinse is So Silver by Matrix. Other concerns are the coarser texture of gray and lack of shine. Sebastian makes a product called Laminates that smooths and protects.

A process called low-lighting (opposite of highlighting), which is a coloring process, is especially good for women whose salt-and-pepper hair is turning all to salt! It draws out and enhances the natural color while weaving it in with the gray—and improves the texture at the same time. This has to be repeated every four to six weeks.

**TROUBLESHOOTING** I remember shooting a commercial once in my living room in Los Angeles. It was a very humid day, but the air conditioner was making too much noise, so the director turned it off and opened the windows. My hair style changed right on camera! Weather, sleeping the wrong way, not having time to wash the hair or fix the kinks that occurred overnight or just bad luck can cause a bad hair day, and a bad hair day can cause a bad day, period.

Braids, ponytails, headbands and so on are pretty in themselves and can help camouflage a bad hair day if your hair is long enough. As for other accessories (see pages 140–145), hats are always stylish—and exude a sense of confidence. Scarves, too, are a great accessory, and you can weave them into all hairstyles, except those that are very short. Barrettes are great, but have to be considered as part of your *jewelry* attire as well as a hair pick-me-up. Here are a few other quick fixes:

**ROOTS SHOWING** The worst! In between touch-ups, Roux's Fanci-Ful color rinse works as a color "Band-Aid" on roots. It comes in lots of colors and does the job instantly. Apply it by pressing on dry hair with cotton, then blow-dry. One bottle lasts for years, and I always decant the original bottle to keep a small one in my travel bag. Another product that works is called Touch-Up. You put it on like mascara, and it's available at better drugstores.

**BAD BANGS DAY** Bangs always grow out before the rest of the hair needs cutting. If you have time, stop in and see your stylist; most will trim the bangs right there, and for free. Otherwise, cut your own, using a good hair scissor from a beauty-supply or cutlery store. (Drugstore hair scissors aren't sharp enough.) Cut bangs when they're wet, one inch longer than you want them to be; they'll shorten when they dry.

**SPLIT ENDS** This is the signal that you need a trim, but until you can schedule it, dabbing a little almond oil on damp ends of the hair before styling will help.

**HAIR STATIC** Dry weather, in particular, can make hair crackle with electricity. Spraying hair spray on your hairbrush before brushing helps to control flyaway hair.

**COWLICK** First try blow-drying *against* the cowlick, in the opposite direction. If that doesn't work, ask your hairdresser to apply a perm solution to the root, which will keep it in check.

**HUMIDITY HELP** To help prevent curly hair from frizzing (or just-curled hair from falling), wear a heavy silk scarf knotted under the chin, Jackie-O style, when going out. It's a classic that really looks great.

**FRIZZY HAIR** Sebastian Laminates makes a product called Silicone Serum, which, mixed with a little silicone-based gel, cuts down on frizziness dramatically. Rub the gel into your hair, concentrating on the middle to ends. Once the product is distributed in the hair, take a strand at a time and twirl it around your finger, then let go. Do this all over your head and let it dry naturally, or use the diffuser attachment on your blow dryer. *Don't* comb, tease, spray or fuss with it. Instead, take more gel, rub into the palms of your hands and shape the hair the way you want it. This will give you pretty curls instead of wild frizz.

**BABY-FINE HAIR, THINNING HAIR OR BALD SPOTS** Human hair extensions, available in twelve shades, are available to add length, thickness and volume. They're called Secret Hair, and they're created by successful hairdresser Jose Eber (1-800-832-5300).

**UNWANTED HAIR** Tried-and-true Nair, a depilatory, is less expensive and less painful than waxing, and looks better than bleaching for unwanted hair over lips and on arms. Stray hairs on breasts should be cut with cuticle scissors. To remove hair in the bikini area, apply creme rinse, then shave carefully with a disposable razor. Use razors as well for legs and hair under the arms. Electrolysis is another method used to remove hair, *usually* permanent but not always. It's painful, time-consuming and expensive. It's done by placing a needle into the hair shaft down to the root, then emitting a mild electrical current through the needle. A newer method is called G-H-R: guaranteed hair removal. G-H-R doesn't use a needle but sends the current through an insulated tweezer into the hair shaft, causing a chemical reaction that halts the production of new hair. After any hair-removal process, apply any over-the-counter cortisone cream to soothe any irritation. (Call Faces in Los Angeles, at 1-213-852-1166, for more information.) Unless you have very coarse facial or breast hair, I prefer dipilatories or bleaching.

**DANDRUFF** Head & Shoulders has been around for years, and is still great for dandruff. Tar, sulfur, selenium or salicylic acid are ingredients to look for in a dandruff shampoo. If the condition persists beyond a few washings, see a dermatologist.

**HAIR LOSS** Pregnancy, stress, hormone changes and genetic predisposition can cause hair loss in women. Rogaine, the product advertised to treat baldness in men, works for women as well. Minoxidil is the ingredient that does it, and your dermatologist has to prescribe it. For more information, call Rogaine, at 1-800-647-9595.

**W**hen I was starting my makeup line, my chemists saw a small "ingredients revolution" coming in nail care—possibly the first since Charles Revson launched his vast empire with Revlon nail polish, testing the colors on his own nails. I hadn't decided whether to do nail colors myself, especially given the good brands and colors already available, but they convinced me.

Formaldehyde and toluene are the ingredients traditionally used in nail polishes to make the nail harder and prevent splitting and breaking, but reports that they cause birth defects have caused them to be banned in California; the rest of the country is following suit. As with the latest skin care and makeup, the newest formulas my chemists were talking about concentrate on *nourishing* the nail as well as covering it with color. I use calcium and protein to treat nails along with coloring them. Other nourishing ingredients to look for are aloe vera and vitamin E, which is sometimes used in a base coat to nourish the nail and provide more flexibility.

Flexibility is the key to preventing chips, and a good base coat—not the brand of nail enamel—is essential not only to ensure adhesion but also to prevent chipping. If the base coat isn't flexible enough, the nail will be too rigid to hold the polish: *It's not the polish that chips; the nail itself chips when it hits a hard surface.*

As for color, if you want your manicure to last a week, give or take, be very careful with color: A tone tinted too blue or too orange is likely to clash with at least something you'll be wearing during that week, and nail color is most noticeable when it

# NAILS

clashes. The easiest manicures to carry are those you don't have to think about. Long nails are out. Short and well manicured is the look that's healthiest for nails, and the most versatile, embellished in any of the following ways:

**NAIL BUFFING** This is the method used to create a natural shine. A little buffing cream—Revlon and Sally Hansen make good ones—is applied to each clean, dry nail. Then a buffer, which is long, narrow and covered in a natural chamois cloth, available at beauty-supply shops—or order a Buffing Bar from Garden Botanika, 1-800-968-7842—buffs each nail back and forth, about fifteen times per nail. This treatment lasts from a few days to a week, but longer when used weekly and the shine builds up.

**CLEAR, NATURAL ENAMEL** A great, classic look.

**LIGHT, NUDE-COLORED OR PINK ENAMEL** To create a neutral palette that goes with everything.

**CLEAR RED ENAMEL** Makes a statement that's very European—a great look on short nails.

**FRENCH MANICURE** Clear or see-through pink nails with a wet white nail pencil (Sally Hansen, Revlon and Nails Again make good ones) brushed underneath the nail all the way to the skin line. French-manicure kits come prepackaged at drugstores with the pale pink and white polishes and instructions. Very clean-looking.

## ROUTINE CARE FOR NAILS/HANDS/FEET

Some routine hand and nail care is *defensive,* to protect the nails against the abuse of daily living. Always wear rubber gloves when washing dishes, for instance, and work gloves for housework and gardening. Pop-top cans can damage or split the nails—better to use a knife. In the same way, using your nails to slice open envelopes can split them; use a letter opener instead.

Nails and cuticles need moisturizing protection the same way skin does— every day. Rub moisturizer over nails when using it on your hands. To soften cuticles and prevent them from splitting, rub almond oil, Vaseline or a cuticle massage cream into them every night. Revlon and Nails Again make good cuticle creams; Nails Again products are available through QVC or by calling 1-800-755-5009. Even rubbing in hand cream while pushing back your cuticles whenever you moisturize your hands is good. Soap and a natural-bristle or stiff nylon nail brush is still the best way to clean under nails. (There's nothing worse than dirty fingernails.)

Apart from regular pedicures (see below), a little special care can prevent foot troubles. I know; I learned these lessons standing on my feet hour after hour in my retail store. Dr. Scholl's foot balm, massaged into the balls and arches of the feet, soothes tired, aching feet as promised, and orthotic shoe inlays (custom-ordered from a podiatrist or Eneslow in New York, 1-212-477-2300; they cost about three hundred and fifty dollars) are well worth the investment if you work on your feet for many hours or walk a lot. Bio-Fit Arch Supports, at thirty dollars, are also good inner soles for shoe comfort. They're available from the Self-Care catalog (1-800-345-3371). If you see signs of cracking between your toes, which suggests the beginning of a fungus, apply Desenex (and always make sure to dry carefully between the toes); cracked heels call for a dose of Vaseline or Crisco and socks at bedtime. A large, flat nail file, together with a good foot exfoliator such as Pedi Scrub when bathing, is a good way to keep feet smooth. Cut toenails straight across just *before* your shower or bath, when nails are rigid; they cut better then. Keeping toenails short helps to prevent ingrown toenails, not to mention torn hose.

Nails reflect overall health, and ridges, white spots and excessive splitting are among the signs that something is out of balance. A supplemental diet for nails (see page 199) may be all you need, but see your doctor if the condition persists.

The rise of neighborhood manicurists/pedicurists in most cities makes a former luxury affordable: Now most of us can get a professional manicure or pedicure for about ten dollars, give or take. Most manicurists are reputable—and you can avoid mistakes in choosing nail color; they'll let you test. In some states, New York for one, customers are required by law to bring their own manicure kits for health reasons. Tweezerman (1-800-874-9898) sells a complete assortment of professional nail and grooming implements, and they'll also sharpen tools you already own.

Even if you decide that you prefer to do a manicure yourself, it's a good idea to have it done once professionally, just to see how it's done step-by-step. Treat your teenager, too, to a good manicure so that she can learn as well, with or without polish. (Nail buffing is a great look for teens.) One woman I know, in despair over her daughter's nail biting, treated her to a manicure. Her nails looked so much better, even stubby and bitten as they were, and she was pleased enough with the results that she stopped biting her nails on her own.

Even if you get a professional manicure and/or pedicure every week or so, it's useful to know how to do it yourself, in case you need to when traveling or for whatever reason. The at-home manicure will take ten minutes without polish, fifteen minutes *with* polish.

Good polish or enamel (they're the same thing) should last six to eight months. The more they're exposed to heat and air, the more they thicken and become useless. The best way to store them is in the refrigerator. For polish to work, it has to be the same consistency as when you

## CHECKLIST FOR A SAFE MANICURE

If you're relying on the manicurists' equipment, make sure they sterilize their utensils between clients with an ultraviolet heat sterilizer and a wet sanitizer containing Barbacide liquid or Ultronics. Emery boards and lotion cups should be disposed of after each client, and other equipment should be disinfected in the following way:

❑ *Washed* in clean, soapy water.

❑ *Rinsed* in clean water.

❑ *Dried*. (This is important so that the disinfectant solution doesn't get diluted with water.)

❑ *Soaked* for ten minutes in the disinfectant.

❑ *Dried* before next use.

Be sure, too, that the manicurist isn't overzealous in trimming cuticles, which should be clipped at an absolute *minimum*.

bought it. Nail-polish thinners don't work and are a waste of money. Diluting with polish remover doesn't work either, because it results in a "thinner," lighter shade. Remover is meant to remove the polish, then is washed off, so it's not good for nails when mixed with polish and left on all week—it weakens nails. As for colors, there are more nuances of color available than any woman needs, and new promotions all the time to bring in new business. As with lip colors—which, by the way, haven't had to match nail colors for *years*—choosing nail colors without testing is a risk. Experiment with special colors for special occasions or outfits, but a go-with-everything red, pink or nude-tone neutral is best for all-around use.

The steps are the same for nails of both fingers and toes—and you can get away with doing a full pedicure a little less often than a manicure; you'll be able to tell when you need it.

**BROKEN NAILS** Sally Hansen's nail glue, available at any drugstore, will save your nails. File down after using until the repair matches your own nail.

## TROUBLESHOOTING

**FAKE NAILS** Even if your own nails are in bad shape, keep away from fake nails, which won't help a bit. Fake nails cover the natural nail bed and inhibit the growth of nails by suffocating them. They also take two or three months to grow out, which leaves an unattractive line of demarcation between the real and the fake.

**WRAPPING** Another bad idea. Wrapped nails usually look lumpy, and require that the glue be applied directly to the nail, which is bad for the nail bed.

**TO MAKE SHORT, PUDGY FINGERS LOOK LONGER** A trick I learned to help with my own short, pudgy fingers: Apply polish down the center of the nail, leaving a slight margin on each side. This creates the optical illusion of elongation.

# TIPS FOR AT-HOME MANICURE

The steps for an at-home manicure are the same as those in a good manicurist's shop, and you'll need all the same equipment. At the drugstore, Tweezerman offers a very useful five-piece manicure set that includes a nail brush, clipper, cuticle clipper, file and cuticle pusher. And here are the steps:

❏ *If your hands or nails are stained,* dip fingers into a grapefruit or lemon to clean them.

❏ *Remove old nail color.* For the quickest removal, choose *instant* polish remover, and *one without acetone,* which dries the nails and is harsh on cuticles. Cutex and Revlon make good removers that come in tubs—just dip the nails in and the polish comes off. They are also available in travel packets.

❏ *File nails.* Buy good emery boards: The big, coarse ones are better than the small ones, with small grains. File in one direction only, never back and forth from side to side, which makes the nails split. A sawing motion is what you want to avoid.

❏ *Soak the nails.* To soften the cuticles and make them pliable, mix a gentle cleansing soap such as Ivory liquid with warm water and soak the nails for three or four minutes. Afterward, use a nail brush to clean over and underneath the nails. If there are any rough corners, calluses or stains, rub them with a pumice stone.

❏ *Treat the cuticles.* Massage in a little cuticle cream or oil.

❏ *Shape the cuticles.* With an orange stick, pencil-shaped pumice stone or cuticle pusher, carefully push back all cuticles. If necessary, and I mean *really* necessary, use a sharpened cuticle clipper (which clips), a cuticle nipper (which slices) or cuticle scissors (which cuts) to cut away any loose cuticles or hangnails. A dull clipper or nipper—ouch!—will pull and tear, so keep them sharpened by taking them to a cutlery or beauty-supply shop.

❏ *Apply polish.* Use a base coat, then two coats of color and an acrylic top coat to seal. Apply the color itself carefully: not too thick, which will peel; not too thin, which won't adhere. Brushing color *lightly,* left and right, over tips will provide added chip resistance. If you make a mistake with polish, dip an orange stick in polish remover and erase it. There's something about nail color that encourages us all not to let it fully *dry.* To prevent that, use Sally Hansen's Dry-Kwik or Revlon's fast-drying spray. They really help.

**PEELING NAILS** See page 199 for a supplement to help the nails, and keep them polished, which will encourage binding.

**NAIL BITING** Apply Sally Hansen's Nail Biter according to directions.

**WEAK NAILS** See page 199 for a supplement to help the nails, and soak them often in warm oil. Be careful, too, when filing. Rounding the edges too energetically weakens nails; the edges should only be rounded gently.

**CHIPPED POLISH** A quick fix: File the raised edges of the chip, then add a coat of color.

**FOR VERY HARD TO REMOVE CALLUSES** Rub a Blackstone pumice stone over deep calluses—it really works. (Available at better drugstores, or order through Williams Lab, P.O. Box 101, Oradell, New Jersey 07490.) This pumice stone is amazing, and well worth ordering if you can't find it in the stores.

**FOR AN INGROWN NAIL** Cut the ingrown section of the nail into a small *V* and it will grow back in correctly.

**FOR DEEP CORNS** See a podiatriast for very deep corns, or you will make them much worse.

**DEEPLY LINED, VEINED, OVERWORKED HANDS** It's a drastic measure, but you can have them "plumped up" with collagen shots.

A friend of mine recently asked me whether I wanted *three* electric toothbrushes. Her dentist told her they were bad for her—after she'd been using them for years! Every mouth has different needs, and you should feel totally comfortable with your dentist, able to ask him or her any questions you have about routine dental care. Advances being made today in cosmetic dentistry are amazing, and if there's anything about your smile you feel uncomfortable with, you should also feel comfortable discussing cosmetic dentistry. The smile is the absolute centerpiece of a woman's face, and if yours isn't beautiful already, there are many new ways to make it so.

More and more hygienists are recommending having the teeth cleaned professionally every *four* months, instead of every six months. Insist on it. That extra cleaning each year can keep your teeth and gums in optimum condition, so that, apart from flossing and thoroughly brushing every day, you won't have to worry about them at all. Mouthwash is not essential, although if you feel a cold coming on, a Listerine gargle is a good precaution.

Daily flossing removes plaque between the teeth and under the gum line, and eliminates the formation of tartar, the substance formed by plaque buildup and the leading cause of gum disease and tooth loss. Unwaxed floss is usually recommended because it does a better job of grabbing the plaque, but if your teeth are set tightly together (or if you have restorations), you might be more comfortable with a waxed floss. Break off a strand of floss long enough

**TEETH**

to wrap around both forefingers for resistance. Slide the floss through each tooth—up, down, around; and don't overlook the molars.

Always use a soft-bristle toothbrush, because medium or hard bristles can encourage gum-tissue recession. As for toothpaste, check the ingredients. Baking soda, however highly touted, has never been shown to brighten teeth. Some abrasive toothpastes, like those formulated for smokers or promoted as whiteners, can wear away the enamel. Calcium peroxide is the *good* whitening agent and won't hurt the enamel. Sensodyne is a good toothpaste.

To keep breath fresh all day, eat parsley after every meal—it really works.

Such hormonal changes as puberty, pregnancy and menopause can affect the gums, and actually make gum disease likelier to occur. See your dentist if your gums feel sensitive, and if your daughter is going through puberty, check to make sure her gums feel okay in between professional cleanings.

---

## PREVENTING GUM DISEASE

Some years ago my dentist thought I might be at an early stage of gum disease—and I went into a panic, seeing ahead trouble, pain, surgery, irreversible damage and lots of dentists' bills. From him I learned a trick for removing plaque (a trick I've since taught to *other* dentists), which I do every morning. This massages away the plaque that builds up overnight, every night, and I've never had a problem since I learned it: Every morning, *before* brushing your teeth, *put a wet, cold washcloth over your second finger and rub gently around your gum line* (upper and lower) twice, reaching left and right all the way back. Then brush your teeth and, *especially your tongue*, which is practically a breeding ground for plaque and bacteria. Tongue-brushing really freshens the breath.

---

Christie Brinkley, Daryl Hannah, Joan Rivers, Goldie Hawn—beautiful smiles. I think of great

## TROUBLESHOOTING

smiles as "Los Angeles smiles"—gleaming white teeth, well-done lips. Possibly this is because Los Angeles is virtually the world's headquarters for cosmetic dentistry, which is becoming more and more popular as the procedures become easier to bear.

For example, not long ago I spoke to Dr. Harold McQuinn, a Beverly Hills dentist (to the stars!) who can now change a facial profile or bite in two visits. Instead of capping a tooth at a time (which can take a year to eighteen months), he puts you in the surgery center in his office and caps all the teeth at once. People from all over the world fly to Beverly Hills, stay two weeks and leave with a Los Angeles smile. As with any medical procedure, a first and second opinion is necessary. Be sure that the dentist shares your aesthetic concerns (you don't want a set of mismatched teeth, for example) and has performed the procedure many times before. For referrals in the Northeast corridor, call 1-800-DENTIST; elsewhere, call your local hospital and ask specifically about cosmetic dentistry.

**CROOKED TEETH** This is a big problem in adolescence, and there are improvements being made all the time in braces for kids (tooth-colored wires and thinner wires are two examples). In adulthood, crooked teeth can also be a problem, because teeth shift forward as we age. For adults, braceless orthodontics are a breakthrough. Removable retainers, meant to work eight to twelve hours a day as long as needed, can be fitted in a week or two.

**DISCOLORED TEETH** *Bleaching,* an increasingly common procedure, brightens the teeth for about six months, and can be done in a dentist's office or at home under a dentist's supervision. (I myself am leery of the bleaching kits you can buy, because there haven't yet been studies done on how the enamel reacts long-term.)

**CHIPPED, CROOKED, MISALIGNED OR GAPPED TEETH** There are three methods for correcting these flaws. *Caps,* or *crowns,* (the words are synonymous) are porcelain jackets that cover the tooth or teeth after the enamel has been reduced. These can last forever. A *veneer* works on essentially the same principle, except that it covers only the front of the tooth and lasts, on average, ten years. *Bonding,* which requires no enamel reduction, is a resin wrapped around the tooth. This last method is the least expensive. On average, it lasts two or three years, but it can last up to fifteen years.

# CHOOSING YOUR COLORS

# HOW TO USE YOUR COLOR CHARTS

## MAKEUP

1   Each color has a number or numbers below it to help you coordinate your makeup. It's easy. Wear ones with ones, twos with twos, etc.

2   You can match the numbers of one or two harmonizing eye shadow colors and one coordinating eyeliner color.

3   You can also use eye shadow as eyeliner when applied with a brush, wet or dry. Make sure the color is keyed to a complimentary eye shadow color.

4   You will notice that some of the eyeliners share the same number. It doesn't mean you can't wear them together. It only means you can wear each color with like-numbered shadows, blushes and lip colors.

5   Choose blush colors with like numbers as well.

## CLOTHING

1   Your color chart is divided into Basic (universal) colors—that is, colors anyone can wear—and your custom colors, those colors that are particularly flattering to your eye color and skin tone.

2   Your darkest custom colors, together with any of the universal colors, work best for suits, pants, stockings, and overall body wear.

3   The lighter custom colors are your most face-flattering accent colors. Use these colors for blouses, sweaters, scarves—those articles of clothing that you wear closest to your face.

# HAZEL/GREEN EYE SAMPLE COLOR PALETTE

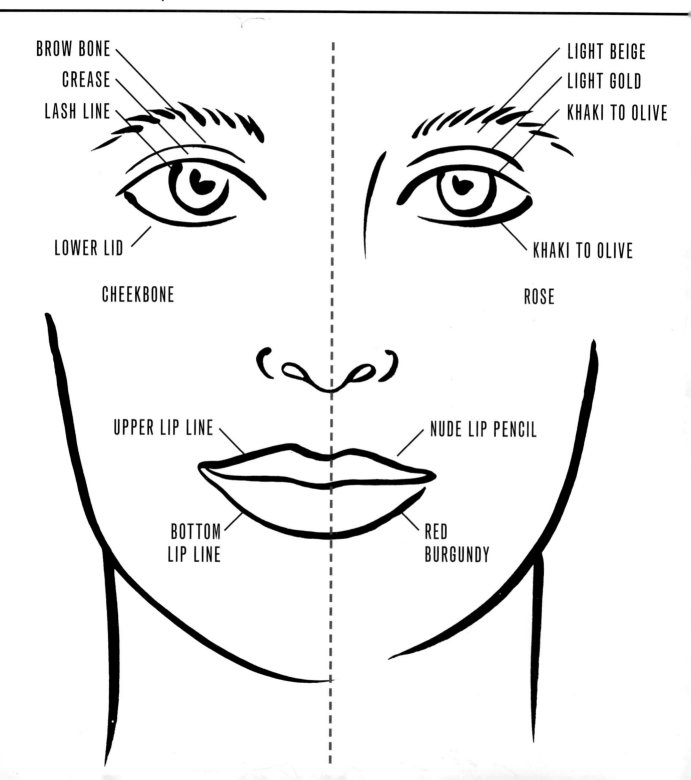

BROW BONE
CREASE
LASH LINE
LOWER LID
CHEEKBONE

LIGHT BEIGE
LIGHT GOLD
KHAKI TO OLIVE
KHAKI TO OLIVE
ROSE

UPPER LIP LINE
NUDE LIP PENCIL
BOTTOM
LIP LINE
RED
BURGUNDY

# If your eyes are... BLUE/GRAY

# MAKEUP

## EYE SHADOW COLORS

For the upper lid and crease:

| LIGHT BEIGE | TAUPE | LIGHT MAUVE | LIGHT ROSE | PALE GRAY | LIGHT CORAL | BABY BLUE | LIGHT PINK |
|---|---|---|---|---|---|---|---|
| 1, 2, 3, 4 | 1 | 4 | 2 | 3 | 1 | 3 | 2 |

Colors to line the upper and lower lids:

| MEDIUM BLUE TO NAVY | DARK TAUPE | PLUM | CHARCOAL GRAY | BLACK |
|---|---|---|---|---|
| 3 | 1, 3 | 2, 4 | 1, 2, 3, 4 | 1, 2, 3, 4 |

## LIP COLORS

  TO    TO

| PEACH | PINK | FUCHSIA | MAUVE | LIGHT RED | RED WITH BLUE UNDERTONES |
|---|---|---|---|---|---|
| 1 | 2, 3 | 2, 3 | 2, 3, 4 | 1, 3 | 1, 2, 3, 4 |

## BLUSH COLORS

| PINK | ROSE | BRONZE |
|---|---|---|
| 2, 3 | 2, 4 | 1 |

# FASHION

## BASICS (universal)

| DENIM BLUE | CAMEL | NAVY | IVORY | GRAY | WHITE | BLACK |

## CUSTOM COLORS

| LILAC | BABY BLUE | VIOLET | ROSE | TAUPE |

| MAUVE | PINK | TURQUOISE | PERIWINKLE |

### THESE ARE YOUR CUSTOM COLORS.

As a general rule, the *darkest colors* in your chart will, together with any of the UNIVERSAL COLORS, work best as your base colors for overall body wear and stockings.

The *lighter colors* are your most face-flattering accent colors for blouses, sweaters and scarves.

### HOW TO USE YOUR COLOR CHARTS.
#### MAKEUP

1   Each color has a number or numbers below it to help you coordinate your makeup. It's easy. Wear ones with ones, twos with twos, etc.

2   You can match the numbers of one or two harmonizing eye shadow colors and one coordinating eyeliner color.

# If your eyes are... BROWN

# MAKEUP

## EYE SHADOW COLORS

For the upper lid and crease:

| LIGHT BEIGE | CORAL | GOLD | BRONZE | TAN |
|---|---|---|---|---|
| 1, 2, 3, 4 | 1 | 2 | 4 | 3 |

Colors to line the upper and lower lids:

| KHAKI GREEN TO OLIVE | MEDIUM TO DARK BROWN | TEAL | NAVY | BLACK |
|---|---|---|---|---|
| 1, 3 | 1, 2, 3, 4 | 2, 3 | 1, 2 | 1, 2, 3, 4 |

## LIP COLORS

| ORANGE | TERRA-COTTA | HOT CORAL | MEDIUM RED | DEEP RED | MEDIUM PINK | BRIGHT ROSE | LIGHT BRONZE |
|---|---|---|---|---|---|---|---|
| 2, 3 | 3 | 1, 2, 3 | 1, 3 | 1, 3 | 1, 3 | 1, 3 | 3, 4 |

## BLUSH COLORS

| PEACH | LIGHT BRONZE | PINK |
|---|---|---|
| 2, 3, 4 | 2, 3 | 1 |

# FASHION

## BASICS (universal)

DENIM BLUE    CAMEL    NAVY    IVORY    GRAY    WHITE    BLACK

## CUSTOM COLORS

CELADON GREEN    TEAL    BROWN    PEACH    ROYAL BLUE    RUST    RED    YELLOW

BRONZE    KHAKI GREEN TO OLIVE    BURGUNDY    PINK    HOT CORAL    PURPLE    GRASS TO HUNTER GREEN

## THESE ARE YOUR CUSTOM COLORS.

As a general rule, the *darkest colors* in your chart will, together with any of the UNIVERSAL COLORS, work best as your base colors for overall body wear and stockings.

The *lighter colors* are your most face-flattering accent colors for blouses, sweaters and scarves.

## HOW TO USE YOUR COLOR CHARTS.
### MAKEUP

1 Each color has a number or numbers below it to help you coordinate your makeup. It's easy. Wear ones with ones, twos with twos, etc.

2 You can match the numbers of one or two harmonizing eye shadow colors and one coordinating eyeliner color.

# MAKEUP

## EYE SHADOW COLORS

For the upper lid and crease:

| LIGHT BEIGE | LIGHT ROSE | LIGHT GOLD | LIGHT PINK | TAUPE |
|---|---|---|---|---|
| 1, 2, 3, 4 | 2 | 3 | 2 | 1 |

Colors to line the upper and lower lids:

| KHAKI GREEN TO OLIVE | PLUM | TEAL | DARK TAUPE | BLACK |
|---|---|---|---|---|
| 1, 3 | 2 | 1 | 1, 3 | 1, 2, 3, 4 |

## LIP COLORS

| DUSTY ROSE | MOCHA | RED ROSE | RED BURGUNDY | RED BROWN | ROSE PINK | DEEP ROSE | TO | FUCHSIA |
|---|---|---|---|---|---|---|---|---|
| 1, 2, 3 | 1, 3 | 1, 2 | 1, 2, 3 | 1, 3 | 2 | 1, 2, 3 | | 1, 3 |

## BLUSH COLORS

| PINK | BRONZE | ROSE |
|---|---|---|
| 2 | 1, 3 | 1, 2, 3 |

# F A S H I O N

## B A S I C S (universal)

| DENIM BLUE | CAMEL | NAVY | IVORY | GRAY | WHITE | BLACK |

## C U S T O M   C O L O R S

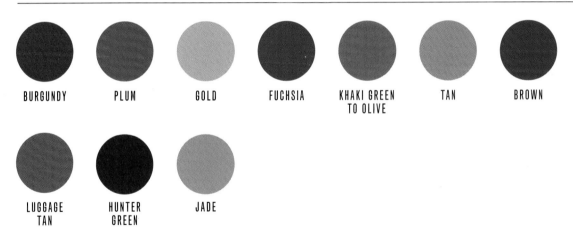

| BURGUNDY | PLUM | GOLD | FUCHSIA | KHAKI GREEN TO OLIVE | TAN | BROWN |

| LUGGAGE TAN | HUNTER GREEN | JADE |

### THESE ARE YOUR CUSTOM COLORS.

As a general rule, the *darkest colors* in your chart will, together with any of the UNIVERSAL COLORS, work best as your base colors for overall body wear and stockings.

The *lighter colors* are your most face-flattering accent colors for blouses, sweaters and scarves.

### HOW TO USE YOUR COLOR CHARTS.
#### MAKEUP

1 Each color has a number or numbers below it to help you coordinate your makeup. It's easy. Wear ones with ones, twos with twos, etc.

2 You can match the numbers of one or two harmonizing eye shadow colors and one coordinating eyeliner color.

# M A K E U P

## EYE SHADOW COLORS

For the upper lid and crease:

| LIGHT BEIGE | LILAC | TAUPE | LIGHT ROSE |
|---|---|---|---|
| 1, 2, 3, 4 | 1 | 2 | 3 |

Colors to line the upper and lower lids:

| KHAKI GREEN TO OLIVE | CHARCOAL GRAY | WINE | DARK TAUPE | BLACK |
|---|---|---|---|---|
| 2 | 1, 2, 3, 4 | 1, 3 | 2, 3 | 1, 4 |

## LIP COLORS

| DUSTY ROSE | DEEP MAUVE | RASPBERRY | BERRY PINK | DEEP ROSE | PLUM |
|---|---|---|---|---|---|
| 1, 3 | 1, 3 | 2, 3 | 1, 2, 3 | 1, 2, 3 | 1, 3 |

## BLUSH COLORS

| DUSTY PINK | ROSE |
|---|---|
| 2, 3 | 1, 3 |

# FASHION

## BASICS (universal)

| DENIM BLUE | CAMEL | NAVY | IVORY | GRAY | WHITE | BLACK |

## CUSTOM COLORS

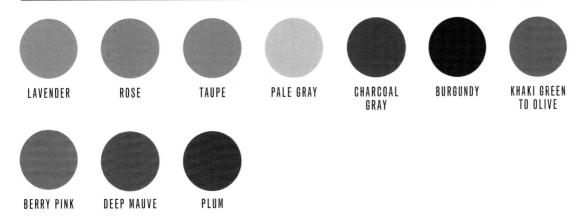

| LAVENDER | ROSE | TAUPE | PALE GRAY | CHARCOAL GRAY | BURGUNDY | KHAKI GREEN TO OLIVE |

| BERRY PINK | DEEP MAUVE | PLUM |

## THESE ARE YOUR CUSTOM COLORS.

As a general rule, the *darkest colors* in your chart will, together with any of the UNIVERSAL COLORS, work best as your base colors for overall body wear and stockings.

The *lighter colors* are your most face-flattering accent colors for blouses, sweaters and scarves.

## HOW TO USE YOUR COLOR CHARTS.
### MAKEUP

1  Each color has a number or numbers below it to help you coordinate your makeup. It's easy. Wear ones with ones, twos with twos, etc.

2  You can match the numbers of one or two harmonizing eye shadow colors and one coordinating eyeliner color.

# If your eyes are... DARK

# MAKEUP

## EYE SHADOW COLORS

For the upper lid and crease:

| TAN | CORAL | BRONZE | GOLD | DUSTY ROSE |
|-----|-------|--------|------|------------|
| 1, 2, 3, 4 | 3 | 4 | 2 | 1 |

Colors to line the upper and lower lids:

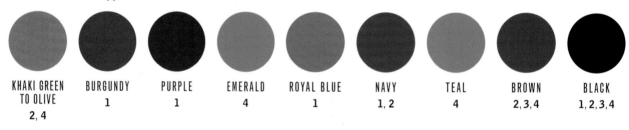

| KHAKI GREEN TO OLIVE | BURGUNDY | PURPLE | EMERALD | ROYAL BLUE | NAVY | TEAL | BROWN | BLACK |
|------|------|------|------|------|------|------|------|------|
| 2, 4 | 1 | 1 | 4 | 1 | 1, 2 | 4 | 2, 3, 4 | 1, 2, 3, 4 |

## LIP COLORS

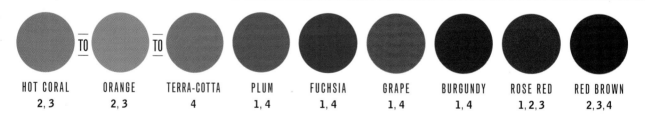

| HOT CORAL | ORANGE | TERRA-COTTA | PLUM | FUCHSIA | GRAPE | BURGUNDY | ROSE RED | RED BROWN |
|-----------|--------|-------------|------|---------|-------|----------|----------|-----------|
| 2, 3 | 2, 3 | 4 | 1, 4 | 1, 4 | 1, 4 | 1, 4 | 1, 2, 3 | 2, 3, 4 |

| MOCHA | BROWN |
|-------|-------|
| 1, 2, 3, 4 | 2, 3, 4 |

## BLUSH COLORS

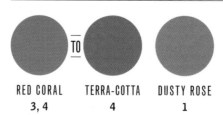

| RED CORAL | TERRA-COTTA | DUSTY ROSE |
|-----------|-------------|------------|
| 3, 4 | 4 | 1 |

# FASHION

## BASICS (universal)

| DENIM BLUE | CAMEL | NAVY | IVORY | GRAY | WHITE | BLACK |

## CUSTOM COLORS

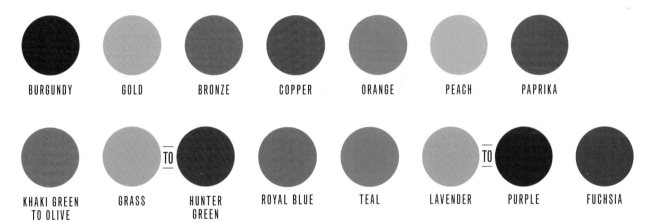

| BURGUNDY | GOLD | BRONZE | COPPER | ORANGE | PEACH | PAPRIKA |

| KHAKI GREEN TO OLIVE | GRASS | TO | HUNTER GREEN | ROYAL BLUE | TEAL | LAVENDER | TO | PURPLE | FUCHSIA |

## THESE ARE YOUR CUSTOM COLORS.

As a general rule, the *darkest colors* in your chart will, together with any of the UNIVERSAL COLORS, work best as your base colors for overall body wear and stockings.

The *lighter colors* are your most face-flattering accent colors for blouses, sweaters and scarves.

## HOW TO USE YOUR COLOR CHARTS.

### MAKEUP

1   Each color has a number or numbers below it to help you coordinate your makeup. It's easy. Wear ones with ones, twos with twos, etc.

2   You can match the numbers of one or two harmonizing eye shadow colors and one coordinating eyeliner color.

# UNIVERSAL COLOR MIXES

The universal colors are the colors for us all, the neutrals that serve as the canvas, which then gets "painted," so to speak, with our own custom colors. Because they're neutrals, they go with everything. But just because denim jeans and gray sweatshirts go together well is no reason to *wear* them together every time.

The universals really come to life paired with unusual, off-the-beaten-track colors. Plus, the more ways you mix and match the universals, the more outfits you can make from one simple classic piece. Now that you know your custom colors, have fun mixing them with these basic colors.

## BASIC COLOR MIXES

### WEAR CAMEL WITH:

green
peach
burgundy/black
black/royal blue
gray/white
peach/red
peach/gray
gray/yellow
white
baby blue
royal blue/yellow
hunter green/dark gray
grass green
burgundy/white/black

### WEAR NAVY WITH:

tan/black
black/yellow/pink
gray/camel
red/gray
tan
yellow/tan

gold
hunter green/purple
gray/olive green
gray/burgundy
white/baby blue

### WEAR IVORY WITH:

gold/gray
white
tan/gray
beige
baby blue/black
powder pink/brown
celadon green/brown
yellow/brown
leopard
rust
gold
white/tan
white/rust
gold/khaki green/brown
black/white
dark green/burgundy
celadon green/gray
peach/brown
beige/brown
tan/black
black/brown

### WEAR GRAY WITH:

fuchsia
camel/white
peach/gold
green/black
red/black
tan/white
green/yellow/red
peach/tan
teal blue/camel
yellow/tan
red/navy blue
white/tan
black/brown/white
brown/camel
green/tan
grass green/paprika
baby blue/burgundy

### WEAR WHITE WITH:

camel/gray
pink/baby blue
navy/baby blue
green/black
red/black
fuchsia

tan/gray
red/green
hunter green/yellow/royal blue
tan
lavender/pink
gray/black/brown
burgundy/black

### WEAR BLACK WITH:

purple
copper
coral
green/gray
white/green
white/red
orange
tan/burgundy
yellow/peach/coral
green
tan/royal blue
royal blue/yellow/pink
blue denim
fuchsia/royal blue
turquoise/gold
lavender/red
peach/white
gray/brown/white
olive green
olive green/brown
burgundy/white

# DRAMATIC COLOR MIXES

## WEAR BROWN WITH:

gold
peach
gray/black/white
camel/gray
black/olive green
khaki green
baby blue

## WEAR PURPLE WITH:

red
black
pink
hunter green
yellow
red/green
hunter green/royal blue
khaki green/fuchsia

## WEAR FUCHSIA WITH:

gray
white
black
royal blue/black
turquoise

khaki green/purple
olive green

## WEAR PEACH WITH:

brown
burgundy/camel
tan/red
tan/gray
pink/black
camel/gray
khaki green/tan
yellow/coral/black

## WEAR RED WITH:

peach/tan
green/white
navy/gray
olive green/yellow
purple
gray/black
white/black

## WEAR YELLOW WITH:

ivory
brown
purple
peach/coral/black
black/royal blue/pink
gray/green/red

hunter green/royal blue/white
gray/tan
royal blue/tan
khaki green/leopard print
burgundy/lavender
khaki green
orange
pink
olive green/red

## WEAR BABY BLUE WITH:

tan
gold
gray/burgundy
ivory

## WEAR PINK WITH:

purple
white/baby blue
black/yellow/royal blue
turquoise
lavender/white
peach/black

## WEAR CELADON WITH:

brown/cream/rust
navy/burgundy
gray

black/soft yellow
peach

# OTHER MIXES THAT LOOK GREAT:

Green/camel
Copper/black
Coral/green
Turquoise/caramel
Rust/teal blue

# CLASSIC COLOR MIXES

Black/white
Pink/brown
Red/white/blue
Navy/gray
Yellow/navy
Celadon/brown
Peach/gray
Yellow/gray

# LIP COLORS TO WEAR WITH FASHION COLORS:

| FASHION COLOR | LIP COLOR |
|---|---|
| **BLUE/GRAY EYES:** | |
| Pastel pink to rose | Pinks, rose, fire-engine red, neutrals |
| Taupe | Any |
| Violet to lavender | Pink to fuchsia, mauves, blue-reds. neutrals |
| Mauve | Pinks, neutrals |
| All shades of light to medium blue, never royal | Pinks to fuchsia, neutrals, rose |
| Light to medium gray | Any |
| Turquoise | Pinks, peach, neutrals |
| **BROWN EYES:** | |
| Yellow—bright and warm | Orange to terra-cotta, coral, fire-engine red, neutrals, rose, pinks |
| Peach and coral | Orange to terra-cotta, coral, fire-engine red, neutral |
| Warm browns | Any |
| Beige | Any |
| Rust | Orange to terra-cotta, red-brown, fire-engine red, neutrals |
| Bronze | Terra-cotta, red-brown |
| Red | Light to dark red (choose according to wardrobe) |
| Burgundy | Rose, pinks, dark reds |
| Royal blue | Pinks, rose, dark reds |
| Clear pink | Neutrals, pinks to roses |
| Deep purple | Rose to fuchsia, dark red |
| Khaki and olive green | Fire-engine red, red-brown, neutrals, orange to terra-cotta, rose |
| Grass, emerald and hunter green | Rose |
| Green | Fire-engine red to dark red |
| Camel | Any |
| All other shades of blue | Pinks, reds, rose, neutrals |
| Celadon green | Pinks, rose, neutrals |
| **HAZEL/GREEN EYES:** | |
| Burgundy | Pinks, rose to fuchsia |
| Browns | Any |
| Hunter green | Reds, rose to fuchsia |

| FASHION COLOR | LIP COLOR |
|---|---|
| Gold | Neutrals, red-browns |
| Camel and tan | Neutrals, red-browns, rose to fuchsia |
| Khaki and olive green | Rose to fuchsia, red-browns, neutrals |
| Fuchsia | Pinks, rose to fuchsia |
| **ASIAN EYES:** | |
| Burgundy | Any |
| All shades of gray | Any |
| Light to dark rose | Any |
| Taupe | Any |
| Olive green | Reds, roses |
| Lavender | Neutrals with rose or wine undertones, pinks to rose |
| **DARK EYES/WOMEN OF COLOR:** | |
| Camel | Any |
| Lavender to purple | Blue-reds, neutrals with rose or wine undertones, rose to fuchsia |
| Khaki green | Red with brown undertones, cinnamon to brown, rose to fuchsia, orange to terra-cotta |
| Grass and hunter green | Deep blue-reds with wine undertones |
| Royal blue | Blue-reds, rose to fuchsia |
| Peach, coral, orange | Neutrals with brown undertones, coral and orange to terra-cotta |
| Red | Choose red according to fashion color |
| Fuchsia | Rose to fuchsia, neutral with rose undertones, blue-reds |
| Burgundy | Rose, blue- to wine-reds |
| Gold | Neutrals with brown undertones, red with brown undertones, cinnamon to brown, orange to terra-cotta |
| Bronze | Cinnamon to brown, red-browns, neutrals with brown undertones |
| Brown | Brown-red, rose, fuchsia to grape, mocha to cinnamon to brown, orange to terra-cotta |

**UNEVEN TEETH** *Contouring* is the process that aligns teeth and makes them even. (Some people also have prominent gums carved away with this process, but I would advise against ever tampering with gums.) Essentially, the teeth—assuming the enamel is thick enough to withstand the treatment—are sanded down to match the teeth around them.

**RECEDING OR PROTRUDING JAWLINE** If, as sometimes happens in the aging process, the lower jaw begins to recede or protrude, it can change the appearance of the face and profile: This condition is called temporomandibular disorder (TMJ for short). TMJ therapy is a conservative—yet highly effective—reversible "splint" therapy, during which improper joint alignment is corrected with orthodontics, porcelain crowns and adjustment of the bite. The final result is a healthier bite, a pleasing full facial profile and the bonus of less facial wrinkling.

**RECEDING GUMLINE** The method of gum-line restoration is called facial composite. Among others, a 3M product called Sylux Plus, which comes in shades to match natural gums, is applied to build up the receding gum line. For filling in gum edges, 3M also has a new gum-restoration material called Z100.

# PART 2

# HOW DO I DRESS?

**W**omen's *Wear Daily* once ran an article about our store that said we had the highest rate of sales per square foot of any store in the country. At Giorgio, space *was* at a premium (especially when we first started, with only eight hundred square feet to sell from), and there wasn't room for anything that wasn't needed.

Just like a woman's closet.

Closets fill a very emotional need, because *we are what we wear—and how we wear it.* I heard it for years in my job as "retail psychologist," and years ago I used to say it, too: "I have nothing to wear." What the statement really means is, "I have nothing to wear that I *feel good* in." Most of us actually have plenty to wear. Sometimes there's so much bunched into a closet that you can't see what you have—out of sight, out of mind. Often it's just a question of *putting together what you already have in a new way.* Sometimes the clothes are there, but maintenance has slipped. No one ever feels great wearing a safety pin where a button should be, a skirt with a Scotch tape patch where the hem has fallen down (except in emergencies) or a skirt with the waistband rolled over to adjust the length. Or maybe you really are missing some key pieces, and need to begin editing and filling in your closet now—*not* going out and replacing a closet full of perfectly good clothes.

# CLOSET SHOPPING

It wasn't until I began to "run" my closet as creatively and efficiently as I ran my store that I discovered I always had something to wear. The principles are exactly the same. Develop an overriding fashion sensibility, or image. Take inventory, regularly. Get rid of the clothes that aren't paying their rent. Pay attention to needs as they change—subtly—from season to season. Present the merchandise so that it looks inviting and can be *seen*. Take good care of the inventory. Turn your closet into *your* own personal clothing store, in other words. Then go shopping.

## TAKE INVENTORY

At Giorgio, I used to close the store twice a year to take inventory, and now I do the same thing at home: I close my bedroom door twice a year, and spend the afternoon alone, taking honest inventory of my clothing and accessories—stockings, gloves, hair accessories, underwear, *everything*. Honest inventory means trying on each and every garment and looking in the two-way mirror. Don't take the chance that the silk blouse you haven't worn in a while that looks fine in its dry-cleaner bag now will have shrunk (or you might have grown a little) three months from now, when you need it at the last minute.

You know more than you think; we all do. You know which clothes in your closet are those you feel good in and *wear*—really wear—and they're probably those in a color you know you look good in, a fabric that's easy, flattering and comfortable to wear and have a great, easy fit. Clothes that fit your image, clothes that fit your lifestyle. Wouldn't it be nice if you felt as good in *all* your clothes as you do in your favorites? Taking inventory—beginning to edit away those clothes that don't work and replacing them with clothes that do—is the way to set that goal in motion.

Part of this ritual necessitates taking stock of *yourself* in your clothes as well, and for this you need a two-way full-length mirror, which you can rig up easily by putting a portable full-length mirror (available for about twenty dollars at a hardware store) in front of and facing your regular mirror with you standing in between, so that you can see yourself perfectly back and front, the way other people do. (I was always amazed by how many women don't "look both ways" before buying.) You also need a giveaway box—for clothes that no longer fit your body, your image, your lifestyle. Another box should hold clothes you like but don't fit right; these can be salvaged by a tailor. Add another basket for clothes missing the right coordinate pieces to make them work, and a *pad and pen* to make a list of things you need to buy to make outfits out of "odd pieces." It's a list you'll keep with you.

*Try on everything—every blouse, every belt, every slip, every shoe—and scrutinize the back of each outfit as carefully as the front, with all the buttons and zippers closed.* Don't overlook anything: It's the only way to learn what fits you *now.* The object is to have a closet full of clothes you can depend on—clothes as reliable as good friends. Give away the items that no longer work—the equivalent of a retail store's final closeout sale. Except for classic evening clothes that can last forever, a closet full of clothes you might wear "someday" is a closet that contains absolutely nothing to wear in the here and now. I can guarantee you that the only clothes worth having in a closet are those that are as often as not *out* of the closet.

If an article of clothing fits but just doesn't *feel* right, the problem almost certainly has to do with the color or fabric. No matter what it cost to begin with, if it's already hanging in your closet, spending a little *more* to get the look or the fit right isn't necessarily throwing good money after bad. Before you get rid of it, see whether you can turn it into the garment you had in mind when you first bought it.

> ## TIPS FOR SMART SHOPPING
> ———
> **The first four things a good shopper looks at when considering a garment are (in this order):**
>
> ❑ **Color**
> ❑ **Fabric**
> ❑ **Fit**
> ❑ **Cost**

**COLOR** Reconsider the clothes that *do* still work but might need updating with new companion pieces; *keep an ongoing list of fill-in and replacement items you need.* Keep the list with you, so that you can buy as you go along. Clothes you're bored with might not seem so "tired" if they were mixed and matched another way, with a new color or companion piece. While your clothes are all out of the closet is a good time to try to reaccessorize them before putting them back. (See the color section for charts suggesting color matches for new *and* old clothes.) If the cost of a new blouse or scarf is all it takes to make a classic look and feel fresh, it's well worth it. Finally, hang your clothes back in your closet as *outfits*—tops, bottoms and belts all together on one or two hangers—the way I presented outfits at Giorgio. They're ready to wear, and you won't have to think about them when dressing.

**FABRIC** Quality is something you feel as well as see, and you feel it in the fabric. You can turn a garment inside out to see how it's made, but you can tell even sooner how it will look by the way it hangs: *Hanger appeal* is the term in the trade. (If it's an inexpensive garment, you can forgive hanger appeal and choose anyway, based on where you'll be wearing it and how it looks on *you*.) Fabric has to have a good *feel* to it, even if it's a synthetic blend.

The most versatile fabrics (see pages 101–104 for a discussion of fabrics) are those you can wear pretty much year-round, adding or taking away layers as necessary. With versatile year-round basics, all you have to add are a few very light pieces for high summer and a few tweedy or heavier wool pieces and turtlenecks for the depths of winter.

If, when you're taking inventory of what you already have in your closet, the fabric is what seems to be the trouble, consider the elements. If the outfit is scratchy when you try it on, possibly you're not wearing the right *undergarments* to muffle the scratchiness. Try a sheer pair of pantyhose under your regular pair to protect you against itchy pants, and a shrunken T-shirt under an itchy sweater. If an outfit exaggerates your own lumps and bumps, a taffeta or Lycra panty slip might make the garment hang the way it's meant to. (See pages 108–109 for buying undergarments.) If it's a tweed suit that just feels or looks heavy, maybe the skirt would look better on its own, without the heavy jacket but set off by a wool sweater with enough "presence" to balance the tweed.

Maybe, too, the jacket on its own would look less heavy with a plain-colored skirt or pair of pants. Take a linen suit, on the other hand, where the jacket feels okay but the skirt wrinkles almost from the moment you put it on (even with spray starch, which helps, linen wrinkles). To disguise the wrinkling, try the skirt with a light cotton tunic sweater for a more casual look, and wear the blazer, which won't wrinkle quite as much with other, less wrinkle-prone skirts and pants, separately.

Fabrics that require constant adjusting—pulling, tugging, reshaping—are never going to feel or look right. If you can *compensate* for a fabric's shortcomings (different top, different bottom, different jacket or blazer), then you might salvage the garment. If not, you've learned a fabric lesson: what *not* to buy next time. Maybe you can do a trade with a friend, or wear it and forget it.

**FIT** One of the most surprising lessons I learned right away at Giorgio was that many of the most elegant women sometimes spend more money on the alterations than they do on the garment itself! Clothes should glide, drape, over the body, never hug or require pulling or tugging to keep them in place. When you're taking inventory is a good time to do a *check on the fit of every garment,* always in the two-way mirror. Sometimes a tailor might have to adjust the fit; sometimes you can do it yourself. Check, for example, all the hooks and eyes, to see that they are tightly sewn and easy to fasten and unfasten. Does too much décolletage show? If so, sewing stores sell two- or three-inch-long wire strips, called stays, to sew or pin inside the front of the dress, which then tuck into your bra. To keep you from worrying about or fiddling with your bra straps, pin or sew in lingerie straps (again—the sewing store has them), which are loops about an inch long with snaps at one end to secure the bra straps. (My customers were always delighted to learn these tricks.)

Finding a tailor you can work with is essential; luckily, many dry cleaners have good ones. Try them out with a simple hem first to see their work.

Tailors are neither intimidating nor expensive, and simply by taking clothes that *almost* fit perfectly into a tailor for a nip or a tuck might turn them into the outfits you hoped for when you bought them in the first place.

When making your list of new and replacement items you need, consider the buys that can give you the most mileage: skirts, pants, blouses, shoes and jewelry. A new pleated black skirt, for example, can make new suits out of all your jackets. Even a bandana tied at the neck (see page 143) can change the look of an outfit *entirely*.

And while you're shopping in your own closet, you might browse through your man's closet. Maybe you don't need a sporty new blazer, after all. Maybe you can borrow one of *his*, the way French women do, and wear it with the sleeves folded back for a casual look on weekends. Other items to "borrow": all sweaters, ties, scarves, shirts (for jeans, to wear with leggings or at the beach) and socks. Men always have great socks!

## SEASON-TO-SEASON CHANGING NEEDS

As co-owner of Giorgio, I would travel the world to buy for my store. I'd choose the designs I liked, and then, because we were based in Southern California, I'd also choose lighter-weight fabrics and usually lighter, softer colors as well, in which I wanted the designs made up.

## HOW TO ANALYZE FIT

If a perfectly okay garment just doesn't feel right, analyze the fit in the two-way mirror, from the shoulders down:

❑ *Shoulders.* **The most important area for fit is the shoulders: That's where all the tailoring is—the "hanger" for the clothes. Clothes should feel easy but not sloppy over the shoulders. If they feel tight or constricting, have the seams let out; if too loose, have the shoulders raised.**

❑ *Sleeve length.* **Sleeves should just cover the wristbone. If the shirt is worn under a sweater or suit, a little cuff should show.**

❑ *Wrist fit.* **Snug enough not to slip past your watch and wrist-bone line.**

❑ *Body contours.* **Nothing should cling; nothing should gap. If necessary, have seams over the hips, along the torso and under the arms taken in or let out.**

❑ *Hems.* **Must be even, always. Scrutinize them carefully from the side view, especially on less expensive clothing. A machine-made top-stitched hem shows an inexpensive finish; to make an inexpensive item look better, have the hem redone by hand.**

At first I was surprised to discover that my East Coast and European customers also liked the lighter-weight fabrics all year long, but then it began to make sense. For one thing, many of us travel much more than we used to, and year-round fabrics are easier to layer and more versatile for travelers. For another, climates are not predictably hot and cold. Most important, perhaps, is that we consumers stopped being so "season driven" when it came to buying clothes, and started buying, and wearing, what and when we wanted to. What we want is a *basic* wardrobe that can carry us through the year, with a few seasonal flourishes as needed.

We are becoming more like European shoppers, filling in, repairing and editing, rather than replacing. We are collecting classics to carry us through year after year, rather than being victims of seasonal whims. As a result, switching your closet from a winter to a summer mode (or vice versa) shouldn't involve emptying everything out and filling it up again. A well-stocked closet won't ever look tired and limp at the end of any given season. Instead, it will look ready for the *next* season.

Classic. Timeless. Seasonless. Giorgio Armani, one of the great enlightened designers of our time, made a fortune building on these principles. By building on them, you, too, can *save* a fortune—and always find something to wear, right in your own closet.


## ORGANIZING YOUR CLOSET

Another lesson from my retail days: Customers never bought what they couldn't *see.*

When it comes to organizing your closet, what you *see* is what you'll wear. You have to be able to mix and match with your eye before you can do it successfully with your clothes. Accessories such as belts, scarves, jewelry and stockings organize well in drawers, baskets or on hooks. The more accessibly your clothes are presented, the more easily you'll find exactly the right thing to wear. When color-coordinating tops and bottoms, be sure to check the colors against bright, natural daylight or under a normal (never fluorescent) bulb of at least 150 watts. Always use a high-wattage bulb in your closet. Even the best eyes can't detect color tones without bright light. Colors need not match exactly, but they *must harmonize*. So must the textures harmonize. A heavy heather flannel won't work with a smooth worsted, but it *will* work with a textured tweed or herringbone.

Most good hardware and houseware stores have closet sections with shoe racks, plastic storage boxes, good hangers and sponge sleeves to use over hangers (to keep slippery clothes in place). The Hold Everything stores and catalog (1-800-421-2264) are an entire business devoted to getting us *organized*. It works.

Belts can best be seen on belt hangers or pointed "arms" in brass or chrome, which are mounted onto the closet wall or on the back of the closet door—great and often neglected storage space. Scarves can be pressed and rolled neatly into baskets (baskets are great organizers). Hats can be stacked, with hat number one well stuffed with tissue paper to maintain its shape. Hanging pocket organizers or small baskets will show your earrings and pins at a glance, while wall hooks will display your necklaces the same way they're displayed in stores. Shoe racks keep your shoes in order. If space is limited, store two shoes on each rung. Store stockings by separating sheer from opaque with a piece of cardboard between the two—makes it *much* easier to find the right ones in the morning.

For the cost of a good sweater, you'll be able to set up a *great* closet. And then you'll actually be able to *find* the sweater.

## MAINTENANCE

To give you an example of how long clothes can last, lately I've started to buy vintage couture clothing from Paris. I've collected designs by Chanel, Mainbocher, Givenchy, Balenciaga, Pierre Balmain, Christian Dior, Jean Patou and Madame Grès. (This has become a *passion!*) The workmanship—details such as buttons, trim, fabrics and design—is impossible to find today; they're exquisite. When I buy the clothes, I take them to my tailor and custom-fit each one. As it is, these clothes have already lasted a lifetime, and if I take proper care of them, they'll last another. So will most clothes, if you buy classic styles—and take good care of them.

I suppose there are R and R days when we all want to curl up in tattered sweatpants and retreat from the world, but I always feel better if I can face myself, my mirror, my husband and anyone else who happens to come along without apologizing. *What* you're wearing is part of the battle, certainly. But *how* you're wearing it is, perhaps, even more telling. Maintaining your clothes is as important an element of style as choosing your clothes, a principle that applies as much to dressing-down attire as it does to black tie.

Keeping clothes clean, pressed, mended and in ready-to-wear condition is also another way to ensure that you'll always find *something* to wear right in your own closet. Some products and tips to help:

**STEAMER** For about two hundred dollars, give or take, you can buy a steamer, the best way to remove wrinkles from clothes—not to mention curtains, tablecloths and bedspreads—while they're hanging on the hanger. (The Joan Cook catalog, 1-800-935-0971, carries them.) We had one at Giorgio, and as every new article of clothing arrived, it was steamed before being placed on the display racks. A steamer takes up no more room than a vacuum cleaner, and it will pay for itself many times over. For example, many women dry-clean their clothes every time they begin to look rumpled, when all they really need is a good pressing. Dry cleaning is not only expensive but also hard on clothes. A quick steaming presses them perfectly, without the wear and tear of all the chemicals dry cleaners use.

**IRON** A regular nonstick steam iron. For most fabrics, steaming is better than ironing: Never iron directly on gabardine or velvet, for example. To be safe, put a dish towel between the garment and the iron for protection; this will also prevent a shine on fabrics like wool and silk. For a professional steaming effect, spritz a little water on top of the dish towel. For crispness and body, use spray starch on shirts, and especially on anything linen (spray starch helps *a lot* with linen). To clean a steam iron, use equal parts of white vinegar and water. Steam several minutes, disconnect and let stand for an hour. Then empty and rinse well.

**LINT REMOVER** Either a big, fat adhesive roller or the red-felt kind, available at hardware and housewares stores. They also do a quick job of removing pet hairs from furniture and car upholstery.

**SWEATER COMB** Also available at hardware and housewares stores. "Comb" the sweater to remove wool balls and fuzz. An alternate, if riskier, method is to shave the sweater very carefully with a disposable razor.

**WIRE BRUSH** For suede shoes and bags.

**PLASTIC DRY-CLEANING BAGS** Save them. Wrapping fragile whites in these bags protects them. Also, clothes packed in suitcases between layers of this plastic don't wrinkle (see page 223).

**TO REMOVE A BAD SPILL** For a red-wine or food stain, *immediately* pour *fresh* bubbly club soda generously directly on the stain and rub aggressively with a terry-cloth towel. Repeat until the stain comes out. (Works on rugs, too.)

**TO SPOT-CLEAN STAINS ON CLOTHING** Goddard's Dry Clean spot remover, available at hardware, housewares or drugstores, is great for removing spots and stains, and especially good for makeup-stain removal.

## FOR A QUICK PRESS WHEN TRAVELING

Do this only when you're visiting a place where water is abundant. Turn hot water on full blast, close the shower curtain and hang garments in the bathroom. Leave the water on for ten to fifteen minutes, until the room is steamy, then turn the water off. Leave garments in the steamy room for an hour or two to relax the wrinkles.

**TO SPOT-CLEAN STAINS ON SUEDE** Lay the garment on the floor and sprinkle a lot of Johnson's baby powder directly on the spot. Leave it on for twenty-four hours *without touching*. Then shake, shake, shake off the loose powder. (*Don't* rub it off.)

**TO PROTECT SHOES, HANDBAGS, COATS** Scotchgard fabric protector will make them water and dirt repellent. Spray it on before wearing the first time. On shoes, spray the soles as well.

**FOR STICKY ZIPPERS** This works for clothes, suitcases, whatever: Run a piece of candle wax up and down the zipper's teeth.

**FOR GENERAL CLEANING** Use a washing machine when indicated on a garment's label, but *don't use the dryer unelss you want your garment to end up two or three sizes smaller.* Instead, hang or lay out the garment to dry naturally. Even cottons need a light pressing with an iron before wearing. Use a delicate fabric soap such as Woolite for sweaters, then lay them out carefully on a terry-cloth towel to dry.

**CARING FOR SHOES AND HANDBAGS** Shoes show wear almost immediately if you don't take care of them; they'll last for years if you do. Polish shoes and handbags as often as necessary, and have shoes reheeled and resoled *before* they get very run-down as a measure to protect the shoe itself, which can outlast countless new heels and soles. To preserve good bags and shoes, first clean with saddle soap, then apply mink oil two or three times a year to preserve and prevent drying out. Vaseline gives a great shine to patent leather (be sure to wipe it off well). For leather, if you're in too much of a hurry to polish properly, spray furniture polish on shoes and wipe clean, or rub with Nivea lotion. For nicked heels and toes, Magix color touch-up, available at shoe-repair stores, will cover the nicks. If shoes get wet, dry them stuffed with newspaper to keep the shape. Tennis shoes can be machine-washed; do the laces separately. *Dry naturally* stuffed with crinkled paper (not newspaper—the newsprint can rub off) to re-gain sizing. (Never put them in the dryer.)

**STORING OUT-OF-SEASON GARMENTS** To store out-of-season garments, fold *clean* clothes carefully. Delicate fabrics go into tissue paper or dry cleaner's plastic. Fold on shelves or pack away, preferably into a cedar chest. No-odor moth cakes are the best way to keep moths away from winter woolens; summer clothes should be put away over the winter in a clean, dry place. Air the clothes next season, and press or steam before wearing. They'll be as good as new.

**C**ustomers who came into Giorgio regularly every three months or so would exclaim every time that there was so much in the store that was *new.* It was true, in a way. We had to stay on top of all the fashions and trends, or someone else would; the stakes on Rodeo Drive were high.

But the truth was that if *new* was what you noticed at first glance, *classic* was the real draw. The perfect gabardine skirt. Pants made to drape a real woman's body comfortably and gracefully. (I became a pattern model myself because I have hips, and the skinny pattern models chosen all too often are built like little boys.) The blazer that works with everything, season after season, year after year. The silk shirt that really fits. "New" feels great this season, perhaps, but by next season it often feels dated. Classic, on the other hand, feels great for a long, long time. I'd take a closetful of classics over a closetful of the latest fashions any day. From the chaotic look of the high-fashion industry today, so would most women.

Back in my Giorgio days, fashion editors and designers worked together to set the trends. Someone from *The New York Times,* for example, might call a designer to ask, "Are you doing anything Spanish for fall?" The next day sketches would arrive and later appear in print of Spanish boleros with full-length taffeta skirts or matador pants with passementerie and beading on the legs. And women would buy them. If Saint Laurent showed tuxedos, women bought them. If

# FASHION: A CLASSIC APPROACH

Oscar de la Renta and Valentino showed mid-calf lengths, women bought them. If the designers proclaimed higher or lower hemlines, we did as we were told, *no matter what we looked like in the new length or fashion.* The industry, composed of fashion makers and fashion media, was all-powerful.

Sometime around the mid-eighties, give or take, the consumer began to change. I can remember, for example, the season Paris touted so-called alligator shoulders—huge, wide ones, and pretty absurd-looking. American women passed, and the look disappeared before it ever happened. Same thing with skirt lengths. Women now wear them up, down, mid-length; we keep them where we like them. All shapes and styles are in, especially if the look is classic. We are collecting good-quality classics instead of replacing styles each season, much the way elegant Europeans have always shopped.

What caused the change? A confluence of factors. Feminism, for one thing. Independent women feel more confident about making their *own* fashion decisions, less willing to be dictated to. Various downturns in the economy have inspired a caution among consumers that seems likely to be permanent: Now it seems flagrantly wasteful to replace our clothes every season. Also, many more of us are working from home today, and comfortable, attractive work clothes have taken the place of the boilerplate "power" look of ten, fifteen years ago. For home-based professionals, dinner and party clothes—along with a few great things to wear to meetings, lunches and so on—are the significant buys.

What does this evolution of the consumer really mean? There have been articles lately deploring the end of the fashion industry, the decline of standards in fashion. To me, because I know the industry, it seems that the designers doing most of the complaining are those still designing from ivory towers, for women who are virtually obsolete.

The designers who are thriving, on the other hand, design for the way we live *now*—and they see the new fashion freedom as a challenge. Because women want *not* to have to go out and buy a lot of new clothes all the time, the clothes we *do* buy become all the more important. As a result, we pay more attention to *quality,* and we want our clothes to go the distance.

If fashion once dictated style ("Here's the look you'll wear this season"), now the opposite is true. *Style* is our own look, the image we present to the world, as personal as a signature, and today the statement of what we want comes from *us:* "This is *my* look. Show me what you've designed to fit *my style.*" A woman who—with respect to fashion—knows who she is can go into any store, glance through a rack of high fashion (or "low" fashion, for that matter) and see at a glance the clothes that will fit her image, her sensibility, her *style.* A woman with style looks natural—*at home*—in what she's wearing. She wears the clothes; they don't wear her.

Let's say that ten women walk into The Gap one day, and they *all* buy classic khakis and a white cotton mock turtleneck, a neutral fashion canvas with tons of potential. *Style* is how each of these ten women will interpret the khakis and turtleneck to make the outfit her own: with blazers, jackets, sweaters or vests; with jewelry; with shoes and handbags; with hats, scarves and other accessories; with hair and makeup. Assuming each of these women knows her own personal style, in the end you'll see ten very individual looks—which is what fashion freedom is all about.

When style takes precedence over fashion, it endures. Sure, your look will expand and evolve, change to fit the times, your changing lifestyle needs, changes in your body. But the essence of your style will remain the same. Your clothes will *last*. And designers who create with this contemporary philosophy in mind will pay attention to substance as well as style—the shape of the female body, with clothes that hang right; silhouettes that flatter; clothes that are versatile, lasting and easy to wear.

Fit is everything. Don't test a garment by standing still in it in the dressing room. Walk in it. A good designer understands how the body moves, and clothes should drape and glaze well in motion. Think how you'd accessorize it. Figure out before you buy it the right shoe height and whether you have the right shoes and the right underwear to make it work. You want to build on what you already own and wear. If you have to start over, top to bottom, with everything you buy, your wardrobe will never work together in the all-of-a-piece way it should.

If fit is everything, *size means nothing*. Every designer (especially Americans, for some reason) cuts every size differently. Many times, too, the *same* designer cuts different styles differently. Sometimes it's a matter of quality control, and some fabrics "make up" differently—but basically it's human error. At Giorgio, I resized everything that came into the store to fit our personal standard, but when I shop now I know I can wear sizes from 6 to 12, European 36 to 44. Always try on everything first, and don't get upset if you're a size 8 buying a 12. Whatever your true size, *always choose clothes that fit one size larger than you are*. Pants, dresses, skirts, everything. You'll look thinner, for one thing. Also, repeated cleaning can shrink clothes—not necessarily right away, but definitely over time.

Only you and your mirror can decide the right skirt length—the length that works best for you. Don't just look at skirt lengths. Look at your legs, front and back, with all the different possible lengths. For daytime, just below the knee (the length Chanel *always* showed), mid-knee or just above are the three classic hemlines. Four inches above the knee works with flat shoes, opaque tights and a young spirit. Eight inches above is cute for kilts with heavy tights, small figures, good legs and weekend activities *only*. This is never a professional look. (I've heard the remark, "You're young, you can get away with it," and I disagree. Start building your life, style, image and wardrobe from the beginning; it's harder to change later.)

In-between lengths are a disaster. Mid-calf should not cut off your calf in the middle—it *has to cover the back of your calf* to work. It's a fun length, great for soft, full summer skirts worn with sandals or flat shoes. Long has to be *long*.

## PROPORTION

——

**Proportion is absolutely
*key*. It brings all the
elements of an outfit
together—the top half,
the bottom half, the shoes.
The weight and textures
of the fabrics don't have
to match, but they have to
harmonize. High heels
with a mid-calf skirt, for
example, are all wrong.
A one- or two-inch heel
(a thick heel, not a thin
one) is okay for a little lift,
but a thin stiletto-type heel
can't "hold" the weight of
a big skirt. One way to tell
is to *walk in the outfit*. If
the shoe is wrong, your
gait will be awkward.**

Ankle length is fun for at-home wear with flats or a formal occasion with mid- to high heels, but *never on the street.*

Be careful, too, with pants—99 percent of us simply don't look as good in pants as we do in skirts. Period. This is not to say that we shouldn't wear them; they can be right much of the time, although they'll never replace skirts. Choose pants with an easy fit—*one size up*—and pair them with an oversized shirt or sweater or a hip-covering jacket or vest (men's are the best). "But I thought I couldn't wear wide-leg pants. I'm too short" is another refrain I heard often at Giorgio. Wrong. If wide-leg pants are slim over the hips, they'll work for women of any height and look great for parties or entertaining at home. (They look wrong for street wear, however.) With wider pants, the top should be close to the body, tucked in, with the waist defined by belt or waistband, making a graceful silhouette.

Running Giorgio made me realize how important it is to *keep it simple.* For example, if I ordered a lot of merchandise in prints, they all seemed to clash even within the store, giving it a Mardi Gras atmosphere, which was *not* what I wanted. Elegance is understated, and prints presented in a big way generally make too much of a statement. Worn judiciously as accents, however, they can give an alluring complexity to an outfit, but be careful. Rule of thumb: Delicate prints enhance small faces with small features; larger prints set off stronger features and rounder or stockier faces.

Stripes and polka dots are always good looks—they looked good on a rack at Giorgio surrounded by almost anything. Paisleys make great scarves and shawls. Gypsy prints are also perennial favorites, on summer skirts to be worn with pretty white peasant blouses. And my favorite classic print of all time is leopard (my makeup packaging is leopard!), which works for handbags, belts, shoes, gloves, trimming—even blouses, T-shirts and sweaters.

*The right image for you reflects how you want to relate to the world and other people.* Whether on location in jeans and a blazer, crisply dressed in the studio or photographed in evening clothes, Diane Sawyer *always* looks like Diane Sawyer. Dressed up or dressed down, Christie Brinkley always looks like Christie Brinkley. Hillary Rodham Clinton, on the other hand, has faced unrelenting criticism from the press for changing her look too often, as if she's trying to figure out—with changes in hair, fashion, makeup—who exactly she's supposed to *be*. Unfairly or not, if a woman's image keeps shifting, other people think she's somehow shifty—and this holds true in real life, too, not just among the rich, famous or powerful.

There are, essentially, three important fashion looks today:

❑ *Out and about* is *the* great American look—sexy, understated, both indoorsy and outdoorsy, casual. It's a crisply pressed shirt, well-fitting jeans, ankle or flat boots and a blazer. It's a casual skirt, low shoes and a sweater. It's the look that takes us to the grocery store, running errands, picking up and dropping off children. It's our at-home daytime look, and it takes us through weekends, to museums and galleries and movies. The look is well supplied by The Gap, Banana Republic, J. Crew and numerous other stylish catalogs, all of which do a great job of offering it at reasonable prices.

❑ *Out in the world* is the look that presents you to the world *professionally*—daytime dress-up, for the office, important meetings, presentations, job interviews. It can also be a dinner look, on its own or dressed up with an upgrade of blouse, handbag, jewelry or accessories. It is *not* true that to get ahead in the corporate world you have to dress like a man; good taste, well groomed, dignified will carry you into any boardroom. This look should never be stiff, but always attainable, accessible, unpretentious. Among the great mid-priced labels to look for are Ann Taylor, Ellen Tracy, Anne Klein II and any of a number of great mail-order catalogs.

❑  *Glamour look* is for *after dark* only—an evening look that can be interpreted in any number of ways: soft and flowing; colorful and dramatic; revealing or not. It's a nice-dinner-out look, a party look, what you might wear to a wedding or an awards ceremony—any special occasion. As has often been said, a good-quality black dress will take you, literally, *anywhere*. However, it's *not* the only color that does, although you'd never know it from the look of most New York stores. The femme fatale look is also well suited to color, so don't just automatically settle for black. This (see pages 122–124 for classic evening interpretations) is a fantasy look, the softest, most dramatic and feminine of all, no matter how you express it.

Which of these looks feels like you? We're all a little of each, and need a space in our closets for each of these looks to face with confidence every occasion that will probably arise in our lives. Each of us, however, is *primarily* one of these, and whichever one feels most like you reflects your *overriding fashion image*. In the spectrum comprising your entire wardrobe, your fashion energy and budget should go toward developing the image *you* want to project.

I learned this lesson in a big way when I left Giorgio and moved back east. My life had been in the fashion industry, and so had my image. My clothes were great—but they were dramatic, high fashion, reflecting my business and my image in the industry. Back east, I married a Harvard professor, lived in Cambridge, a university town—and still had a closet full of high-style Los Angeles clothes. Wearing them would have made me feel out of place, and made my husband and the people around me feel uncomfortable. I changed my overriding look in about a minute to out in the world. The occasion and the lifestyle dictate the look. My Giorgio femme fatale look still emerges in the evenings, but my life now in New York and Washington is a different "fashion pie," with bigger slices for out and about and out in the world.

When we shop, too many of us tend to choose pretty things haphazardly, which, however pretty they may be, and however pretty they may look, may have nothing to do with the way we actually *live*. I have a friend, for instance, with a closet full of perfectly good out-in-the-world career clothes—and "nothing to wear." The trouble is she *used* to work in an office, but now works out of her home. And she's right: Who would sit all day in a home office wearing a suit, stockings and heels? No one. Gradually she's rebuilding her wardrobe—and her image, by translating her clothes to her new lifestyle—with tailored sweaters, more blazers, crisply pressed shirts, and clean, well-fitting jeans and casual skirts. The new image—and new fill-in pieces—are finally beginning to "match" her life and make fashion sense given the way she lives now.

What I always tell my friends who have "nothing to wear" is to *pretend they're the stylist for the movie or theater production of their own life*. Then dress the actress for the role. Having the courage to look at yourself this way, as if you were someone else, requires total honesty—but it *will* help you find your image. Does the expensive slouchy cashmere sweater make sense? Maybe not, if you're a workaholic who rarely relaxes, even on weekends. But probably so, if your life is spent transporting children and working at home. Your image, your life and your wardrobe have to work together or they won't work at all. You'll feel good in what you're wearing only if it fits what you're doing, and you'll feel good doing what you're doing only if you feel and look good in what you're wearing. Spend the most money on what you'll *wear* the most. Spend the most energy on *your image*.

## FABRIC

At Giorgio, if I liked the style and fit of a design but not the fabric, I'd have it made up for us in a fabric I did like: Fabric is very important. As with makeup and skin care, it's important to read the labels to see the composition of the fabric and what kind of care it requires. With fabric, you can't always tell just by looking and feeling. In very small print, for example, you might see 80 percent wool and 20 percent angora. If you're allergic to angora (and mohair: itchy!), as I am, this might inform your decision to buy—or to pass.

Gabardine and thin to medium lightweight flannel are the best fabrics with which to build a basic wardrobe—suits, skirts, pants. They're virtually year-round, they drape and wear well and they last.

Pure 100 percent cotton is wonderful. Washing instructions notwithstanding, it wears better if it's hand-washed, and *always* looks better if it's neatly ironed.

Other fabrics:

**RAYON** Rayon itself is a synthetic, and there are many rayon blends. Some feel great to the touch and wash and wear terrifically. Skip the ones that don't feel right to the hand; they won't feel right on the body either, and they won't clean well. I particularly like rayon crepe and silk rayon.

**POLYESTER** This synthetic has come a long way, and now there are polyesters such as Qianna that have a "good hand"—good to the touch with a graceful way of draping. Read the cleaning instructions carefully.

**LINEN** I choose very little linen because as much as I like it, linen simply wrinkles too much and too quickly. Ironing with spray starch helps a little. In general, linen is better worn *on top*. It's always a disaster to sit in.

**LEATHER** Apart from bags, shoes, belts and gloves, leather is a fabric I carried very little of at Giorgio. A sporty leather jacket in classic black or brown is nice to have—and I *did* stock some great jackets. Occasionally, too, you can come across good straight, lined skirts to wear with tights and a sweater. But leather pants *never* fit properly and don't flatter even the best figures.

**SUEDE** Luxurious, delicious, feels great on the body. It's also expensive and *most perishable*. The best colors are the neutrals, beige to brown. Colored suede always looks fake to me. As for black, the color rubs off on everything, even if they tell you in the store that it won't. (I once had a black suede evening bag rub off on my white gown at an important dinner—disaster!) I love it in jodhpurs, mid-calf skirts, jackets, gloves, shoes and handbags. Ralph Lauren always carries a good selection of suede.

**MELTON** *The* wool for coats. It's warm, sturdy and has great body.

**VELVET** When you can afford to add something new, a velvet suit goes a long way in black, brown, navy or burgundy—and the jacket alone will work as a blazer. There are three types of velvet: Cotton velvet is the sportiest, and a heavier matte version is best for suits; silk or rayon velvet is softer, with a little sheen, and is great for dresses; pane velvet, which has a little roadlike pattern to it, is the softest and shiniest and is best for at-home wear.

**SILK** A lovely fabric for blouses and scarves, but thin silk dresses can be disastrous. They show every ripple and wrinkle terribly.

**CREPE** Much better for dresses than silk. It has body, drapes well and doesn't wrinkle nearly as much.

**JERSEY** Available in a matte wool or rayon version. The designer Halston reinvented this formerly dressy fabric for daytime, and his tailored but molded jersey shirtdresses were famous for their fit. With jersey, fit is everything, so scrutinize carefully, front and back, before you buy. A Lycra panty slip or a taffeta slip really helps to smooth out the line.

**SATIN** Be careful with satin, which can look cheap. Satin separates are always safer than a full satin dress look. Black, brown or navy satin pants or skirts are always right for evening. Satin shirts in pretty colors go with velvet, gabardine or wool bottoms.

**NYLON** A little nylon woven into an otherwise pure cotton, cashmere or wool sweater won't hurt, but too much of it will detract from the purity of these fabrics. The shine and feel will tell you. In general, avoid it if you can.

**LYCRA** For leggings worn with big shirts or sweaters—a very flattering, casual at-home look for most women. Stretchy Lycra is also miraculously well suited to exercise and beachwear, but not becoming on anyone when made into skirts or dresses: *way* too obvious.

**CASHMERE** For sweaters, scarves, caps and gloves, the ultimate collectible! Another luxury is to add a matching trouser or legging. Cashmere dresses cling and thus are harder to wear; they belong on very thin bodies. Halston was famous for his cashmere evening gowns—a very new idea at the time—in primary and pastel colors with matching coats. These are classics. For all its elegance, you can easily hand-wash cashmere in Woolite or Ivory liquid just like any wool sweater, then lay it out to dry naturally on a terry-cloth towel.

## SHOPPING: WHEN TO SPEND, WHEN TO SAVE

There are so many fashion rules out there, and many of them, I learned at Giorgio, can be broken with sensational results. I'd often hear, for example, "Green? I've *never* worn green." As it turned out, a rich emerald green was always one of our fastest-selling colors. With so many choices, it's a shame for anyone to get stuck in a rut. Give yourself time when you shop. Try on the rich emerald green, the off-the-shoulder look you think you can't wear, a sweater that follows the torso. Knowing your style is learning when to say yes, and when to say no—and the dressing room in the store is where you practice, and *the mirror is your tool.*

To avoid making mistakes when shopping, rule number one is to *go shopping alone.* It's the mirror you want to communicate with, not a friend. We all bring our own needs with us when we shop, and ours are the needs we have to satisfy. *Trust yourself, and the two- or three-way mirror.* And try shopping in your closet first—you may not need a new outfit after all.

One of the reasons it's good to keep with you an ongoing list of items you need is so that you won't be distracted by a pretty blouse or special promotion. It's essential to buy with the aim of *filling in* a wardrobe, not just adding to it in a random way. Your list will keep your closet with you at all times, so that you can look at potential new purchases in the larger context of what you actually *need.*

The discounting business has grown huge, and in many ways they're doing a great job. *If you understand your own style, trust the mirror and know about fabric and fit, you can enjoy great savings by buying discount.* But never buy for the price. Only buy sale or discounted items if you would be willing to pay full price for them.

## In general, the items worth *spending on* include:

❏ *Handbags*—good basic leather ones. They get dragged around all day, used a million times; they're noticed and subjected to more wear and tear than you realize. Cheap ones wear out faster, and there's no way to repair the damage. A good leather handbag, though, can be polished and repaired as needed, and can last twenty years.

❏ *Blazers*—classics that should last for years. Ask anyone who's ever owned an Armani or Ralph Lauren blazer.

❏ *Shoes*—worth spending on for all the same reasons as handbags. Even more important, *shoes absolutely need to fit correctly* or you can do real, permanent damage to your feet, not to mention your energy level.

❏ *Suits*—very important; the look that says you mean business whenever you're wearing one.

❏ *Coats*—the first thing people see. Like blazers, an uncluttered wear-over-everything coat will last forever. (You can always find *great* buys on winter coats every year at department stores beginning a month or so after Christmas. They *won't* be out of style next year.)

❏ *Jewelry*—not diamonds necessarily, but *good costume jewelry.* By spending a little more, you'll look as if you're wearing the real thing, and good costume jewelry can last for years.

## Items to *skimp on:*

❏ *Summer clothes*—these get limp after a couple of seasons, no matter what you do to take care of them. Buy simple light fabrics (try discount stores) in great summery colors and simple styles, then forget about them.

❏ *Weekend casual clothes*—khakis, shirts, T-shirts and so on: comfortable, classic and not worth making a designer fuss about. It's more chic not to.

❏ *Scarves*—check out designer scarves at a good department store, then look around for great knockoffs at discount stores. You'll find them.

❏ *Stockings*—L'Eggs, for example, is one great supermarket brand, and they fit and wear very well. Wear sheer natural, or black, gray, taupe, brown or navy (always choose the darkest navy you can find; it's hard to match navies) opaques for daytime wear; black or natural sheer for night. For women of color, there is a line of pantyhose called Color Me Natural that provides a full range of beautiful colors from mocha to ebony. (Call 1-800-925-3447 for the store nearest you.)

❏ *Socks*—one of the fun purchases. White, tan and navy 100 percent cotton are the basics, and colors such as red, yellow, burgundy, peach and hunter or celadon green are whimsical to wear with pants. Argyles are good, too.

❏ *Underwear*—simple cotton panties and cotton-knit camisoles, all available even at the dime store.

❏ *Watches*—there are great copies around, of classic Cartier tanks and the oversized Bulgari.

If this dress code sounds boring, it's not. It depends on fit and fabric; the style is goes-with-everything classic. Pay close attention to the *cut.* Brooks Brothers, for example, will always be conservative, because that's what they're known for. But they offer very wearable striped tailored shirts (surprisingly hard to find!), nice blazers and a good basic straight, lined sheath, all reasonably priced. (For their women's catalog, call 1-800-274-1815.)

Private-label suits—which bear a store name, such as Saks, Barney's or Bloomingdale's, rather than the designer's name—are less expensive than designer labels but higher fashion than, say, Brooks Brothers. They're generally excellent buys. The Carlisle Collection offers, through private consultants, very simple, chic career suits in lots of pretty colors and fabrics. (To find the consultant in your city, call 1-212-246-4275.)

*Your eye color* determines the colors that look best on you. (See the color section for color palettes and charts showing thoughtful color mixes. These personalized charts will show you how to use color to make your wardrobe uniquely your own.) However, for building a wardrobe, we all start with the *universal colors,* the basic colors for suits, skirts and pants—the *neutral* canvas upon which to build with blouses, accessories, et cetera. As a general rule, lighter colors look best with darker suits; here is where your individual colors come into play. Build your basics with the universal colors, and you'll *always* have something great to wear.

The universal colors work on all eye colors and skin tones—they're classic, and they're neutral. Using universal colors as your *base* color, here is how to build a wardrobe:

**SUITS** Choose gabardine or lightweight flannel in basic, universal colors, depending on how many suits you need, to develop a year-round collection. Suits can be sexy, too, when worn with a soft silk blouse or a camisole, T-shirt or turtleneck.

---

## BASIC UNIVERSAL COLORS

—

- ❑ **Blue denim**
- ❑ **Camel**
- ❑ **Navy**
- ❑ **Ivory**
- ❑ **Gray**
- ❑ **White**
- ❑ **Black**

**PANTS** Choose a classic two-pleated straight-leg style. Black, brown and navy gabardine will take you anywhere, and thin gray flannel is a spectacular dress-up or dress-down look; you can wear gray flannels dozens of ways. Add white cotton for all-around use in the summer, khakis and jeans for sportswear and weekends. Fit is all important (see page 86).

**SKIRTS** Pleated, classic straight or slightly A-line skirts are the most versatile and flattering to all figure types. As with pants, black, brown and navy gabardine plus a good gray flannel will *always* look right. (See page 87 to read about hemlines.)

**BLAZERS** A must. A medium-weight navy flannel blazer will get more wear than practically anything else you own. It goes over pants, from jeans to gabardine, skirts, plain T-shirts, even simple shirtwaist dresses. Single-breasted looks best if you're size 12 or up; double-breasted is a great look for smaller sizes.

**BLOUSES AND SHIRTS** Tailored white cotton and blue chambray long-sleeved shirts are *essential* all year long; I have three of each of them, and they're always in use. (The Gap and Banana Republic sell good classic ones.) Neutral stripes go with everything, including jeans, and are a good crisp tailored look: a gray and white striped shirt and a blue and white striped shirt will match *all* neutral suits, pants and skirts.

To change a daytime look for dinner, switch to a white or cream silk or satin man-tailored, long-sleeved shirt or crew-neck blouse, or a pretty beige lace or organza blouse, all of which require an unadorned camisole underneath.

**T-SHIRTS** White, white and more white—for underneath just about anything (big shirts worn with leggings, sweaters, when you need just a hint of white showing), to layer for warmth, to wear with jeans and summer skirts. Hanes, available

---

## LIP COLORS TO WEAR WITH THE BASICS

Make the universals personal by taking care with lip color:

- ❑ **Blue denim**—any except orange and coral
- ❑ **Camel**—any
- ❑ **Navy**—any except orange and coral
- ❑ **Ivory**—any
- ❑ **Gray**—pinks, coral, reds, roses, neutrals, no orange
- ❑ **White**—any
- ❑ **Black**—pinks, reds, roses, neutrals, no orange

everywhere in packages of three, are my favorites, and The Gap sells good ones, too. Buy one or two sizes larger, as they always shrink. Keeping them *pressed and hung*, never folded or scrunched in a drawer, makes all the difference.

**SWEATERS** In universal colors and your personal colors, as many as you can afford, and definitely a few 100 percent cotton ones, which are year-round classics. (See page 127 for choosing the most flattering necklines.)

**UNDERWEAR** Very important, and too often neglected; straps, panty lines or nipples showing is *always* careless-looking and a real mistake. (I was always answering questions about underwear at Giorgio. There are products out there to solve everything; it's just a question of learning about them.) In general, for all the colors available, nude, white and black are all you really need. (Dye white with Lipton tea to make nude. Boil a big pot of water, stir in six to eight teabags, drop in bra and panties and leave for six to eight hours, depending on the "nude" tone you want.)

A satin camisole (with very little or no lace) belongs under every T-shirt and blouse for a more "finished" look. Another option is a nude bodysuit; the Green Mountain Mercantile catalog (1-802-362-2575) sells good ones. Warner's Nudes collection, available in department stores, offers good bodysuits in all skin tones, from very light to black coffee.

For revealing or summer dresses, Garnet Hill (1-800-622-6216) offers a great cotton strapless bra, and lingerie straps, available in sewing shops, will hold straps in place once and for all. Some women, of course, "solve" the problem by going braless. Your choice—but clothes always fit better when you're wearing a bra, which also gives *you* a better shape and contour. The perfect bra to wear when you want nothing to show but don't feel like wearing a camisole or slip is a camisole bra made by Wacoal and available at department stores.

To *add* a little cleavage or extra support, try Shape Up self-adhesive pads, which come in support fit or padded—they're like shoulder pads for the bust. (Cosme Search sells them at 1-800-448-4468, extension 55, or 1-619-481-2118.)

For realistic breast enhancement, order Curves invisible breast enhancer. Made of silicone gel, they're lightweight and can be worn swimming (Self Care catalog, 1-800-345-3371, style A3790, $150). The Wonderbra is a new name for the old-fashioned push-up bra, which adds cleavage and five pounds of rubber. The best selection of padded bras, in all sizes and for all different shapes, is available in the Frederick's of Hollywood catalog (1-800-323-9525). For all bras, *try them on and look at them under clothes.* Sizes vary, and there's nothing more uncomfortable than an ill-fitting bra.

Panties (buy one size bigger!) should be comfortable, and not show any lines, ever. To avoid lines, wear *thong or G-string* panties under pantyhose.

Slips are terrific, to help suits and dresses fall correctly, to finish a sheer look, to smooth out fabrics that cling and to keep itchy fabrics from itching. I think every woman should own two taffeta half-slips, one nude, one black; they're easily found at department stores. A full-length satin slip is another feel-good (and look-good) option; the Winter Silks catalog (1-800-648-7455) sells them.

The contemporary update of the old-fashioned girdle are the new slimming garments made out of Lycra—slips, panties, et cetera. If you'd feel better wearing one, why not? They're very comfortable and do make a difference. Bodyslimmers by Nancy Ganz (with versions for fanny, stomach or waist) is one good brand (for the store nearest you, call 1-800-426-SLIP). The newest "disguise" for a drooping fanny is a comfortable, lightweight "hip bra," currently sold only in Japan—but it should make its way here soon.

For warmth in very cold weather, there's nothing like silk long johns. These can be expensive, but Winter Silks sells an inexpensive and attractive version: very warm.

For special needs, consult the Intimate Appeal catalog (1-602-747-5000). Their control pants liner (style 42294) will slim you down two sizes, for example, and their pants liner (style 42183) will give you an all-over smoother line. The garment-shield mini-camisole (style 41375) absorbs perspiration. They also carry mastectomy forms and bras.

SHOES No gold or silver for daytime, ever. Black, brown, navy and luggage tan are the go-with-everything basics, plus bone or taupe (never white) to wear with white or light colors in the summer. Flat or low heels are basically all you need for daytime, unless you want a mid-height heel to dress up an important daytime occasion, such as a lunch or presentation. Little ballet slippers are practically de rigueur with leggings and a big shirt or sweater for at-home wear. And red shoes can be stunning with black, gray or beige. (See also pages 126–127 for fun shoes to add for different looks.)

Ideally, shoes should always feel great in the store and just as comfortable when you get them home. They don't always, however, but they *can* be stretched. Dr. Leonard's Health catalog (1-800-785-0880) offers good, inexpensive stretching inserts. For even better stretching, spray Kiwi's Shoe Stretch on the leather, first inside, then outside, the shoe. Insert stretcher, and leave in place for twenty-four hours.

## COLLECTING CLASSICS

I can remember my mother telling me (and telling me and telling me!): "Don't wear white after Labor Day and never white shoes except tennis shoes or sandals." These and all her other rules, much as I might not have wanted to pay attention to them at the time, came to echo later on, as I was making my way in the adult world.

As we become less consumption-oriented, perhaps our children will follow suit so that teaching them the principles of fashion won't be such a tug of war. European girls have fads, too, but their overall look is more classic (like their mothers have always been), less extreme.

From what I've seen, the dress-code problem with teenagers is more difficult in cities like New York, Chicago, Washington, D.C., Los Angeles and San Francisco, where kids are exposed to so much more so early. Private schools with dress codes are one answer, if you can afford it: Where all kids are made to dress alike, they don't feel they have to compete. But my stepchildren went to public school, and I know that kids are kids and will break rules constantly, mostly to test how far they can go. Their father and I initiated a dress code early on, and did everything we could to enforce it. All we could do was our best to teach them the classic principles of fashion and good grooming. When they would say, "My friends don't do this, so why do *I* have to?" our only answer was, "Because I care about your learning the things you'll need to know as an adult. If you choose not to practice these principles when you're on your own, that's your decision. But I care about you, and my responsibility is to know you've learned the right way." It's a struggle, but the lessons usually *do* sink in sooner or later.

The best way to teach good taste is by example. Young girls are, above all, curious, and they'll watch as you do your nails, apply makeup, shop for cosmetics and clothes, organize your own closet, choose how you want to present yourself to the world. The more they'll let you work *with* them to develop their own look, the better. The more you can make grooming fun, the more they'll take to it. They do want to learn. But they also want to express themselves, and if you let them, *within the bounds of the dress code you've established,* they'll learn. For example, a little trendier on weekends is fine for adolescents—a bit more makeup, flirty skirts, funky jeans.

Keep stylish catalogs such as J. Crew, Tweeds and Clifford & Wills around the house; teenagers won't be able to resist looking. Rip pictures out of magazines showing outfits that you think would be especially flattering on your daughter. *Exposure* is a teaching tool.

Wear, collect and pay attention to the classics yourself, and one of these days even the most stubborn teenagers will also come around to them.

**POLO SHIRTS** This enduring casual has been around since Lacoste first came out with it in 1927, and is a stylish variation on the T-shirt theme. The Lands' End catalog (1-800-356-4444) offers a terrific version in wonderful colors for men and women.

**COTTON TURTLENECKS** For year-round wear—under sweaters or vests, by themselves, as an extra layer for warmth. Lands' End makes the best ones for

112

men and women I've ever come across, in wonderful face-flattering accent colors (see the color section for *your* best accent colors).

**WALKING SHOES** Much more graceful than the look of running shoes with out-in-the-world clothes are classic oxfords. Bass (1-800-950-2277) does a great version, comfortable and handsome, in sturdy nubuck suede, available in black, brown and, for summer, beige. (Wear opaque hose or socks over your stockings in colors to match the shoes.) Available with or without a rubber sole, they're very reasonably priced and will last forever. The perfect all-weather shoe. Don't forget to spray with Scotchgard.

**NAVY CREW-NECK SWEATER** To me, it's a fashion must-have: a navy crew neck in light wool or cashmere. I bought mine years ago in the men's department, and dress it up or down. You can wear it with *any* color shirt underneath; with pearls and a gardenia (real or fake) on the shoulder; with a slim black skirt or pants and a white shirt with collar and cuffs showing underneath; tied over the shoulders, schoolgirl-style; with colored beads (amber, celadon, garnet, jet, sapphires) and crisp white cotton pants; with any color pants or jeans twelve months a year.

**SEERSUCKER SUIT** One of the coolest looks for summer. Try a blue and white striped seersucker suit with a powder-blue shirt and navy tie (Brooks Brothers sells a nice one), natural legs and navy, black or luggage-tan pumps.

**PIN-STRIPED SUIT** After collecting the basics, there's nothing like adding on a pin-striped suit in a medium to lightweight wool: very crisp-looking, and always feels right. Charcoal-gray/white, navy/white or navy/burgundy are the color mixes to look for—they seem both neutral and high fashion at the same time. Be sure the stripes are no wider apart than one inch.

**A BIG WOOL OR CASHMERE SHAWL** Tossed over a suit or coat, or worn by itself if it's warm enough, big shawls are practical, comfortable, warm and great-looking. Black, brown and gray are the best neutral colors to look for, plus white for the summer. And if you love them enough to collect them, burgundy, navy and camel are colors you'll wear time and again. Benetton sells a good, inexpensive one.

**SEQUINED T-SHIRTS** A pastel blue, pink or raspberry sequined T-shirt is a surprisingly simple classic that dresses up gray flannel or silk, and cream, black or navy pants or skirt.

**VELVET COAT** A mid-calf black or brown velvet coat is indispensable for evening worn over short or long dresses or suits. One such coat will last you a lifetime. In addition to coat departments, try thrift or secondhand shops, which, if you're lucky, sometimes have a good selection of classic fashion collectibles.

**RIDING BOOTS, ANKLE BOOTS, COUNTRY CLOGS AND MOCCASINS** All tasteful and comfortable casual looks. Riding boots and full-legged jodhpurs (the ones with the protruding sides) can camouflage a hip problem; it's one of the looks Ralph Lauren made classic for casual street wear. Ankle boots dress up jeans in a minute, and Top-Siders are a super look for hanging around in the country. I love soft Indian moccasins for wearing at home. They're surprisingly hard to find, but you can always order them from World Traders of Maine (1-800-603-0003).

**OVERSIZED MEN'S CARDIGANS IN WOOL OR CASHMERE** I have one each in gray, camel and dark red, and I wear them all the time as casual jackets over both skirts and pants. A really cozy look, and they feel wonderfully warm when wrapped around you.

**BEACHWEAR** Gottex cuts very flattering styles for real-life women, as does Norma Kamali. I've also found very flattering two-piece suits in prints or solids in the Joyce Holder catalog (1-800-245-4647). The bottoms have tummy control, generous full-cut backs and flattering high-cut legs. They come in split sizes—style 30 for the top and style 700 for the bottom. Unitards, boxers from J. Crew or exercise shorts worn with racer tops (like midriff bras) are a cute look for the beach and swimming, especially for full thighs. *Always* wear a big men's shirt on top, and a great Panama or sun hat, for protection against the sun.

**N**o black with navy! No black with brown! No dark colors in "light" cities like Los Angeles, or light colors in "dark" cities like New York! No cuffed pants if you're short! No belts if you have a large waist! So many rules—*and all of them false.* Black with navy is a great look, and so is black with brown. You *always* wear the colors that are right for you, and let the place, occasion and your own common sense dictate when each of *your colors* is right. Shorter, taller, heavier, thinner: Almost nobody has an absolutely perfect figure. We all have to customize our wardrobes so that they work for us, not against us, and so that *we feel good in everything we own.*

Once again, your mirror will show you what you need to look out for. Get to know your body well. From time to time reassess it, wearing only a bra and panties, in front of a full-length mirror in good lighting. Shapes change with more or less exercise and with age: "Gee, I wasn't aware that my hips had grown two inches"; "I'm longer-waisted than I realized"; "My shoulders are much narrower than my waistline." Once you get to know your shape intimately, and accept it honestly, the rest is pretty simple. *Accentuate* the good parts, and *camouflage* those that aren't as good. Build a basic wardrobe of classics, then add the flourishes to express the *image you want to project to others.* Choose great accessories (see the next chapter) to create and enhance *your individual look.* Wear the colors that bring out the sparkle in your eyes. Refine the look even more by tailoring lip

# YOUR WARDROBE: A CUSTOM APPROACH

color to fashion color (see the color section). Then forget about what you're wearing, and focus instead on what you're *doing*.

## YOUR CUSTOM COLORS

During my years at Giorgio, I was constantly asked *what colors* to put together with *what other colors* for a finished look that is both elegant and professional. Color confusion was a real problem. Some women were still wearing the colors their mothers had worn, or the colors their mothers had dressed them in as children. Many women, afraid to try new colors, stuck to the neutrals—the *universal colors* (see page 106) that look great on all of us. But neutral-on-neutral worn all the time isn't very sexy and can look (and feel) pretty drab.

After successfully styling thousands of women, I finally figured out the principle behind what I was doing instinctively—and only then knew *exactly* how to use the color formula to enhance my own wardrobe, and, later, in my makeup line: *Your eye color is the key to choosing the colors that look best on you.*

---

## HOW TO USE THE COLOR CHARTS

First go to the color chart that represents *you* in the color section. The colors shown there will be the face-flattering colors that will *compliment* you and *harmonize* any look you choose to wear. These are your *custom colors*. As a general rule, the *darkest colors* in your chart will, together with any of the universal colors, work best as *your base colors*, for overall body wear and stockings. The *lighter colors* are your *most flattering accent colors*, for blouses, sweaters and scarves.

Then look at the index that suggests *color mixes*—ways to draw several colors together (some predictable, some truly surprising—but they work!) for texture and complexity. There are mixes for all the *universal colors*, plus *dramatic mixes* I kept on charts for my customers at Giorgio. Again, choose the mixes that flatter your eye color and skin tone. Finally, there's an index featuring *classic color mixes*. Lots of neutrals here, colors every woman already has in her closet—tried-and-true ways out of a color rut.

The more ways you can reinterpret and reinvent your classics with your colors, the better your wardrobe will work *with* you, and *for* you, and the further it will go.

---

If you go to Europe, you will see how well the women there understand this principle at work. When choosing sweaters, blouses, scarves, whatever, women don't hold the colors up to their suits, necklines or the skin tone of their faces or necks—*they check the color against their eyes.* Even European men know to hold new ties up to their eyes to see how they look, not up to their shirts, the way American men usually "try on" new ties. It's the eye color that matters.

## A GLOSSARY OF LOOKS

No woman needs a lot of clothes, but every woman needs to be able to create *a variety of looks* from the clothes she *does* have. With, say, two skirts (navy and gray), one gray pant, a navy blazer, two blouses, two sweaters, pearl earrings and a necklace, you would always look chic and as if you had a lot of clothes. A suit jacket can be worn over pants, skirts, dresses. Wear nothing underneath; wear different blouses or sweaters underneath; wear a camisole underneath and change the jewelry: That jacket becomes the basis for, literally, dozens of different looks. *It's not the quantity but the careful choice of classics that makes a wardrobe work.*

The looks that follow are starting points to stimulate your imagination for developing new ways to put old favorites together. There's lots of denim—a true classic that expresses the way we live now. Also, it's great to mix with other classics, such as pearls, Chanel-type jackets, cashmeres and good wools, real or costume jewelry, blazers and silk shirts. There are probably more formal looks suggested than anyone needs, but at Giorgio, I found that dressing to the nines makes a lot of women nervous. Pick the evening looks that feel like you.

And these are looks to have *fun* with.

## STAYING IN/SPORTY/CASUAL

One of the great pleasures of the day is coming home to relax, shedding work clothes and changing into something comfortable but still stylish, so that you *feel as good at home as you do when you're out.* Even if you work at home all day, it's good to switch moods and gears by changing clothes for the evening. And at-home activities require several different looks—entertaining looks; sexy looks; curl-up looks for *you alone;* relaxed looks for *close to home.* Some suggestions:

❑ For summer, make a *sarong skirt* out of a big batik tablecloth by wrapping it around your waist (see page 143). Add sandals, a T-shirt and gold or ethnic jewelry. Throw a large piece of face-flattering silk over your shoulders as a shawl—a great look for a weekend lunch with friends.

❑ For the beach, boating or hanging around on weekends, white jeans, a *brightly striped T-shirt* worn in or out (J. Crew has great ones) and espadrilles is a sunny, relaxed look you don't have to think about.

❑ Curl up comfortably and sexily for an evening in *leopard tights* with an oversized black or beige sweater or a big white shirt with a tank top underneath. Black leather looks good with leopard, too—and sexy for discos; very *feline.*

❑ For daytime resort wear or summertime at home, wrap a big square piece of *chiffon* sarong-style (page 143), tie it at the shoulder and wear it with a strapless bra over leggings.

❑ *Black leggings* with an oversized men's white cotton or blue denim shirt. Belt it low with a black leather belt.

❑ For a quick *summer shawl,* and a high-spirited look, try a custom-colored plaid picnic or Indian blanket draped over your shoulders.

❑ *Ski pants,* black or brown, also look sleek off the slopes, for casual wear, with a long or short (depending on your shape) sweater on top.

❑ For a day at home, tuck a *striped T-shirt* into jeans, then add a simple leather belt. If you have to go out, throw on a blazer and a sailor cap from an army or navy surplus store. If it's warm, just wear a blue denim workshirt as a jacket and add a baseball cap.

❑ A *cotton peasant blouse* looks fresh in summer worn with jeans or a big cotton skirt and colorful beads.

❑ Casual and dressy at the same time: Black pants or skirt, matched with a pretty blouse in one of your custom, face-flattering colors.

# 118

*Bronze or gold ballet slippers or sandals* give the look accessibility. Colorful ballet slippers are widely sold (French Sole, 1-212-737-2859, has all colors), or you can spray-paint white ones with paint from the shoe-repair store.

❑ For *entertaining:* Crepe, chiffon or velvet pants with a chiffon or silk blouse is a classic at-home look, as is a stark-white cotton shirt with black or navy crepe pants or an ankle-length black skirt (try it with a tan or burgundy belt) and a pearl necklace and earrings.

❑ Black jeans, gray turtleneck, red-plaid *lumber jacket*—a rosy-cheeked outdoors look.

❑ Other *chic ways to hang around in denim:* Wear your denim shirt buttoned and outside your jeans, with a narrow brown belt—and a great pin or choker at the neckline. Or substitute a navy crew-neck sweater tied around the waist instead of a belt. Wear a tailored shirt in one of your custom colors tucked into jeans, and add a blazer if you go out—very crisp. Denim workshirts worn with jeans look especially bright with a white T-shirt underneath and a scarf at the neck. A denim shirt looks casually stylish with olive-drab pants; brown belt and shoes add complexity. *All* denim colors—black, white, tan, lighter or darker blue—mix well together; mix and match for variety.

## OUT AND ABOUT

For the office, shopping, working in or managing the home, pants, mid-calf skirts, shirts and sweaters mixed and matched is still the best look. Diana Vreeland wore gray flannel pants and a cashmere sweater just about every day of her career—there's nothing more chic. She added her signature ivory accessories; you can add yours (see next chapter). Comfortable, pretty, easy to move around in—these are looks for *active lives.*

❑ Even miles from a horse farm, a great year-round look is *jodhpurs,* riding boots and a turtleneck, worn with a cardigan sweater.

❑ Wear *two short-sleeved T-shirts,* one on top of the other, in two of your custom colors—doubly warm, doubly face-flattering, doubly cute. Roll the sleeves up individually so that you can see both colors. Good with jeans or khakis for running errands or for casual days when you're in and out.

❑ A great *American look:* khaki pants, white shirt, denim jacket. A black and white polka-dot tie gives it an Annie Hall twist. A *sexy variation:* jeans, white shirt, black leather jacket or a tailored blazer. Accessorize (see following chapter) to make the look *you.*

❑ For the weekend or a casual dinner, wear your jeans or khakis and a face-flattering custom-color or white T-shirt with a *Chanel-style jacket* and very tailored jewelry: understated and looks great.

❑ The more *complete a denim look,* the sexier and more effective it is. For a true-blue denim look, try a blue denim workshirt tucked into jeans with a plain or western black leather belt, a blue bandana knotted at the neck (page 143) and a black or navy blazer or jacket. Accessorize with gold or silver earrings.

❑ A *safari jacket* is a really nice extra to have. (The J. Peterman catalog—1-800-231-7341—sells stylish ones.) Belted in brown leather with a slim black skirt, tights, low pumps and simple gold jewelry, it can take you out and about to lunch and all kinds of daytime appointments. For perfection, add a straw safari hat.

❑ Army or navy surplus stores sell *sailors' summer jackets,* which never go out of style, worn with a striped T-shirt and navy or white pants.

❑ Pair your tailored blue denim shirt with black or white jeans, a black or brown belt and shoes. A scarf or piece of jewelry goes at the neckline, so that the touch of brightness is close to the face.

❑ Other ways to *wear denim out and about:* Suede is great with denim—try brown or tan suede pants or a jacket with denim shirts or jeans; layer with a T-shirt in white, beige, ivory or pale gray. Ralph Lauren makes lovely soft chamois shirts (I learned to pass on any chamois pants—they stretch and bag), which look luxurious tucked in or out of jeans. One surprising mix is a denim shirt with rust pants, black shoes and belt and an ivory sweater or blazer on top. Turn denim into a casual suit—with a tweed blazer and a tweed or black leather newsboy cap; with a houndstooth blazer and a wool cap; with a white shirt, simple gold jewelry and a red-plaid jacket. One of my out-and-about uniforms is my peach Versace blazer, jeans, white shirt or turtleneck, black or brown loafers, a good scarf and sporty jewelry—and it's the jeans, somehow, that give the look its energy.

## OUT IN THE WORLD

The professional look should look *personal,* not corporate-boring. It should also be flexible: Take off the suit jacket or change the sweater for a more casual look, or dress up the suit to transform it to an evening look. To do so, change the sweater to a pretty silk or lace blouse; substitute a clutch for the daytime handbag; switch opaque hose to sheer natural, black, gray or brown; change low pumps to mid- or high heels; dress up the jewelry—and voilà!

❑ To customize a trim tailored *shirtwaist,* wear a T-shirt in one of your custom colors (see the color section) underneath. Works well, too, under a V-necked sweater.

❑ For a winter dinner at a neighborhood restaurant or a casual evening with friends, bundle up in slim black ski pants, a black turtleneck, and throw over it a colorful ski jacket—*bright* looks crisp and fresh in the cold.

❑ Using your colors to customize, mix *subtly striped* shirts with a *glen plaid* or *pin-striped* suit. This gives the suit an unexpected femininity!

❑ *Festive dinner out:* There's nothing more classic than a lacy white shirt, black wool pants and a pretty belt in satin, suede or silver or gold leather.

❑ *Men's ties* are just as flattering to women if the colors are right. Try a red or black one with a white or powder-blue shirt worn with a gray or navy pin-striped suit. Great with seersucker. Sparks up the classic look!

- *Summer standard,* for lunch, cocktails or dinner: Try a black T-shirt or cotton sweater with white linen, cotton or crepe pants or a skirt, draped with lots of white pearls.

- *Restyle your daytime black* dress or suit and shoes by wearing it with *navy opaque stockings* and navy or black shoes. Do the same with brown. Very stylish.

- ❑ A cool lunch-in-Malibu look for a hot summer day anywhere is a short white pleated skirt worn with a short-sleeved cotton sweater, mid-heel gray pumps and a straw hat.

- ❑ Try a *black shirt and yellow tie* with a gray pin-striped pantsuit. Add a white flower to the lapel.

- ❑ Ways to *wear denim out in the world:* Dress up jeans with a white shirt, pearls and an "alligator" belt and loafers, then finish the look with a feminine wool or cashmere vest or jacket in gray, brown, navy or a soft custom color. Gray flannel pants with a blue denim shirt and a tan or navy blazer is a look so masculine it actually looks even more feminine when a woman wears it. Wearing mid-heel pumps with jeans is another sophisticated look; a silk shirt and pearls or pretty beads and earrings dresses up the top half. Substitute tighter, sportier, more casual black jeans (denim or velvet) for regular black pants for a casual dinner, worn with a velvet tunic or a lush wool or cashmere sweater and a mid-heel pump.

## GLAMOUR

Parties, lovely dinners out, special occasions, black-tie events—the glamour look is for after six, the time to have the most fun with makeup, electric curlers and the clothes that make you feel most feminine while still feeling natural, at home with what you're wearing. If you're most comfortable in very tailored clothes, for example, you won't feel right in ruffles and feathers for evening, but you *will* feel like yourself and look great in a simply draped crepe dress or maybe dressy velvet pants, blazer and a silk or satin shirt.

We did a lot with glamour at Giorgio, and I learned that a correctly, classically interpreted evening look can last *forever;* I still have, and wear, almost all of my evening wear from those days. So, buy with care and a thought to the long term. Some of the looks that endure:

- ❑ For a *young girl's first glamour look,* prom dresses should be chosen in a look to last a long time for black-tie wear. Full-length black, white or off-white are classic and pretty choices, in an off-the-shoulder, strapless or slip-dress style; taffeta, satin and crepe are fabrics that will wear well. Add white kid gloves to the elbow, "pearl" earrings and choker, black or cream satin mid-heel pumps. For comfort and a smooth look, underwear should be secure, and stockings should be natural or, if the dress is black, black. Long hair worn up is elegant, and so is a *little bit* of makeup.

❑ Young French girls love *black fishnet stockings* and wear them under pants, jeans or with black dinner dresses—*trendy* and Left Bank. (At home, throw a big sweater over the same fishnets and wear with ballet shoes as an alternative to leggings.)

❑ Everyone, regardless of weight, can wear a *chiffon illusion top* with a bodysuit underneath—very feminine when they glaze your silhouette. Pair it with dressy black pants or a skirt. A *black taffeta skirt,* for example, lasts forever. A burgundy or green silk or satin belt adds a lovely contrast.

❑ *Pink* is wonderful—and unusual—at night, and set off very well by gunmetal or bone shoes. If your legs are good, definitely go a little *shorter for party wear.*

❑ If red's your color, a *wonderful red dress,* with natural hose (not red) and red or black shoes, makes a great entrance and is a welcome variation on the wear-black-everywhere theme. Add a black bag and pearl or "diamond" earrings, and that's it.

❑ To make a wear-everywhere *basic black dress* into a look-twice outfit, wear it with natural hose and *red shoes.*

❑ *Make your bustline the "accessory"* by wearing a push-up bra under a well-tailored suit or coatdress and very little in the way of accessories: a confident, grown-up look.

❑ For a sleek, high-fashion formal look, pair *black sequined pants* with a black cashmere sweater. High heels and simple rhinestone button earrings complete the outfit.

- For black tie or a *special holiday* look, top a long satin or velvet wool skirt with a red cashmere sweater set. Sparkly earrings give the outfit a *glow.*

- Black satin pants worn with a *gold sequined cardigan,* tailored (no blouse underneath), is very sleek, particularly with black high heels.

- A *gold or silver lamé blouse,* simply tailored, will dress up a slim black skirt and stockings for dinner.

## ALL SHAPES, ALL SIZES

"But I thought I could *only* wear . . ." and, "But I thought I could *never* wear . . ." were two of the phrases I heard most often at Giorgio. My answer always was, "Try it on and see for yourself." As often as not, the customer went home happy and looking fabulous in something she thought she could *never* wear. There are a few tricks to enhance and to camouflage, and a few general guidelines. Otherwise, it's you who, with your mirror, decides.

STOCKINGS AND SHOES Starting at the bottom, women have a lot of trouble with shoes. "What kind of shoes do I wear with this outfit?" and, "What kind of stockings?" were always two of the big questions. Stockings are easy: *Match the stocking to the shoe or to the bottom of your hem.* Or wear a natural sheer, which is always right. Very light off-white opaque or sheer stockings look good in the summer with black, white or navy in place of natural.

In general, high-heeled shoes look great for evening, although never more than two and a half or three inches high with evening pants—you'll walk funny. For daytime, choose chunky little heels or flats, a "men's" lace-up oxford or a loafer. During the day you're active, walking fast and running—no matter what you're doing. Anyway, an active look for daytime is always the sexiest. Glamorous shoes belong in the evening, with sensuous evening looks. The rule-of-thumb rundown:

- ❑ With *miniskirts:* flat shoes.

- ❑ *Above to just below the knee:* one- to two-inch mid-heel pumps for daytime. Higher, if you like, for evening.

- ❑ *Mid-calf:* flats, one-inch pumps or knee-high boots for daytime. For evening, a high heel is appropriate and graceful, especially with a slim-lined skirt.

- ❑ *Ankle length:* Never for daytime—looks dowdy. For evening, a mid- to high heel will carry the look.

- ❑ *Evening formal:* Mid- to high heel only; never flats.

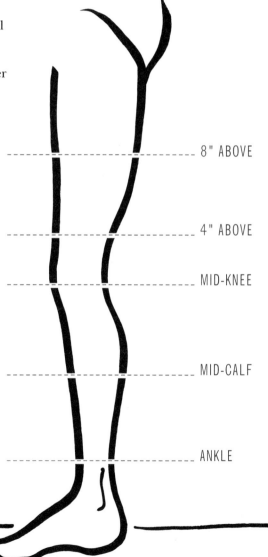

8" ABOVE

4" ABOVE

MID-KNEE

MID-CALF

ANKLE

# 126

Your shoe wardrobe is determined by your lifestyle; if you don't hike, you won't need hiking boots. But, in addition to the classic shoe wardrobe (page 110), acquiring the right shoes will always make you feel better in what you're wearing. Some add-a-shoe styles that are close to essential:

- ❑ *Running shoes:* For running and exercising, but never for street wear.

- ❑ *Sporty shoes:* The L.L. Bean catalog (1-800-221-4221) has a sturdy collection of boat shoes, snow and hiking boots and casual shoes. Timberland and the Lands' End catalog (1-800-356-4444) sell real boating shoes (in brown and tan, which are the only *real* boating-shoe colors), which also work for casual street wear.

- ❑ *Tennis shoes:* A clean, fresh-looking tennis shoe with brightly clean laces is American sportswear at its best, and perfect for jeans, khakis, shorts or culottes, but never to the office. To me, white is *the* color and Keds is *the* brand. They're also cute with white ankle socks and a cotton summer dress for weekends and country wear—a look for all ages. If you're not wearing socks, those little socklets called Peds keep the shoes fresh.

- ❑ *Leather loafers:* In brown, black or luggage tan. They're good with pants, skirts and jeans, with socks or no socks or tights in the winter.

- ❑ *Boots:* Black or brown riding-type boots with a wide, flat heel in a good leather are all anyone really needs. Wear under mid-calf skirts, or wear trousers *over* the boot leg for an ankle-boot effect.

- ❑ *Tuxedo pumps:* For me, little "men's" black patent-leather tuxedo pumps with wide, flat grosgrain black bows are indispensable! I wear them all the time—at home with pants and mid-calf skirts, and with out-in-the-world dresses and suits year-round. The Brooks Brothers catalog—1-800-274-1815—sells them.

- ❑ *Sandals:* Brown, black or luggage-tan fisherman sandals worn with or without socks are great for sportswear, beachwear and with jeans and khakis. (Flip-flop rubber thongs are shower shoes. They fall off on the beach, so they're useless there, and they look horrible on the street.)

❑ *Espadrilles:* These rope-soled canvas shoes don't last very long, but they're comfortable and inexpensive, and they look great with casual pants and skirts. Navy, white, red and beige are the most useful solid colors.

❑ *Ballet slippers:* Very popular today, great with leggings and at-home wear and widely available in a variety of colors, including silver and gunmetal for evening.

**NECKLINE** Think of the neckline on a dress, sweater or blouse as a picture frame; the neckline and *your* facial shape (see page 129) should *contrast* to frame the face—no square necklines against a square jaw, for instance.

❑ *Crew, or jewel, necks* are probably the most classic necklines, and they should be designed to be close to the base of the neck. A gap on either side of the neck showing skin is not as attractive as a clean, close, "tight" neckline. If you have sweaters or T-shirts with a wide crew neck, fill in with a simple choker or scarf to demarcate the neck.

❑ *Mock and full turtlenecks* are dress-up or dress-down looks for year-round, and translate well in fabrics like cotton, wool and cashmere. Cowl necks are another choice, but not as clean and usually not as flattering a look.

❑ *U-necks* are deep and low, but can be very flattering because they cover the *unflattering* hollows between shoulder and bottom of neck.

❑ *V-necks* also cover those hollows. If they're tight and close, they're a great look.

❑ *Halter necks* look great on most women, provided the shoulders are well formed. Make sure, though, that the garment covers, or is altered to cover, those little pads of fat we all have under our arms.

**SHOULDERS AND UPPER ARMS** Broad or square shoulders are strong-looking and attractive, particularly if they're in balance with your hips and lower torso (Too broad? See page 130.) For *average, tapered and sloped shoulders,* shoulder pads are great! They come in small, medium and large, and they're worn directly on top of the shoulder; pin them and check the mirror before sewing to make sure they're the right size, comfortable and in the right place. They make all the difference in how a garment hangs, and in presenting a strong *contour.* Be sure to remove shoulder pads before laundering.

*Set-in sleeves* look best on most figures, and they should always fit the shoulder perfectly, with or without a shoulder pad. On a *raglan sleeve,* the seam extends from the neckline to the armpit, leaving a drape of extra fabric under the arm, which can camouflage a little bit of extra weight. Set-in is by far the crisper look. A *caftan* sleeve is a straight-lined raglan in which the armhole is dropped, and should be worn only in a gracefully styled at-home dress or for entertaining. *Off-the-shoulder, slip styles and sleeveless* can be worn by anyone with good shoulders and upper arms—and the right lingerie: no straps showing.

**FROM THE WAIST DOWN** A full hip, derriere or thigh should not wear a tight pant or skirt. Choose A-line, dirndl or full. If the skirt is pleated, the pleats, called kick pleats, should start low—at the bottom of the hip. Be sure when wearing pants, even if they're just jeans, that your fanny is comfortably covered. Then put on an oversized men's shirt or sweater, or a tunic. It's a good look anyway, even if you're slim. All pants should be hemmed as long as possible without touching the floor: makes the legs look longer, and everyone likes that. The wider the pant leg, the more even the line. For a narrow pant leg, you'll want a slight break in the front, longer in the back.

## THOSE NINE MONTHS

During the first six months, you'll be comfortable in men's shirts and sweaters worn over maternity pants and skirts. If it's summer, you'll be lucky—buy inexpensive full pinafores and off-the-shoulder gauzy dresses that you can belt later on. These are soft and pretty looks. Thankfully, maternity clothes aren't all ruffles, bows and Peter Pan collars, the way they used to be, so during the colder months, buy simple, tailored clothes to see you through—the less complicated, the more flattering. In the final months, a special baby girdle will give you support and help to prevent stretch marks.

One of the first things I learned from my movie-star customers is that hemming your jacket at

crotch length is *not nearly as flattering* as choosing just below the derriere as the cutoff point, especially if you're under five feet six. It can be a difference of an inch or two, but it can make *all the difference.* Similarly, a jacket shouldn't be worn *above* the hips unless you're very thin and wearing a sophisticated Spencer jacket with widish, pleated man-tailored pants. Whether you're *camouflaging flaws* or *enhancing your strong points,* let fit and proportion be your first consider-ations. *Always check your two-way mirror.*

Arbitrary rules can be instructive as guidelines, but they're not set in stone; you and your mirror are the final arbiters. For example, I'm five four, and I love pants with cuffs although they're against the "rules" for women on the short size. If the pant leg isn't too wide and the cuff is one or two inches wide, they look fine.

The same goes for the monochromatic "rules": Sticking with monochro-matic colors will make you look taller, and black will make you look thinner. True, but that doesn't mean that a large woman has to forgo a black tunic-style sweater over white slacks because monochromatics are more slimming. Buying one size bigger, covering the fanny and wearing light, pretty colors next to the face will draw you out nicely, too, so please don't adhere to monochromatic rules at the expense of looking feminine and expressing your own style.

So, these are guidelines, not rules. *Don't rule out anything that catches your eye until you and your two-way mirror have given it a try.*

**ROUND FACE** V-necks and square necklines are especially flattering to a round face. Round necklines emphasize the roundness and are best avoided.

**SQUARE JAW** Avoid round and square necks. V-necks work an asymmetrical magic on a square jaw—they really soften it.

**NARROW FACE, POINTED CHIN** No V-necks, which pull the chin down. Instead, wear round or square necklines.

**DOUBLE CHIN** Turtlenecks are a good camouflage, and so are mock turtles. Draping a scarf around the neck attractively (page 140) will help as well.

**LONG NECK** Lucky you. Carried with confidence, long necks impart an Audrey Hepburn kind of gracefulness. Don't try to disguise it. Choose any neckline that suits your *face*. You can wear them all.

**SHORT NECK** Avoid turtlenecks, except for the low mock turtle, which will give your neck the illusion of *length*. Lengthen, too, with *long accessories, beginning at the neckline*. (See next chapter.)

**BROAD SHOULDERS** Keep away from shoulder pads (remove them, if necessary) and necklines that cut straight across the torso from shoulder to shoulder. V-necks and deep round necklines, if they suit the shape of your face, will draw the eye in and away from the shoulders.

**NARROW OR SLOPING SHOULDERS** Shoulder pads to the rescue! Collect all sizes and wear them as often as possible, gearing the size to the proportion of the outfit. For a casual look, tie a custom-color sweater over your shoulders, which will be both face- and shoulder-flattering. Avoid halter tops.

**PEAR-SHAPED** Add shoulder pads whenever possible. A wider shoulder line *on top* balances out the pear shape on the *bottom*.

**BIG STOMACH** A slightly full or dirndl skirt, belted at the waistline, will draw the eye away from a big stomach.

**VERY HEAVY LEGS** Wear a darker stocking whenever possible. Even when you're buying a neutral sheer, you can buy up to three shades darker than your "natural" shade to make the legs look slimmer.

**VERY SKINNY LEGS** When wearing a neutral sheer, go a shade or two lighter than your "natural" shade. Opaques in dark colors make skinny legs *disappear—* dark sheers are better.

**BIG BUST** To camouflage, avoid ribbed or heavily textured fabrics, and anything horizontally striped.

**SMALL BUST** To "add" a little to it, wear ribbed or heavily textured fabrics, and try horizontal stripes on top.

**TOO SHORT** "I'm five two, and clothes are always too overpowering for me" is another problem that came up all the time. It's a *proportion* question. Be sure your shoulder line sits smack on top of your shoulders; otherwise, it will make you look shorter still. Jackets should be shortened to just cover the fanny. You *can* wear cuffs on pants if you want to. And mid-calf skirts are okay, as long as they're long enough to cover the back of the calf.

**A LARGE WAIST** Silhouette-flattering A-lines will *drape* and suggest a waistline. Large waists *can* wear belts, but they should be narrow and not buckled too tight.

**TOO HEAVY** It's a myth that women size 14 and up can only wear loose-fitting "fat" clothes. For years at Giorgio I would ask designers to make small-size designs in sizes 14 to 18 for our larger clientele. And little by little, styles in larger sizes are getting better. If you're large, you're large. You're not going to hide it with an overblouse or an all-black wardrobe. You'll just look dull and styleless. Wear pretty colors and styles you feel good in. Hold posture tall, keep hair and makeup up to speed, smile. That's what people will remember you for.

The legendary columnist Hedda Hopper was known for always wearing a hat. To this day, whenever I think of Barbara Bush, I picture her signature choker, composed of those three strands of pearls—classic. Diana Vreeland's distinctive look was as much a part of her identity as the way she signed her name. Every day she wore a cashmere sweater, flannel pants and (long before anyone knew about endangered species) two ivory cuff bracelets, a big ivory tooth claw on a gold neck chain and earrings.

That's one way to approach accessories: Take a signature look and make it your own—let it *define* you and become an integral part of your look. I know a woman, for example, who wears pearl earrings every day, rain or shine, blue jeans or black tie. They're classic, and the look works for her. Another friend always wears one chunky long necklace consisting of twenty-four strands of seed pearls and no other accessories—never a bracelet, earrings or pin. A third woman I know always wears twelve to twenty-four simple thin bangle bracelets, either gold or silver, depending on what else she's wearing. Those are her signature accessories, tailored but with a twist of femininity that's always recognizable as *hers.*

The other way to approach accessories is to collect them to *stretch your wardrobe,* to wear different accessories to reflect *different moods and occasions*—sporty, glamorous, casual, sophisticated or sexy.

# ACCESSORIES CREATE STYLE

We all have accessory looks we prefer, that really add to and interpret the image we present to the world. *This becomes your style.* I personally love the look of a gold or silver link choker under a shirt collar, for example, with the buttons all buttoned up. I love simple cowboy bandanas tied at the neck, and have them in every color I've ever been able to find. I love the look of men's ties on women, worn with a suit or more casual pants. I love white flowers to pin just about anywhere, all classic looks, as classic as well thought-out clothes. And all are feel-good, fun-to-wear accessories.

Scarves, shawls, gloves, hats—we always had a complete collection of great accessories at Giorgio, and over the years I learned how to "package" the clothes we offered together with the accessories that would enhance them; I used to "dress" the hanger from head to toe. What surprised me most was how many women would buy *everything* from the display hanger, because it looked so good together. Sure it did, I always thought, but I suspected that these women as often as not already had the accessories they needed right at home. If you buy and collect accessories to go with your image, then they will go with your clothes.

Good accessories are classics that never go out of style; there were standard accessories we reordered—and sold—at Giorgio year after year. Some of my favorite costume jewelry—little summer necklaces of shells and beads, for example—go back twenty years or more, when I bought them from vendors on a beach in Mexico. Bright bangle bracelets, great for casual summer lunches, last forever, as does wonderful costume jewelry from wherever you find it. If you *buy costume jewelry with the same strict criteria you'd use for buying real,* it will wear just as well and last just as long.

## TO ACCESORIZE, GET ORGANIZED

Half the battle, I learn when I "accessorize" my friends, is *shopping in your closet for accessories you already have.* A woman will never find the right scarf if all her scarves are bunched into a drawer or box, unpressed and unappealing-looking. A jumble of necklaces tangled into one big knot will never yield anything to wear. The same with gloves, hats and mufflers all bunched together beyond vision and reach on a closet shelf. The more you can organize and separate your accessories into baskets, boxes or whatever works for you, the more often you'll find just the accessory you need.

Not long ago I was poking through a basket of a friend's accessories as she was sorting it out, and I came across a very beautiful cameo pin that I'd never seen her wear. When I asked her about it, she said it had been her grandmother's, and she liked it well enough, but wasn't it too matronly? Where would she wear it? I offered a number of suggestions, and the one she liked best was on her denim jacket, where it's remained ever since. Classic juxtaposed with casual is a great look, always a sign of individual expression. *Mixing and matching gives accessories and the outfits they enhance the most mileage.*

Accessories can also save the fashion day at times when you need them to. I remember one weekend when my husband and I were visiting friends for one night. They had told us that we would be having a very informal dinner at home, and I'd brought along a pair of black denim jeans to wear with a cotton shirt, a sweater and a couple of pieces of stay-at-home costume jewelry. The plans changed, as plans will, and suddenly we were going out to a dinner party. It didn't matter, really, but if I had brought along some slightly dressier accessories, maybe a silk blouse (and thrown the sweater over my shoulders) and slightly dressier shoes, I know it would have felt more like a party to me that evening. Accessories dress you up or down, particularly if the clothes you start with are classic canvases, and now I always *travel with a plastic zipper-top bag containing a choice of accessories in case plans do happen to change.*

The best way to keep track of the accessories you have already is to sort them all out and try them different ways every time you go through your closet (see page 83). If you really need a new muffler or handbag, add it to your ongoing shopping list. As for how many accessories are enough, prudence dictates buying only what you need, unless you fall in love, which happens often with accessories.

Tag sales, thrift shops, antiques stores and outdoor markets when you travel are all great sources for accessories, as are standard department and discount stores. Museum shops (particularly the galleries at the Smithsonian Institution in Washington, D.C.) are increasingly offering a wide selection. And shop ethnic neighborhoods—Little India for scarves, linens, jewelry, tablecloths; Chinatown for baskets, fans, kimonos, pagoda hats (great for sun protection); Mexican neighborhoods for peasant shirts and Native American jewelry. The accessories that turn out to be the most fun to wear always seem to be those that are also the most fun to acquire.

## JEWELRY

However creative many of my Giorgio customers were with fashion in other ways, I found that with jewelry, many women tended to play it tailored and safe—gold, silver, pearls—thereby missing out on a lot of creative looks, with beads, a variety of costume jewelry, even a satin ribbon worn round the neck as a choker. (To clean jewelry—except pearls and beads—use an old toothbrush and toothpaste.)

The question women have asked me most often is whether to mix silver and gold. It's a judgment call each time, but mixing can be very effective. To start with, more and more jewelry is being made with both silver and gold—watches, rings, earrings. In general, if you can give equal weight to silver and gold—for example, three gold bangles and three silver ones—mixing works. If not, it's better to stay in one family or the other—whichever predominates in the jewelry you plan to wear.

**EARRINGS** Which earrings to wear is the most important jewelry decision there is because they're closest to the face, and it takes a full-length mirror to show whether the proportion is right. In general, for daytime wear, gold or pearl buttons are standards for everyone. Also classic are coin earrings; hoops in small, medium or large (Spring City Craftsman, 1-800-262-6026, has a huge selection of hoops, pierced and unpierced); rhinestone stars (Saint Laurent knockoffs); fake solitaire stones in rhinestone, ruby, emerald or sapphire; and

> ## A TIP FOR BUYING ACCESSORIES
> ——
> **When buying anything from hats to pins, check in a *full-length mirror* to see how they look and whether the proportion is right with your overall look. General guidelines are pretty much common sense: Smaller, fewer accessories if you're small, and vice versa; taller or bigger women can sometimes carry off and look sensational in bigger, bulkier pieces. *The only real "rule" is that when you're in doubt, leave it off.***

pearl, ruby or emerald "fringes." Noticeably dangling earrings are distracting for weekday wear; they're better for weekends, evenings or at-home looks.

To *customize* your earring wardrobe, if your face is round or your jaw wide, choose a semismall or flat earring, slender drops or oval buttons. If your face is oval-shaped, a round medium-sized earring—a big circle with a pearl in the middle, for instance—will be very flattering. If your face is triangular, fill in the lower cheeks with a pear-shaped earring, wider at the bottom than it is on the top.

If your ears aren't pierced, you may find that some earrings pinch. A good costume jeweler can loosen them, but first try Comfees eyeglass temple-bar pads, available at any major drugstore. Apply one or two to the back of the earring clip. If you do decide to pierce your ears, be sure that the hole goes into the *middle* of the lobe and not too low; otherwise your earrings will droop.

**NECKLACES** *Chokers* don't usually work on short, thick necks, and they may or may not be the best look for long faces and necks. Big-busted women generally look best in necklaces that stop at the breastbone (a good look for all women) and tall women like the balance that necklaces thirty-four to thirty-six inches long give them. On the other hand, I've seen women break these rules every which way—to great effect. For instance, the classic choker for a suit neckline is a heavy link chain in gold or silver, ideally with a bracelet to match (antiques jewelers sometimes have good buys). Or try Mrs. Bush's triple-strand pearl choker, perfect for everyone worn over or under shirt collars and dresses. (Kenneth Jay Lane, 1-212-868-1780, makes hers.) Take time with a full-length mirror to assess how all the different lengths look on *you*.

*Pearls*—real, cultured or even well-made fake ones, both "black" (which are actually gray) and white—are always pretty and always correct, and very chic when the colors are mixed (one black pearl earring and one white one, for instance). But don't let your wardrobe of "beads" stop there. All sizes and colors of beads are always stylish and work with everything, from jeans to dinner wear.

To me, they're the ultimate accessory collectible, and I look for them everywhere I go—in flea markets, open bazaars abroad, street vendors here at home, even fine jewelers all the way up to Cartier. But some of my favorites cost only a few dollars, if that much.

*Caviar beads* are the tiniest, and *seed-pearl size* are small but not as tiny. From there they just get bigger, but all sizes work with everything. Multiple chains of tiny beads is a fabulous look, too. Look for face-flattering colors in your custom palette—cinnabar, amber, silver, amethyst, gold, ivory, tortoise, turquoise, coral, burgundy, all shades of green from celadon to emerald, sapphire, ruby, the jets and clear crystals are among those fairly readily available. Be sure they're all one color. It's a cleaner look. Mix and match them with both the universal colors and your custom palette.

*Chains*—gold and silver, long and short, plain or bearing *one* ornament or charm—complete the classic necklace wardrobe.

**BRACELETS** Simple bracelets that aren't noisy are for daytime wear, or you'll drive your colleagues (and probably yourself!) crazy. Otherwise, bracelets are fun, feminine and sexy—and right now you probably have more bracelets in your bracelet wardrobe than you remember. (It's good to try them in new ways from time to time.) *Cuff bracelets* can be found in the same shades and places as beads, and are just as satisfying to collect and wear. Wrist size permitting, wear two wide ones (up to two inches each) on each arm, or a dozen or more narrow *bangles* on one arm. Skinny bangles rising up the arm in gold, brass or silver also look great in numbers. Wood and ivory beads mix well with silver or gold. Or choose one important-looking cuff, even for daytime. If you ever come across Bakelite bracelets from the forties, buy them—they're collectibles and getting harder and harder to come by. An armful of solid red or green Bakelite bracelets, bangles and cuffs all mixed, to accessorize a very simple black or white outfit is one of the sleekest looks of all time. *Chain-link* bracelets can also be mixed with narrow bangles and look stylish.

# 138

**RINGS** Rings call attention to the hands; again, *it's the full-length mirror that will tell you when they're too much.* I have short fingers and wear only a very slim wedding ring. Baguette bands, gold cigar bands or insignia rings (your insignia or not) are the simplest styles, flattering to everyone. For important rings, a diamond, pearl, ruby, emerald or sapphire solitaire is a forever classic. I don't like big gold and diamond rings (too glitzy), and if I had one, I know I'd take it to a good jeweler and have it turned into a pin.

**PINS** Small daytime pins—such as frogs, stars, butterflies, ladybugs, hearts, Art Deco bar pins—are cute to wear on the collar of a turtleneck, lower left side of a sweater (including cardigans), top button of a shirt or on a blazer or suit jacket. If they look good together, wearing two or three at the same time makes a nice statement. For evening, don't buy dressy pins too small even if you are; they'll get lost. Two and a half to four inches is about right. Wear pins high under the left shoulder, at the center of a V-neck, on the waistline of a dressy dress or on the lapel of a suit.

**CUFF LINKS** Simple cuff links are the easiest and most elegant to carry off. My favorites are little roped fabric knots sold in men's stores, or simple pearl, gold or silver button-type links. Sometimes nice ones turn up in antiques shops. More often, they turn up in the accessory cases of boyfriends and husbands.

### HANDBAGS

I always think of handbags as suitcases to fill your needs as you're traveling through the day. The style and the size are your choice, but keeping it proportionate to *you* is best, as long as it can carry what you need. Leather bags in black, brown and luggage tan will fill most daytime needs—plus they go with everything. If you stick to these basics in choosing bags, shoes, belts and gloves, they'll always go well together; trying to match them is almost impossible to carry off, old-fashioned, unnecessary and less interesting than having them harmonize. For evening, a small black unadorned silk envelope bag can take you anywhere, forever.

A comfortable, proper-sized handbag notwithstanding, I usually find that I need to have a tote bag with me as well when I'm out and about, or out in the world. (It can also carry a change of shoes and accessories for evening.) Just as handbags should be both functional and fashionable, tote bags should be un-obtrusive—the lightest-weight ones you can find in nylon or easy-to-clean canvas (they look horrible when they're dirty). Keep contents accessible by sep-arating them into zipper-top plastic bags of different sizes. In summer, tote bags can get a little prettier if you choose nice baskets with shoulder straps or han-dles; J. Crew (1-800-932-0043) sells an excellent one, as do many ethnic stores.

Extra bags to add for fun are a black, brown or luggage-tan lightweight backpack for travel and weekends—so comfortable to have your hands free—and a fanny pack for hikes and museum-going.

## BELTS

At Giorgio, I carried expensive, ornamental belts with gold or silver buck-les: These were belts that made a fashion statement. In real life day-to-day, gray, burgundy or tan works with all basics and some custom colors to call attention to the waistline more quietly. Even if you have an extraordinary waistline, you want the viewer's eye to discover it on its own, not to zoom in first to the middle of the body before it even notices the face and neckline.

The purpose of a belt is to cinch in the waist (never tightly, so that you can't breathe), marrying top half with bottom. Basic colors for leather belts in-clude black, brown, luggage tan, bone and taupe—all colors that mix well with basic colors for handbags and shoes. (Again, the idea that they have to match is dated. Instead, they harmonize.) In general, choose one-, two- or three-inch belts, depending on your figure: *The slimmer you are, the wider you can go.* A self-covered buckle is the easiest to work with and the most versatile, because it can be dressed up or down.

For softer belts, make your own by buying velvet or satin ribbon two or three inches wide at the fabric store and tying it into a pretty bow at the waist. Choose ribbon in colors accenting what you'll be wearing (see the color section)—the look is great with a soft blouse or sweater and crepe mid-calf skirt or trousers. If you can't find the perfect belt, look under "Belts" in the yellow pages, or check with a tailor—you might be able to have a self-covered one made from the hem of your dress.

### SCARVES

I don't agree with anyone who says (and a lot of people do), "A scarf is the most versatile accessory. It can be worn to tie back hair, as a belt, a necklace, a skirt." A scarf, unless it's a narrow, solid-colored one pulled through belt loops, looks terrible as a belt. No matter what you do to it, a scarf won't *look* like a necklace, although it can be folded horizontally four times, placed around the neck and knotted at the ends to play the part of a necklace; this is a nice accent for under a shirt collar, over a turtleneck or T-shirt or tied into a cowl. Nor will it look much like a skirt, unless you're wearing it over a bathing suit. And it doesn't tie the hair back very well, either, but always ends up making it look sloppy.

A scarf has to look natural, never contrived, in order to work, and the way to make it do that is to keep it looking like a scarf, not trying to turn it into something else. As for color, here's the place to indulge your taste in abstract prints, in grays, black and white, navy and white, burgundy, tan—basics that go with everything. Prints, too, featuring your custom colors, will contrast beautifully with the neutral canvases of suits, pants, skirts. One way to collect instant "scarves" is to buy pretty silk fabrics when you happen to come across them, then take them to the tailor to hem the edges.

❑ *Silk pocket squares* look great in suit-jacket pockets, which women all too often ignore, and give the suit a new look with just a change of the pocket square. Paisleys are classic when used this way. Just grab the center of a quartered square in the middle, tuck into the pocket with points facing down and a pretty, soft pouf results.

❑ *Silk scarves, two or three feet square* are practically indispensable to loop casually over your shoulders after folding once into a triangle. Worn crisscrossed under a coat or jacket, it flatters the face at the neckline. To turn it into a cowl neck—which looks good over almost any neckline—knot it at the side, by your shoulder, or at the back of the neck, then drape into a cowl. To wear as an ascot, fold corners in and fold again, then place at back of neck, loop once in front, then tuck into shirt. It looks smart and pulled together.

- *Mufflers* in soft wool or cashmere provide warmth over jackets and coats, and, if chosen in your softest custom, face-flattering colors (yellow, rose, baby blue—see the color section), also flatter.

- *Shawls* (pages 112–113) can take the place of coats, or be worn over them, for extra warmth and European style.

- To wear a scarf on the head, try making a *headband,* by folding two corners in, fold in again, then wrap from underneath the neck, twisting once at the top of the head (knot, if you like) and tucking in the ends. *To cover the hair,* wear a scarf in the classic Audrey Hepburn style, folded into a triangle, looped under the chin and knotted in back.

❑ Come summer, there are more ways to use scarves as accents. *Cowboy scarves,* or bandanas, are a fun and cool warm weather look—white T-shirt, jeans and a bandana tied around the neck. Making a scarf into a *sarong* as a bathing suit cover-up is also a practical look that has become classic. Using a large scarf or a small tablecloth, hold one end in front of you just a little above the waistline, and start wrapping from behind, going around, behind and around again. When you come to the end, roll the last end and the first end tightly under, forming a kind of waistband. Add sandals, a tank top and hoop earrings. *Gypsy head scarves* are also a classic summer look: Make a triangle and place ends down at your forehead. Wrap over ears, knotting at the back of your neck. Expose the earlobes and add gold button or hoop earrings.

HATS

I love the look of hats, and they're practical besides—warm when necessary, protective all the time and they add to the mood of a look, from casual on up, enormously. To me, classic hats include canvas or denim slouch hats or baseball caps with large visors for out and about; berets in neutral colors (such as off white, red, navy or black) for an everyday out-in-the-world flourish; Panama straw hats for the sun; and round straw daytime hats for summer in off-white, black or navy. Wool or cashmere caps in one's softest custom colors (see the color section) are great for winter. Extras include a tennis hat (a must if you play tennis and *to swim in*) and a cowboy hat for fun. The Gap, Banana Republic and other casual stores have great all-around hats, and the Peterman catalog (1-800-231-7341) offers my favorite big Panama with a chin strap for summer. If you'll be traveling, however, pick a crushable hat to take with you, wearing your straw hat on the plane. You can get cashmere watch caps, available in some two dozen face-flattering colors, from the Vermont Bird Company (1-415-967-3123).

Men's stores, too, are a great source of hats—my favorite is Arnold Hatters in New York (1-212-768-3781). They offer classic fedora, Panama and cowboy hats, along with almost impossible to find oversized Basque berets, which are big enough to enable you to tuck in all your hair.

One hat that's both functional and fashionable (in a forties kind of way) is a terry turban, to keep your hair clean while you're having a massage or to preserve the style while you're bathing. The ones I particularly like are available in fuchsia, blue, white or black from Dr. Leonard's catalog, 1-800-785-0880.

## ACCESSORIES FOR THE HAIR

Be careful with hair accessories. They become part of your jewelry attire, and have to be coordinated with the rest of your jewelry and accessories, particularly because they're within such easy range of sight—right on top of your head. A gold or silver barrette can give a sense of sparkle, but when you start adding to it earrings, necklaces and so on, it becomes too much. For this reason, I prefer tortoise-shell barrettes or combs, which are much less no-ticeable on dark hair (and more subtle than gold or silver, which are better on blondes), and give myself more free-dom with the rest of my accessories. Barrettes, in other words, should blend into the hair.

## EYEGLASSES

My brown-eyed professor friend recently asked me what color frames she should buy, and I said, "Red." She was surprised, but bought some anyway—and loves the lift they've given her.

I love the look of glasses. I love choosing frames and used to wear glasses without a prescription as a fashion ac-cessory even before I needed them. And even back then, I never had much luck finding frames I liked in prescription stores. Instead, to this day, I buy sunglasses I love at the dime store—even brightly colored plastic ones—and then have the optometrist change the lens to prescription. I've found wonderful, inexpensive frames this way, and people are always asking me where I got them.

The shape of the frame matters, and the size of the frames, too, should be proportionate to the size of your face, although I love oversized frames on just about everyone. Frames can be found in round, oval and square shapes, but

---

## TIPS FOR HAIRSTYLING

The hair, when styled or adorned in an unusual way, itself becomes an accessory.

❑ Pull your hair into a low pony-tail with an elastic band, then wrap and twist the tail around the elastic, anchoring with large hairpins. You will have a very sleek, sophisticated *bun*. A little gel or hair spray on top will smooth out the look.

❑ Fun accessory: Buy a long *fake braid* in your own hair color, and attach it under your bun. This is a summery party look—with cottons and peas-ant outfits.

❑ To create a *semibraid*, divide hair in half, and twist each section around the other. Anchor with an elastic band at the end; it's a slightly differ-ent look from the usual braid, and quick to create if you're running out the door.

## CHOOSE EYEGLASS FRAMES ACCORDING TO YOUR EYE COLOR

Tortoise horn-rimmed, wire-rimmed and black are the universal colors that look great on everyone. And custom-colored frames look great, too:

❑ **BLUE/GRAY EYES:**

Blue

Gray

Rose

Lavender

Turquoise

Pink

❑ **BROWN EYES:**

Red

Burgundy

Green

Brown

❑ **HAZEL/GREEN EYES:**

Khaki green

Brown

Burgundy

Fuchsia

❑ **ASIAN EYES:**

Burgundy

Rose

Wine (deeper than burgundy)

❑ **WOMEN OF COLOR:**

Purple

Green

Burgundy

---

*don't select frames based on the shape of your face. Instead, select frames based on the shape of the bone structure around your eye area, from brows to cheekbones.* For example, I wear square glasses even though I have a triangular face. Why? Because the shape surrounding my eye area is square.

When choosing frames, line up the top of the frame with your eyebrows. Then look for your cheekbones and try to find a frame that fits well and sits in a balanced way between the two. Then stand back and examine how the frames look in a *full-length mirror*—the overall look. If you really don't like glasses at all, "invisible" frames—rimless with a thin bridge—are the least noticeable. Otherwise, go for maximum accent value with color. Colored frames are really fun and, as with your custom colors, they are determined by eye color.

**OTHER GLASSES** Sooner or later, most of us need reading glasses; fortunately, there are some great buys—and great looks—around. If you use glasses only for reading, *half-glasses* will probably do the trick. They're usually rectangular, or rectangular with rounded off corners. A neat-looking nonprescription pair in mild, medium or strong magnifying strengths is available in several colors from the Paragon catalog (1-800-343-3095). I also discovered a wonderful thin, flat, tortoiseshell lorgnette *reading glass* to carry in my handbag or pocket at Purdy Opticians in New York (1-212-688-8050)—a real find. Everyone asks me where I got them.

## GLOVES

I love gloves as much as I love hats, wear them as much as possible and am always getting compliments over them, probably because they look so unusual, even dramatic, now that so few women wear them as a matter of course anymore. They protect the hands year-round, and, like hats, they also finish a look. Black, brown, gray or luggage-tan soft leather are the basics, white kid can be used to "upgrade" any lunch or dinner outfit and pale-gray kid is very elegant for dress wear. Soft wool or cashmere gloves in your most subtle face-flattering custom colors (see the color section) are pretty extras to blend with caps and mufflers. And white cotton gloves are still dazzling for summertime when you want to be dressed up.

## UMBRELLAS

Because I always lose umbrellas, the small, inexpensive, foldable ones are the answer; besides, the minute the sun comes out, they fit right into a tote bag. Bright colors are available, too, to brighten up a gloomy day.

## ACCESSORIES: A GLOSSARY OF LOOKS

I love watching teenagers I know learn to express their fashion creativity as they begin their accessories collections. (Accessories are also great gifts for those what-to-buy years.) Teenagers look great carrying big canvas backpacks for schoolbooks. One brown leather medium-sized "dress" day bag of their choice (shoulder bag, or whatever they prefer) and a small black satin clutch for dinner or formal wear are other standard bags most teenagers need. As for jewelry, small pearl earrings, gold studs and small or medium-sized hoops are classic "starter" styles. They can begin to collect what they like in the way of interesting bracelets, strands of flattering beads, Native American earrings, bracelets and turquoise beads. "Diamond" studs or pearl button earrings for dress-up are classic for teens. They can also have fun with scarves, belts and so on—I like to give teenagers a little leeway finding what looks best on them.

**148** There are *no hard and fast rules* for women, either; accessories are a personal thing. Here are some of the looks I put together at Giorgio for my customers and myself, looks I've worn and loved ever since:

❑ Many women feel shy about wearing flowers for some reason, but ornamental ones can be used as accents in dozens of ways. A *fake white gardenia or camellia* (available at fabric and trim shops or, for many times more money, at Chanel) is one of the most versatile accessories of all. Pin it on a crew-neck sweater when you're wearing jeans and you'll dress up the look; add pearls, too, and you're another notch dressier. Wear it on your shoulder, at the center of an appropriate neckline, on a belt. Pin one (fake or real) in your hair just over the ear or on the elastic of a ponytail or at the end of a braid, or on an evening bag. Or try tying a two-inch black satin bow over a low-slung ponytail, then pin the flower in the middle of the bow. For a dramatic look, take ten or twelve of them and pin at random over a sleeveless or strapless black party dress. Or pin two instead, one large and one small, either together or with the big one in the middle of your neckline and the smaller one higher and to the side.

❑ Antiques stores sometimes have *old watches,* which look sensational hung on a narrow velvet ribbon as a choker or necklace. Sometimes they also sell fun antique *eyeglasses* into which the optometrist can insert your prescription lenses. Try hanging the frames closed on a pretty ribbon, velvet cord or antique silver eyeglass chain to make a necklace.

❑ A sexy beach and summer look for all ages: Wrap a dark brown *suede cord* or thong (available at fabric stores) around your wrist, ponytail or braid and tie into a knot. For a dressier look, wrap pearls or pretty beads around your wrist to make a bracelet.

❑ A silver or gold *upper-arm bracelet* (ethnic stores have them) is dramatic with summer evening sleeveless pant outfits or long skirts. (Not with short dresses; the proportion is wrong.)

❑ A Native American silver or silver-plated *conch belt* is classic with jeans or skirts with a pretty shirt tucked in, and silver bangle bracelets and earrings to complete the look. If the belt has turquoise in it, check your face-flattering custom colors (see the color section) for a selection of tops that will work.

❏ For a casual flourish, order a chrome *bobby whistle* from the Safety Zone catalog (1-800-999-3030) and hang it from a black cord or silver chain.

❏ Instant "*key jewelry*" for sports and the beach: Hang the keys you need (up to three or four) on a chain or ribbon to wear them as a necklace. Or clip your key ring onto the center of your bikini top.

❏ *Ring necklaces* are created by looping two or three simple gold or silver rings through a silver or gold chain.

❏ If you find big, flat, round *red plastic earrings* someplace, buy them. They'll look surprisingly chic with a black skirt, sweater, shoes and stockings, a red handbag if you have one, and with red lipstick to match.

❏ *Gold safety pins* can also be whimsically ornamental. Pin one of the large pins horizontally, then, if you want, hang one or two layers of three or four pins each. Wear on the side of a sweater or on a casual jacket.

❏ Hang a *monocle* or *small magnifying glass* on a chain as a necklace.

❏ Mix pearls and a gold or silver link chain to create a custom *choker* to wear over a crew-neck sweater or T-shirt. Or wear under the collar of a tailored shirt. Mix or match longer pearls and chains (24 to 36 inches) to create *necklace ropes*.

❏ Teenagers love to collect *pins,* fun ones, to wear all together on denim jackets, front and back. Pins on jackets (maybe not quite so many!) is a customizing look at any age. Keep your eye out for antique *medal pins,* a nice accent for a suit lapel.

❏ One forever look is that of *crosses:* gold, silver or ivory hung on a chain or pinned at the neck of a shirt. "Diamond" crosses are best set off on a velvet ribbon. Kenneth Jay Lane (1-212-868-1780) has can't-tell-the-difference copies of Chanel's Maltese cross, enameled cuffs in ivory or black, which are stunning on normal or big-boned wrists.

150

- ❏ If it's a look that suits you, *suspenders* in an amusing pattern are fun worn without a jacket. Solid red, brown or black ones will look nice as well, pulling together the look of a tailored pantsuit. For the young in spirit, pin a fresh summertime daisy onto the strap.

- ❏ Turn a black pantsuit into a tuxedo with a *black men's bow tie* against a white shirt, or wear nothing underneath but a *camisole and dressy necklace* for a slinky evening look.

- ❏ *Black lace gloves* look wonderful with filmy black chiffon for black tie or dressy summer occasions.

- ❏ To get into a gardening or working-around-the-house spirit, try a *cotton workman's jumpsuit,* which you can usually find at an army or navy surplus store. A denim shirt or a bright T-shirt goes well underneath.

- ❏ *White knee socks* are classic with walking shorts and sandals or espadrilles. Toss a denim jacket on top.

- ❏ A fresh small red carnation is a nice touch pinned on a black suit lapel with a white tailored shirt underneath.

- ❏ To subtly dress up at-home trousers, wear black or cream *point d'esprit or lace hose* under them, and little black flats.

- ❏ Wildly popular in the forties, with reappearances off and on ever since, *snoods* create a soft, demure look if you look good in them. Cream crochet works for day, and black or brown for evening, no matter what color your hair is.

- ❏ Tie a pretty *scarf* (Hermès style, or any other style you think looks good) to the strap of your handbag or backpack. It gives a note of cheer to the day—plus you may need it later.

- ❏ Laced-up *Roman sandals* are fun with mid-calf skirts, in camel or dark brown, to match your skin tone.

- ❏ *Little baskets,* particularly closed ones, make cheery and unusual handbags for casual summer dinners or vacation wear. Japanese basket stores such as Be Seated in New York (1-212-924-8444) carry a good selection.

- ❑ To add color and finish to the neckline of a suit or coatdress, try a *crisscrossed scarf* in simple off-white silk or satin. Crisscrossing and tucking or pinning it in will anchor it.

- ❑ Make your own *eyeglass necklace* by tying the ends of your glasses with a narrow red or black grosgrain ribbon compatible with your frames.

- ❑ Take red, black or ivory lacquered *chopsticks* and poke them into your bun, crisscross-style—a great look for summer parties.

- ❑ Take a *large cuff bracelet* or *oversized costume watch* (such as a big Swatch) and wear it *over* your shirt sleeve.

- ❑ Soften the functional look of a watch by adding a delicate *silver or gold chain bracelet or two,* depending on the watch color, to the same wrist.

- ❑ Don't forget *buttons* as accessories. To make an ordinary cardigan look designer, for example, change the self-colored bone buttons to pretty gold ones.

- ❑ For hot summer days, I love the look of a *pretty fan* (Chinese markets sell them), which is practical and very feminine. To personalize, spray it with your scent.

In December 1993, *Consumer Reports* ranked sixty-six prestige fragrances for quality and integrity, and "Delicious," my new fragrance, came in third. I was thrilled, but when I told my friends, I was very surprised by the way some of them responded: "How can you measure quality and integrity in a fragrance?" they kept asking. "Aren't they all about the same? Isn't it purely emotional whether someone responds to a scent?"

Instinctive reaction is part of what draws us to a scent, it's true; otherwise there wouldn't be dozens upon dozens out there. But a lot more goes into creating a fragrance's appeal. I like to think of fragrance as an art, not unlike music. You can be drawn to a piece of music (or a fragrance) instinctively, just because it's a pretty tune or, in the case of the fragrance, because it smells good. The more you learn about music, however, the more you demand from it: moods, nuance, complex and harmonious compositions. It's the same with fragrance: The more you know, the more you look for.

In the business, I'm what's known as a "nose." Coco Chanel, Estée Lauder, Charles Revson, Annick Goutal—those who work with perfumers to create the fragrances they want to market—are noses. As for the perfumers, they're certified chemists who have gone to perfumers' school to study the thousands of in-

# FRAGRANCE

gredients that make up a perfume. As part of their training, they also apprentice under a great perfumer before going out on their own. We noses are, in effect, the composers of a fragrance, and the perfumers are the musicians.

I've always loved and responded to fragrance, but my response had always been instinctive: I liked one fragrance and didn't care very much for another, the way most of us respond to perfumes. I can still remember my first gift of scent—the toilet water my mother gave me when I was six and had to have my appendix out. (To this day, I think it's a great idea to introduce young girls early to the classics—the cologne version of, for example, L'Interdit, Arpège, Chanel No. 5.) By age eight, I was hooked—buying perfume oils and toilet water from Woolworth's; as a teenager, I sprayed scent onto my pillow before going to sleep. In my dance-student days, I graduated to bath oil—the least expensive form of perfume. As I grew more sophisticated, in my twenties, I began sending to Paris (it was actually cheaper!) for the classic fragrances. I tried them all: Chanel No. 5 (created in 1925 and still in the top ten), Bal à Versailles, Joy, L'Interdit, Cabochard, Calèche, Fracas, Ma Griffe, Arpège, My Sin. I also tried pure isolated oils like sandlewood and tuberose. Even at that point, though, little did I know how fragrance would later shape my life.

After selling the head-to-toe "total look" in fashion and accessories for years, fragrance seemed to me the next logical step for us at Giorgio. *Fragrance is, above all, a fashion accessory—and an important one: the last thing that goes on before you leave the house.*

I had seen the power of fragrance, an invisible but profoundly potent form of communication, not only in my personal life but also in the store. Some of our customers had vivid signature fragrances, as much a part of who they were as their autographs. For instance, when the unmistakeable scent of Jungle Gardenia floated through the room, instinctively I would turn to look for Natalie Wood or Elizabeth Taylor. I knew, as most women do, that wearing fragrance makes you feel sexier and more beautiful. The pressures of my job also taught me that *scent can really affect your mood.* I discovered, for example, that I felt more serene and was able to concentrate better when I burned scented Riguad candles in my office.

The fragrance business is based in New York and Paris, not in Los Angeles, where I was living. So I wrote on a legal pad what I liked and wanted in a fragrance, and what I knew I didn't like and didn't want. Without yet knowing the language that perfumers use, I tried in my own words to describe what I thought it should smell like.

Creating a scent is not unlike choosing a scent, because for each *you have to have an idea of what you want the fragrance to impart,* the sensibility you want to convey whenever you wear it. In creating what came to be the perfume Giorgio, I had a very clear idea of what I wanted to convey. I started the process in 1978, right in the middle of the feminist movement, when women were struggling to assert themselves toward equality with men. In fashion, the emphatic shoulder pads that were becoming popular gave us a little extra stature as we found our way into every segment of the workplace. I wanted my perfume to do the same thing: be assertive and empowering—make a statement—and at the same time be sexy and feminine. I wanted a fragrance that would make a confident entrance and linger a while upon a woman's departure.

I met with the big fragrance houses on visits to New York and explained what I wanted. The perfumers asked for my marketing plan, demographic study and targeted age group. I said I had none of those but knew what I wanted, based on the one-on-one experiences I had daily with all kinds of women in my own store six days a week; I also believed—as I still believe—that fragrance is ageless. A few perfumers said to me, "It doesn't matter what you put in the bottle. Once it's packaged, it will sell." But I knew better. I knew how fussy our customers were. Finding "my" perfume took more than two and a half years.

The biggest mistake a consumer can make in choosing a fragrance is the first mistake you learn to avoid when actually creating a scent. The first thing a perfumer learns is to distinguish between the notes of a fragrance.

Most fragrances are composed of three sections—the top, middle and bottom. Again, as with music, the notes change as the fragrance "progresses." If the early notes smell good, you'll be likelier to enjoy the fragrance all the way through. But not necessarily: The first few chords of a piece of music can sound just fine, but they sometimes veer off into a song you don't like at all. You have to hear the song—or smell the fragrance—all the way through to decide whether you like it.

The *top note* is the very first scent you smell when a fragrance is applied. It can last anywhere from thirty seconds to two or three minutes. *The top note is important because most consumers buy fragrance based on this first impression, not on the scent the fragrance will ultimately develop into.* The *midsection* comes next—the phase of the fragrance that lasts between five and ten minutes. The midsection generally features notes compatible with the top note, but "arranged" slightly differently, or a different version of the first note. The third section is what we call the *dry down,* composed once again of compatible notes, but varied slightly. The dry down is the fragrance that you're actually buying, the one that will stay in place for the next few hours.

There are several categories of scent from which we choose our fragrances, as profoundly different as musical notes. The *floral* category encompasses the essence of the flowers you'd find in a garden—tuberose, lily of the valley, gardenia, rose, jasmine, orange blossom, carnation, honeysuckle, hyacinth and so on. A fragrance can consist of the scent of a single flower—*single florals,* they're called—or *bouquets,* in

## WEAR A FRAGRANCE BEFORE PURCHASING IT

Walk around the store for twenty minutes to see if you like it as much as you did when it first came out of the bottle. If possible, step outside as well and smell it in the fresh air, where it isn't competing with all the other fragrances wafting through the store. If you like a fragrance after it reaches the dry-down stage, you'll never be disappointed once you get it home.

which the scents of several florals are mingled to create a unique and more complex scent. Diorissimo, Joy and Giorgio Beverly Hills are among the bouquet fragrances.

*Floral aldehyde* compounds are chemical compounds that yield scent. Scents created from chemical compounds are by no means necessarily inferior to those created from natural ingredients—most good perfumes, in fact, use a combination. Chanel No. 5 was the first to use an aldehyde compound in its formula.

Imagine walking through a forest in a light rain, and you'll get a sense of what the *green* scents—such as Lauder's Aliage, Balmain's Vert and Di Borghese—smell and feel like: A crushed green leaf smell is the smell of quintessential green. Pine, mint, tomato leaves and any of a huge variety of herbs can yield the green scents.

Lime, lemon, orange, grapefruit, tangerine, bergamot, neroli and so on comprise the *citrus* category, fresh and crisp. Citrus notes are the predominant notes in many men's fragrances, but they also appear in such women's scents as Hermès and Diorella. As to the idea that unisex scents are new, consider Eau Sauvage, a citrus-based so-called "men's" fragrance, which I smell at least as often on women; I wore it myself for years.

Such earthy substances as oakmoss and sandlewood yield the sweet, soft, warm scents known as the *chypres*. Femme by Rochas, Guerlain's Mitsouko, Paloma Picasso and Versace are among the fragrances in this category.

*Oriental* fragrances are heavier, generally rich and spicy. Spices, exotic resins from the Far East, musk, patchouli and incense make up these exotic scents, and classics in the category include Shalimar, Opium, Youth-Dew and Tabu. An *Oriental chypre* keeps the rich tenor of the Orientals, but it's fresher, brighter, sparkling, perhaps less moody. Here again, aldehydes are used to open up the top note. Passion, Samsara and Tiffany fall into this category.

As for ingredients, more and more chemicals, or manmade ingredients, are being substituted for naturals because of cost and availability; natural ingredients have doubled in cost over the past fifteen years. The production of natural jasmine, sandlewood and rose has been cut back. Many musks aren't available anymore, and the use of ambergris (from sperm whales) is illegal.

Why are perfumes so costly? If natural ingredients are used—and they do smell richer and rounder—they're very expensive. It's costly as well to develop manmade formulas to substitute for natural ingredients. Also, the more intricate the formula, the more scents commingled, the more expensive the perfume will be. Bottling, marketing and advertising costs can also push up the price. But the fact of the matter is that good perfumes are expensive to make, and not marked up as much as you'd think: The fact that competition is so stiff keeps pricing within reason. For the same reason, you can often find great perfume bargains at drugstores, discount stores and chain stores—so look around before you buy.

What makes fragrances work in the long run is a superior blend of ingredients creating notes that are utterly original, sophisticated and pleasing. All the marketing and advertising money in the world mean nothing long term if the consumer doesn't love the scent. I received hundreds of samples in my search for Giorgio and rejected hundreds. I spent hours in laboratories smelling isolated oils to communicate what I liked and didn't like. One day at IFF (International Flavors and Fragrances) I smelled too much at one time, and by the time I left I actually became light-headed—I can still remember how strange I felt walking out the door.

Finally, after two years of searching for just *one* scent, the one right scent, three boxes arrived on my desk from three different fragrance companies. I opened the first one, and put it in the return box right away. When I opened the second box and smelled the fragrance, I said to myself, "Oh, my God, this smells great. Can it be true?" The third box was another reject, so I went back to box number two, which became Giorgio. It wasn't until years later that I learned that this very same fragrance had been turned down by all the big fragrance companies (too strong, too sweet), but even that wouldn't have shaken my certainty. It was highly unusual, too, in that it's what is known as a linear fragrance, which means that it has the same top, middle and bottom notes, and smells the same from the moment you put it on until its last fadeout. Even so, I *knew* this one was right. And you should always feel that same powerful "Eureka!" sensation every time you choose a scent.

Packaged in a stock bottle using our existing yellow and white striped boxes, Giorgio probably had the quietest launch of any fragrance in years. In 1981, we put it on the shelf with Kenneth Jay Lane earrings and Judith Leiber handbags and started to sell it.

Giorgio's launch couldn't have been more modest. To start with, we sprayed it inside the store and left the door open to Rodeo Drive. Spraying a strong fragrance like that around every day eventually makes it waft into the street, which it did—and soon many customers were following their noses right behind it.

Since we had very little in the way of an advertising budget and we were the only store selling Giorgio, we decided to try mail-order ads in a couple of regional magazines, and also began to use scent strips, which were still a novelty back then (we were only about the third to use them). It was then that I learned how deceiving the scent strips can be; they are one way to help you choose a perfume, but they're not always true-smelling. Sampling is the only way to be entirely sure. Still, they can give you a general idea. I wanted my Giorgio strips to smell *exactly* like Giorgio does in the bottle, and formulating the strips was almost as arduous as finding the fragrance in the first place. Finally, a special formula was made, I was satisfied and we placed two full-page ads—with scent strips and, in blatant red handwriting, "CALL 1-800-GIORGIO"—one in *Palm Springs Life* and the other in *Texas Monthly*. The ad was homemade-looking, but the scent strip was sensationally true to life. Soon women and teenagers were tearing out the scent strips, and the magazines had to be shrink-wrapped!

That mail-order ad was the equivalent of our department-store counter, except that 100 percent of the sales came directly back to us, enabling us to afford even more ads. Since we got an unheard-of 80 percent response, the business grew amazingly fast. Those scent strips sold the perfume, and sold it, and sold it—beyond my wildest dreams.

Unlike most perfume launch parties, ours was held *after* Giorgio was already a success in our store on Rodeo Drive, a combined anniversary and fragrance party for my former husband and me. A huge tent, yellow and white striped, was erected in the parking lot across the street. We invited hundreds of people, and hired the Freddie Martin orchestra. Merv Griffin was a wonderful emcee; he introduced us as the mama and papa of Rodeo Drive. A song was sung that was written about us. In the middle of the party a giant Giorgio bottle was wheeled out, and we all sang "Happy Birthday." It was a festive, happy night for me—fragrant, so to speak, with pleasure—and all because of the power of scent.

## USING FRAGRANCE

Scent is linked directly to the brain, capable of evoking memories and emotions more powerfully—and subliminally—than any of the other senses. If you walk into a hotel room and smell mustiness, you may not even know why you don't like it there—but you don't. Everything has its own smell: lakes, oceans, houses that have been closed up, bread baking. Scent can probably connect you to every chapter of your life.

*With a substance as powerful and pervasive as fragrance, it's important to use it subtly, with thought and care.* Many women don't. On one end of the spectrum, for example, you have women who get onto an elevator absolutely reeking of heavy perfume: This isn't what fragrance is meant to do. At the other end of the spectrum is a "politically correct" contingent in rebellion, who claim that secondhand fragrance is as much a health hazard as secondhand smoke. Demanding fragrance-free zones, they cite the blitz of smells that confront (and affront) each of us every day—exhaust, the numerous smells of household cleaners and chemicals, deodorants, shampoos, cosmetics, lotions, you name it. But secondhand fragrance is not a health problem, and fragrance-free zones would be sterile places indeed.

This scent patrol aside, more people are wearing fragrance than ever before, and if your nose is overly saturated with scent, it's probably because the marketplace, too, has become saturated over the past decade or so. The market started to change when the perfume companies that had turned down Giorgio (as too strong, too sweet) were taken by surprise by how quickly it caught on in 1983 and 1984. Giorgio's surge—*Newsweek* termed it "the scent of the century"—also rode a crest of increased consumer spending. Consumers everywhere wanted designer names, status symbols, strong fragrances that would make a statement. Giorgio did, and so did a number of other fragrances launched soon after: Calvin Klein's Obsession, Poison by Dior, Saint Laurent's Paris, Paloma's Picasso, Lauder's Beautiful, Liz Taylor's Passion. More women wearing fragrance, and more women wearing *strong* fragrance: Those were times that did, in fact, make a statement.

So do the times we're in now, but it's a very different statement. We're not proving and projecting our strength as women anymore. Ours is an inner strength now—graceful, tasteful, elegant but still sexy—and I wanted my new perfume to reflect this new aura of our times. By this time I could tell the difference between manmade and natural ingredients, and I decided to go with natural as much as I could, for a classic fragrance, subtle with nuance. I worked with a French perfumer, and explained that I wanted sophisticated for day, alluring for evening—all in one fragrance. It took another two years to smell "Delicious."

I had a great time doing the packaging. I knew I'd be selling "Delicious" along with my skin-care and makeup lines; the makeup is packaged in a leopard-spot motif, which I carried out into the perfume. A powerful, sensual leopard in recline sits on top of the bottle, and the packaging is the mood and color of a soft, ripe peach—all the elements that set apart women today.

American women have begun to change—in choosing fashion, and in choosing fragrance. The overall mood is lighter now, casual/classic, less self-

# "DELICIOUS"

"Delicious" is a floral scent, with top notes of narcissus, mimosa, mandarin, boronia, neroli and black currant bud. Rose, jasmine, tuberose, lily of the valley, ylang-ylang and angelica comprise the midsection, and the dry-down notes are of patchouli, sandalwood and musk. But as soon as I smelled this complex fragrance, and settled in to smell it all the way through, I knew as I had with Giorgio that it was just right. "Delicious" really named itself. I'd try it out on friends, and they'd all say, "Umm, that's delicious!" And when I'd wear it myself, strangers or taxi drivers would ask what it was. I'd say, "It's 'Delicious,'" and they'd say, "Yes, it really is. Where can I buy it?" "Delicious" it became.

*"Delicious"*

conscious, less conspicuous. Working at home, engaging in sports, at ease with who we are, more independent as consumers, we still want fragrance to reflect how we relate to the world, but today we're relating to the world more inwardly, more reflectively, and we want our fragrances a little quieter, too. Of the forty to sixty fragrances launched each year, the newest ones, "Delicious" among them, are definitely more subtle than the strong perfumes of the last decade.

Because fragrance is such a personal thing, there's room in the market for all these moods. A great fragrance has a complexity that transcends the moment of its invention. There's no need to switch scents unless you want to, just as you wouldn't discard all your classic clothes for the newest transient fashions. On the other hand, there's also no need to get "stuck" in a fragrance just because you've worn it forever. Sometimes trying a new scent will provide just the mood enhancement you need.

American women used to have a wardrobe of fragrances: different ones for different moods, different seasons, various times of day. That's changing now. We're beginning to use scent more in the European way, finding a fragrance—or two or three—that expresses our individual personality and using it as a signature. Some women like a light, sporty scent for active daytime wear, splashed on as much for the cooling and freshening effect as for the scent. They might save the fragrance they're most serious about for evening, worn like an important piece of jewelry. There are no rules. *But the fragrances you choose are profoundly important, because they help you tell the world who you are.*

After Giorgio took off, Michael Coady, then the editor of *Women's Wear Daily*, had a rule: No one could wear it until after the daily ten o'clock meeting. I love Giorgio, but the editor is right: Huge gusts of it in a roomful of people before they've finished their morning coffee would be too much! By design, some scents are meant to be overpowering, but even that doesn't mean they have to overpower. *How you wear the scent is just as important as the scent itself.*

Fragrance is a form of attraction, an aura. When you leave a room there should be a hint of you that remains—your fragrance. Clashing fragrances—scented deodorant, hair spray, talcum powder, whatever—work against you. You wouldn't mix your jewelry or clothes without thought. It should be the same way with fragrance. Whatever scents you're wearing should at least be in the same family.

Given the variables—the strength of the scent to begin with, and the concentration—there are no hard-and-fast rules of how much scent is enough; each new scent requires experimentation. The disparity is just as great with men's products (men's aftershave can have a 2 to 4 percent perfume level, while the level in

## SCENT CONCENTRATIONS

——

*Cologne is the weakest,* containing just 3 to 15 percent of concentrated scent. *Eau de toilette comes next,* with a concentration of 8 to 15 percent, *followed by eau de parfum,* with a higher concentration of 15 to 20 percent. *Perfume is the most intense,* with a 20 to 30 percent concentration. In the other fragrance products the percentages that follow represent the amount of perfume:

| | |
|---|---|
| *Scented candles* | 3 to 6 percent |
| *Scented soaps* | .1 to .3 percent |
| *Perfumed body lotion* | .1 to 3 percent |
| *Perfumed body cream* | .05 to 5 percent |
| *Potpourri* | 2 to 3 percent |
| *Body oil* | 8 to 10 percent |
| *Bath oil* | 1 to 10 percent |
| *Bulb disk air freshener* | 5 percent |
| *Bath powder* | .5 to 1 percent |
| *Bath gel* | 1 to 5 percent |
| *Shampoo* | 1 to 12 percent |

men's cologne can be 3 to 12 percent). Sometimes a lighter perfume and a heavier eau de parfum will "feel" about the same. In general, perfume is worn on the wrists, nape of neck and breastbone. The lighter cologne belongs in the same places, and a spray of it on your overcoat, on the hem of your skirt and in your hair will help to leave a sensuous lingering trail behind you. For sports, saturating a cotton ball with perfume or cologne and tucking it into your bra is a sexy way to mix the scent of your choice with the clean, honest smell of a good workout. In the office, stick with cologne only for work and meetings. Don't apply it just before a meeting; the top note will seem too "loud," particularly in a closed room. A spray as you're leaving the house in the morning, then again at the end of the day, might be enough, depending on the fragrance; if it's very delicate, a few more light applications during the day will perk you up as much as a cup of tea will—and make everything else go better, too. For quick pick-me-ups, keep with you a purse-sized atomizer into which you've decanted your fragrance.

---

## PERSONALIZE A FRAGRANCE

*The best way to create a signature with fragrance is to layer the scent.* **Once you've decided upon your signature scent (or two or three), you can leave a subtle lingering trail of yourself wherever you go by layering bath gel or soap, body lotions and creams, cologne, eau de parfum and perfume itself when you bathe and dress. Women are discovering how effective it is to *stretch a fragrance* with these additional products, which are especially popular now. These days, perfume is for the self—to relax you during the bath, awaken you afterward, wrap around you as a way to soften the day for yourself.**

---

## SCENTING YOUR LIFE

The power of scent goes much deeper than scent strips and clever marketing schemes for new perfumes targeted to this audience or that one. For centuries, people have turned to the scents and essential oils of flowers and herbs for everything from healing headaches and curing depression to aiding memory and driving witches and demons away from the house. Today, aromatherapy is the term used for using herbs to heal. Herbal teas are soothing concoctions, and it's the *fragrance* of herbs as much as the taste that enhances the finest meals.

I'm not sure I believe every herbal folk remedy, but I do believe that fragrance is a mood enhancer: When your world smells good, you feel good.

Scenting your environment so that there's *a faint trace of pleasant fragrance trailing through the house* creates a welcoming environment and an escape from the harsh smells of the outside world. (Speaking of the outside world, Avon's Skin-So-Soft, a bath oil, is the most incredible insect repellent there is.)

*To scent your world to suit you, you first have to take control of the scents in your life.* Fragrance-free household cleaning products, for example, are available in the supermarket; just check the labels for the products you need. Using these products creates a fragrance-neutral environment that you can scent any way you like. The best smells in the world are natural—a fire burning in the fireplace, bread baking in the kitchen, a baby just out of the bath. These smells will ring truest if your cleaning products don't scent the air with clashing smells that you're so used to, you don't even notice them.

*Fragrant cut flowers and indoor plants* are great for scenting the air in any room of the house. Provided with proper light, circulating air and adequate watering, they'll emit fragrance beautifully. Consider the size of the plant to the size of the room; the smaller the space, the stronger the aroma. Among the most fragrant plants: scented geraniums, hyacinths, freesias, dwarf citrus and kumquat trees and daphnes.

Let the fragrances that scent your home be those of your own choosing. Potpourri's great for every room but the kitchen. To revive it as it begins to dry out, add rose water, lemon juice, cognac or a little perfume, then toss as if it were a salad. Scented candles are great everywhere, to scent and clean the air. (They're also great for offices, where the air can be notoriously stale; try burning one behind a picture frame.) To infuse your drawers with fragrance, use empty perfume bottles as sachets, or rub some perfume oil onto the wood inside your drawers. Add a few drops of scent to the final wash of lingerie and linens.

And to send your scent anywhere in the world, spray a little cologne onto your note paper and let it dry before writing your note. Your fragrance will remind your friends of you as vividly as your words will.

# PART 3

# HOW DO I LIVE?

**H**ealth isn't the opposite of sickness, nor is it something that needs attention only when a function of the body is off kilter. As with attitude, health is a *choice:* Either you live a life that constantly restores and replenishes the body's energy and resources for optimum health, or you don't. And, as with any other aspect of a beauty regimen, there's a certain amount of discipline involved at first, but choosing health soon becomes second nature. Radiant health makes you feel good, and when you feel good you look good. And feeling good—feeling really good—gives you power and control over your life the way absolutely nothing else can.

My husband is a medical scientist, and I occasionally go to conferences with him and meet his colleagues in the profession. I felt shy at first about meeting all these leaders in the world of medicine, but soon found that I had more in common with them than I'd ever expected. In a way, for two professions that couldn't be more different at first glance, the direction medicine is taking mirrors what's happening in fashion: Both pursuits are about empowerment. No longer are the doctors (or designers) dictating from above. Smart "consumers" of health care (and we're *all* consumers of health care) take an active role in learning about and monitoring our bodies and our health. The best doctors welcome patients who become involved with their own health-care decisions—run as fast as you can from any doctor who doesn't. At one conference I attended, the speaker quoted Albert Schweitzer: "Each

# HEALTH

patient carries his own doctorate inside him. We are at our best when we give the doctor who resides within each patient a chance to go to work."

In other words: Patient, heal thyself. Better yet, learn about your body before something goes wrong—how it feels from top to bottom when it's *well,* so that you can tell right away when it isn't. Be sensitive to your body. Find a doctor who will *educate* you and help you make your own decisions. Prevention, early diagnosis, managing your health—these are the simple and gratifying steps to good health.

I've seen the subtle dynamic linking health, beauty and well-being ever since my days at Giorgio. Some women would just walk through the door exuding good health and energy—the two *always* go together—and these women, I knew, would invariably find the dress they wanted and wear it proudly. A healthy body and outlook transcend the body's outward or cosmetic flaws. Energy shows. You can't see energy, but you certainly can feel it, in yourself and in others. It's rarely discussed but never goes unnoticed. It colors your lifestyle and everything you do: the tone of your voice, the decisions you make, how much you accomplish in a given day. We can choose a high-energy lifestyle or a low-energy lifestyle. High energy is more fun, more productive, more satisfying and well worth the extra thought and discipline it takes. Health, high energy, beauty and well-being are all of a piece, and once you catch the rhythm—the pace of health—everything in your life will really start to connect, maybe even for the first time.

I might not have believed it so passionately when I was, say, twenty years old (and invincible!), but choosing health is the best way to combat the effects of age, and the sooner you start, the better off you'll be. As we get older, our body shape changes slightly; gravity pulls things down, muscle tone gets softer, muscle that was muscle loses tone and becomes slack. Even if the scale doesn't change, your dress size can, simply because fat weighs less than muscle. The *shape* of the breasts, stomach, buttocks, drops a bit, redistributes. Terrible? Inevitable. I prefer the shape of my body now compared with the way it was in my twenties and thirties. It's less round—but there's always a trade-off. What is a constant is that our bodies will change shape slightly, usually with an overall weight gain of five pounds, give or take, over twenty years. No big deal if you're not overweight to start with. And no big deal if you eat well and exercise (see next chapter)—and choose health.

Stress, pressures, extraordinary demands on our time: These are the unprecedented everyday conditions of contemporary life for most women, and the only way I know to combat them is to *take the time to care for ourselves—take the time for health.* I've learned that you can't care for anyone else unless you care for yourself first, and once you do, the stress, the pressures and the demands on your time are challenges you're ready to meet, not obstacles you don't have the energy to overcome. A *high-energy lifestyle* is my goal and the goal of most women I know, and this seems to me to be the only way to get the most out of life. *Stamina* is necessary to live a high-energy lifestyle, and in order to build stamina, you have to *pace yourself* from morning to night. Focus your energy on your priorities. Don't waste it on things that aren't important. Balancing your life builds stamina, and you're the only one who can set the balance. This means time for exercise, time with family and friends, time for restorative walks and meditation, time for sleep, time for fun, time for work . . . *time for life.* But is health really a beauty issue? Yes, because good health infuses life with strength, power—and beauty.

## BECOMING A PARTNER IN YOUR OWN HEALTH

Some years ago I awakened one morning with very blurred vision in my left eye. I'd never even been to an eye doctor and had no idea what the problem was—maybe my eye was dirty and needed cleaning? In any case, I proceeded to exercise and do the rest of my daily activities, then met with an eye doctor at the end of the day. After looking at me, he asked, "What happened? Were you in an accident? Did someone hit you?" "No," I replied. "Who," he asked, "is your internist?" Next thing I knew, he was sending me over to see my internist. I walked the few blocks over, thinking: "Whatever this is, I *know* I'm going to be fine."

When I arrived, my doctor was very concerned, asked me more questions, then said, "You have to go into the hospital right now. You have a blood clot on the retina of your eye." As arrangements were made and I made my way to the hospital, I kept saying to myself, "It's okay." I meditated, I prayed, I kept "seeing" myself with my sight restored. What alarmed the doctors most was that they'd never seen this kind of a clot in a woman in her early thirties—and what made "history" was how my sight improved every day. After five days it was perfect again.

Throughout, the doctors and nurses kept telling me what a good attitude I had but to me there was no choice. I couldn't have had a bad attitude; I needed all the help I could get from wherever I could find it.

Did this attitude heal my eye? I don't know, but I can tell you for sure that my faith, along with the deliberate choice to be positive, helped *me* through the ordeal, which was a big part of the healing process.

Some people believe in the profound connection between the mind and the healing process, others don't, but one doctor I asked about it had the answer that made the most sense to me. "I'm not sure that your mind can actually heal disease," he said, "but I do agree that it helps the doctor help you." Personally, I believe in the mind-body connection even more. I believe that continuous negative thinking breeds a negative state of mind which *can* affect your health adversely, and that bringing to the issue of your own health the same positive energy and enthusiasm you bring to every other aspect of your life can affect your health in a beneficial way. It certainly can't hurt. So why not try?

With doctors encouraging patient involvement and preventive care, and with so much health-care information now available to all of us, this is the best possible time to become partners in our own health. Many doctors I know envision a time soon when medical information will be communicated on-line worldwide, where we can work together with doctors and hospitals on comput-

170

ers right from our homes. In the meantime, there are CD-ROMs available that cover every aspect of your health; medical encyclopedias like the *Merck Manual* ($25.00, 1-800-659-6598) or *Physicians' Desk Reference* (PDR) for information on all medicines; and insightful columns on health in numerous magazines and good newspapers. Local hospitals offer many seminars and community services. All this information can be confusing—even conflicting (there's so much of it!)—but all of it can help you, your family, and your doctor. The more you know, the more you can be involved. It's your health. It's essential.

The first step—and I didn't fully understand this until I married a medical scientist—is to *open up health as a subject for dialogue.* Sounds simple, but most of us don't really discuss health, ask questions, share what we know, avail ourselves of all the information available to us. Men and women should be able to discuss health as easily and openly as they discuss anything else. Health should be a subject for conversations with friends. Parents should discuss health with their children, adolescents particularly. If you're unclear about anything having to do with AIDS, or want to instill how important protecting ourselves against it is in your teenagers, call 1-800-324-AIDS, and talk to someone at the hot line. Take control yourself. Never take someone's word that he or she doesn't have AIDS; before having sex, both partners should always be tested. For up-to-date information on contraception call the hot line 1-800-584-9911. If you're unclear about how to perform monthly breast self-examinations, write to the American Institute for Cancer Research (Washington, D.C., 20069, is the only address you need), and they'll send you the information you request. For any questions about preventing and treating cancer, the cancer information service number is 1-800-4-CANCER. The American Institute for Cancer Research also offers information by phone, including dietary recommendations for preventing breast cancer (1-800-843-8114). Health is something to learn about, not a subject to be hidden away, and the information is available to us all. Fill your house with information about health, and you're that much closer to ensuring a healthy household.

Visit health-food and vitamin stores, if only as an instructive exercise to see what's out there. Often they're filled with brochures about the products (garlic as an age-old and newly popular—not to mention effective—remedy to treat colds, for instance; see page 199). Many of these are advertising brochures, to be sure, but instructive all the same. Check what they say with your doctor, or read one of the many paperbacks about vitamins available today. Many health stores also carry such books. Speaking for myself, I can vouch for what a few over-the-counter supplements can do (see pages 198–199) to make you feel a whole lot better.

Health-food stores are often also gathering places for information and services for people who are health-oriented—not just for "fringe" types, as a friend of mine once suggested, who "only eat bean sprouts." In Europe, for example, women routinely have foot and body massages, visit spas, *restore their bodies,* not as an indulgence but as a matter of health. Increasingly (and happily), this is happening in America, too, and it's getting easier all the time to find feel-good health sources and services. Restorative massages are going mainstream, from the head down and feet up. And the local health-food store is as good a place as any to start learning about them.

Feet first: Happy feet go a long way toward making a happy body, as I learned in my store from standing day after day on aching feet. Foot-massage rollers are available in many health-food stores—terrific to soothe and stimulate the feet. If you have an on-your-feet job, as I used to, the Master Massager for feet (write to Morfam, Inc., 3002 North Home Street, Mishawaka, Indiana 46545, or call 1-219-259-4581) is a daily restorative massage you will love. Foot reflexology—an elaboration on an old-fashioned, all-over foot rub—is a soothing treatment, too, for tired feet. Health-food stores often advertise reflexologists on bulletin boards, and even offer do-it-yourself charts on *where* to rub. One tactic is to offer *him* a great foot rub after a long day or strenuous workout, under the condition that *you* get a great foot rub afterward in return! Soothing oils make reflexology rubs feel even better.

Massages are so popular now that chain stores are offering quickie but deep penetrating rubs as an instant stress reliever. Caparan Salons, Aveda and the new chain of Great American Back Rub stores are among the names to look for. For a more leisurely, private masseuse, check bulletin boards at health-food stores, the phone book or ask at a gym, making sure the masseuse is *licensed*. For do-it-yourself at-home spa equipment, order the Sharper Image Spa catalog (1-800-344-3440) or Dr. Leonard's Healthcare catalog (1-800-785-0880), which carries the Maxi-Rub heavy-duty foot massager—great!

## CHOOSING YOUR DOCTOR

Not long ago, my left middle finger became slightly stiff—not bad enough to require medicine but just not functioning as well as it usually does. When I saw my gynecologist for a routine checkup, he recommended an arthritis doctor. I liked this new doctor right away. I told him I believed in preventive medicine: What could I do to *prevent* crippled and painful fingers? He told me that he usually gets cases too advanced to help, and that he was glad I came to him *early*. He was pleased to explain that if I exercised my fingers with a rubber ball for a few minutes a day, preferably under warm water, this would keep my fingers agile and prevent them from getting worse. I felt like a full partner in managing my health; my fingers are now fine.

Similarly, a friend of mine, at age forty-five, took her health into her hands after being told she needed a hysterectomy because a fibroid tumor she'd had for years appeared to be getting bigger. She was already scheduled for surgery when I suggested she get a second, and possibly a third, opinion: This was a *major* decision.

Sure enough, the second doctor said, "Let's watch it. It's benign and still not big enough to cause any problems." Even more encouraging was the third doctor, who agreed with the second but added, "If we do need to remove it, I'll do it endoscopically, with laser surgery, rather than invasively." Much faster recovery this way—much easier on the patient. In addition, she received medicine to shrink the fibroid. Five years later, the tumor is smaller and she still hasn't had to have the surgery. Always seek two more opinions before undergoing surgery. Help the doctor with the decision. You know yourself better than anyone. Trust what you know.

Plan for emergencies in advance. In an emergency, first try to reach your own doctor, or the backup doctor. *Don't necessarily rely on the emergency-room staff.* If you can see that they're all busy and you're not being attended to, call or have someone call the main switchboard of the hospital and request the department you need. When they answer, *ask for a doctor to be paged immediately to meet you in Emergency.* In busy cities, this will often mean faster attention than waiting for hours in the waiting room.

Don't be afraid, as well, to *ask the doctor to help you monitor your health.* Rudimentary care is not necessarily preventive care, but the more you tell the doctor, the more he or she will be able to take action *before* any problems arise. For example, one very important and fast-growing area of medicine is what doctors are learning about how certain diseases run in families—such as colon cancer in men and women, and ovarian, breast and endometrial cancer in women. The genetic component to Alzheimer's and other neurological diseases is also being studied intently. Why is this important? Because the ultimate in preventive care is genetic testing to see if you have a predisposition toward any of these diseases. And if your chances are higher than average of getting any of them, you'll know to be tested more often than usual to detect any early signs.

## CHOOSING YOUR DOCTOR

*Communication* is everything. A doctor should inspire trust on every level, be willing to be interviewed, *understand* that you plan to take an active role in your own health. Some women prefer women doctors, some like men. Personally, I'm open to age and gender as long as I sense real knowledge—someone who will understand my concerns about preventive medicine, someone who will talk me through every stage of diagnosis and explain all possible side effects of any medication. Ask questions:

❑ **What hospital are you associated with? (Sometimes the doctor is great but the hospital isn't.)**

❑ **How would I find you in an emergency? Can I have your home or beeper number? How do I reach your backup doctor? (Type all information—doctor's name, home number, office number and beeper number—on a wallet card for you and your family.)**

❑ **Can I reach you easily during office hours by phone for answers to routine questions?**

If your mother, grandmother, sisters, aunts or cousins have had any of the types of cancer mentioned above, discuss this with your doctor *now*. Genetic testing is still very new and not yet widely available, but there are laboratories that will perform tests for breast, ovarian and endometrial cancers at the written request of your doctor. They'll also send you information if you call. Two of these are OncorMed in Maryland (1-301-208-1888) and Myriad Genetics in Utah (1-801-582-3400).

Additionally, there is already in place a new test for people who, owing to family history, excess weight or high cholesterol, have a high risk of developing heart disease. The test, called Ultrafast CT Scan, can detect coronary trouble years before it becomes life-threatening—giving plenty of warning and the chance to make preventive life changes. It costs about $375, and is well worth it.

Your internist or family doctor can direct you to other doctors you may need—gynecologist, dermatologist, optometrist, any specialist; different insurance plans present different ways of lining up the doctors you need. In general, the following are subjects you should feel comfortable discussing with either an internist or a specialist.

**GYNECOLOGICAL** Take it upon yourself to perform monthly breast examinations the first week following your period, when breasts aren't swollen, or, if menopausal, do it the first day of every month, or any other specific time that will be easy to remember. *Any* changes in the look or feel of the breasts, at *any* age, should be checked out immediately with a mammogram. Insist on it. Inflammatory breast cancer may show up as a sore, slightly swollen breast. If swelling doesn't go away in a week with the use of antibiotics, a biopsy is needed, as this can be a form of cancer that won't show up on a mammogram. *Many times this is overlooked because it doesn't feel like a lump.*

Most doctors recommend having your first mammogram between the ages of 35 and 39; one every year or two from age 40 to 49; every year after the age of 50. The first mammogram becomes what's called the baseline, the point of comparison for later on.

## PMS

Some women can handle PMS on their own, while for others it's extreme enough to require discussing it with their doctor. Try these often recommended remedies first: Take deep breaths, try to relax, do stretching exercises (see pages 202–204), but not bouncy aerobics; women who exercise regularly have *fewer* premenstrual symptoms. A warm relaxing bath can help, as can a heating pad or hot-water bottle. Avoid salt (makes you retain water), caffeine (can make you jumpy), alcohol (dehydrates you, which makes the body compensate by retaining water). Drinking lots of water, on the other hand, will flush out your system. Clearasil, applied with a Q-Tip, can help fight acne flare-ups, which can be a result of PMS, and a positive attitude can (sometimes) transcend the symptoms. Next step: over-the-counter medication. And if you're still feeling debilitated, talk to your doctor.

While mammograms are fairly routine, having your hormone levels "worked up" is less routine but also very important. At about age forty, have a doctor take a blood test to measure your levels of estrogen and progesterone, along with the so-called "antiaging" hormone, DHEA. These numbers can be tucked away as baseline measurements to be referred to later if you consider supplemental hormones at menopause or if anything goes wrong.

**SMOKING** If you're still smoking—and you already know this—talk to your doctor. It's a medical problem like any other and deserves to be brought out as such. A doctor can explain to you the pros and cons of hypnosis, acupuncture, nicotine gum and the patch, all of which have worked well for thousands of people. Most of it, however, is up to you. Again, trust your instincts; the method for quitting that *feels* right to you is very likely the one that *will* be right.

Be aware that because your metabolism will slow down when the nicotine leaves your system, you're likely to experience temporary weight gain—but only temporary. Even if you don't substitute high-fat snacks, you'll still probably gain some weight no matter what you do, although your body will snap back to itself, more or less, usually within a year. Keep exercising. Drink lots of water and low-calorie cranberry juice. Chew sugarless gum if it helps. (Chew a pencil if it

## QUITTING SMOKING

- ❏ Make public your decision to quit and then stop talking about it. Talking about it only reminds you of how much you miss it. If you need to talk, join a support group. Having announced your plan, stick with it: These days, it's so hard to be a smoker that you'll feel downright embarrassed to take it up again!

- ❏ Try to quit on a vacation, where the stresses of "real life" and all the triggers that make you want to smoke are fewer. But don't use "waiting for a vacation" as an excuse to postpone quitting. Once you make up your mind, do it.

- ❏ Move your life around a bit. Sit in a different place when you have your morning coffee or your evening cocktail—both potential cigarette triggers. If you like to talk on the phone and smoke, avoid those long, heartfelt conversations for a while.

- ❏ If you cheat and have a cigarette, don't give up! Every cigarette you *don't* smoke makes you one step closer to your goal.

- ❏ Every day, put the money you would have spent on cigarettes into a jar. After the first month, go spend it on something frivolous. (Or save it until after the first year, when you can *really* buy yourself a great present!)

helps!) If you're around other smokers a lot, order a Smoke Grabber ashtray (from the Adaptability catalog, 1-800-288-9941), which reduces secondhand smoke and makes it easier for you to keep to your resolve. Keep visualizing yourself as a healthy nonsmoker. And focus not on the weight gain but on the *positives:* your clearer complexion; how much cleaner and healthier you feel; how your clothes and hair don't smell of smoke!

**DIET CONCERNS** Being overweight is, like being a smoker, a medical concern, one worthy of discussing with your doctor. If you're concerned about your weight, bringing it out in the open makes it an issue to be discussed, not a shameful "secret." There are realistic ways to fight excess weight. The first thing you must do is to modify your eating habits entirely (pages 190–194). Learning how to eat right *will* make you lose weight. Talk to your doctor. He or she may recommend a special diet or a nutritionist, who will tailor a diet especially for you—this has helped dozens of people I know.

Another way to deal with weight is not to be too hard on yourself. As we get older, particularly after age forty, weight loss is slow—and losing a pound a week, once you set your diet and mind to it, is great progress. You're not alone; most of us have to fight against gaining weight. Aim for being healthy, fit and strong. And remember that when I was at Giorgio, I "interviewed" a lot of men and found that none of them found the skin-and-bones look attractive. The old trick of posting a photo of *you* fat on the refrigerator helps. Trying my own diet tips (see pages 194–198) helps. Constantly visualizing yourself as the thinner person you want to be helps. Exercise (pages 200–207) definitely helps. And *learning to love the person you already are, the person who is trying to lose a little weight,* helps, too. Loving who you are makes it easier to change what you weigh.

What isn't a good idea are diet pills. Over the years, I have seen many people before, during and after taking diet pills. They often do suppress your appetite, causing sudden weight loss, but invariably the weight comes back (sometimes more of it) the minute you go off the pills. In general, they're not good for you. Almost always, the weight loss is short-term. It's much better to take stock of yourself and learn to modify your eating habits—forever.

**EYE CARE** Too many of us just don't get around to having our eyes tested. Talk to your internist about this, or see an optometrist. Have your *eye pressure* checked at around age forty, and get a thorough eye exam. A good optometrist can tell in advance whether you're at risk for cataracts or glaucoma, and how to keep such conditions monitored *before* they happen. At about age thirty-five, many of us need reading glasses—a good time for a thorough checkup.

**SINUS TROUBLES** Many people have chronic sinus troubles and just live with them, but this, too, is a subject worth discussing with your doctor. I learned about and recommended a simple remedy that has helped a lot of my friends; ask your doctor about it. Often it helps simply to rinse your sinuses out daily with a saline solution prescribed by your doctor, using a baby's nasal-aspirator bulb. Sometimes the solution is just this simple!

**BACK TROUBLES** This is another chronic problem that too many people simply suffer with. Here, too, your doctor can help, by recommending a good back specialist, specific back exercises and massage therapy. Open up the dialogue. Don't suffer in silence.

**A CHANGE IN YOUR SKIN** If anything at all, at any age, changes in your skin—growth of a wart or mole, an odd thickening of the skin, a change in texture—see a dermatologist at once. When you do your monthly breast exam, examine your skin, all over, as well. Skin cancer is a huge problem now, and to be safe, report any changes in your skin to your dermatologist as early as you can.

**WHATEVER ELSE DOESN'T FEEL "RIGHT"** Depression, achiness, fatigue, pains here or there. Talk to your doctor. If you can't, find another doctor you *can* talk to.

### TAKING CONTROL

Stress can come from good things, bad things, big pressures and small, but most often it comes from feeling overwhelmed—and is one of our biggest contemporary health concerns. *Stress prevention* is what keeps feeling overwhelmed at bay, and as someone who runs a business and travels every week from one of my homes to the other, I know that *being organized* is the best way to prevent stress. Is this a health tip? Sure, it is. *Time management is stress management.* If your life is organized, you'll sleep better, feel more in control, find more time to accomplish more and be better equipped to find an area of calm in your life. You'll function better, too—and that's definitely a health issue.

Always keep note pads everywhere—by each phone, in every room, in your handbag, in your car. Once something is written down, *you're in charge of it.* Whether it's a meeting you want to attend, an appointment you might forget or a phone number you need, you'll have it. Think through and visualize the day early in the morning, focusing on what you *must* achieve, what you *might* achieve and what you *don't have to* achieve. Listing your priorities is key to reducing stress.

## TAKE CONTROL TO FEEL IN CONTROL

—

❏ Use a *personal calendar/organizer* daily, listing "to do" priorities, calls to make, numbers you'll need. Crossing off the list puts you in control.

❏ Face daily errands and shopping with a *cohesive plan* for consolidating these rounds. Errands are best handled in one fell swoop.

❏ *Learn to say no*—a big problem for a lot of women: "I'd love to, but I can't. Maybe another time."

❏ Be brief in phone conversations and quick encounters. *Don't waste time.*

❏ *Cook in large quantities and freeze portions* for the future. A freezer full of good food buys time.

❏ Does one task seem daunting? *Break it down* into step one, step two and so on. Take the first step, and usually the second will fall into place.

❏ *Release control* whenever you can by delegating.

❏ Use commuting time to *meditate,* clear your head, get ready for your next role.

❏ Establish *routines,* daily and weekly. Tasks that become automatic don't add to stress; they alleviate it.

❏ *Plan for the expected and unexpected* by having extra keys made, filing photocopies of important documents, putting all tax papers in one file, setting aside time to pay all monthly bills at once. Or do them as they arrive, if you prefer. Just be sure to set up a system that *works.*

❏ *Exude control with your body:* Take deep breaths, deliberately stand up tall, pull your stomach in, consciously relax your shoulders, smile. This is the control stance, and when you take it, you feel it.

## STRESS MANAGEMENT

It's my feeling that stress is one of the biggest health issues of our day, and as someone who tends to worry about things even before they happen, I know what a toll stress can take—I've actually had to train myself to keep stress in check. In the process, I've learned that stress management is a discipline like any other. I've learned it; you can, too. Studies indicate that people who internalize high levels of stress are at greater risk of developing heart disease, ulcers and some forms of cancer.

We *all* have high levels of stress, but it's how we *react* to the stress and demands that counts. One trick I've learned is to ask myself at the first sign of a new stress: Is this something within my control or beyond my control? If it's beyond control—a loved one's illness, a firing, a move we don't want to make, an end to a relationship—avoid exerting more energy (and generating more stress) over something that can't be changed. Accept the change, carry out any positive actions that might help, grieve, visualize life beyond the change. *Find what's controllable in the seemingly uncontrollable.* Focus on the solution, not the problem. Stress can eat you up, but action won't; taking action keeps you in control.

For every stress, there's a positive side and a negative side. Letting stress take control is the negative reaction, but focusing on the positive side keeps you in control. If the stress *is* something within your control, then coping with it, managing it, is the way to overcome it, move beyond it and—in most cases—solve it. With practice, stress management is a discipline anyone can master. All it means is turning negative reactions toward stress into positive, productive ones. For example:

❑ *Frantic.* You're overloaded, so much to do you don't know where to start . . . we all know the feeling. Positive reaction: Stop right here! Frantic gets you nowhere. Go into a quiet place, make a clean list of priorities. For now, put what's dispensable aside, and choose and organize what must be done. Put your energy not into being frantic but into creating your list, the first step toward carrying it out.

❑ *Criticizing.* Maybe you're being negative or critical, or maybe someone else is. Turn the criticism into a dialogue, a discussion. Pinpoint the *real* problem, not the emotional subtext surrounding it. Real problems have solutions. Put the emotional problem aside for now and decide what the steps to take are to solve the *real* problem.

❑ *Money problems.* "We're spending too much" is a statement that can encroach on your well-being like nothing else. Take the abstract worry and *put it on paper.* Make a budget. Discuss the overspending: Is it a temporary problem (for example, overspending at Christmas)? Be firm with yourself and family, and take the steps necessary to live within your means. Panic can be solved only by taking positive action.

❑ *Paralyzed with fear.* Too scared to seek a new job, face a deadline, tackle a new project: *too scared to act?* Ask for help or, at the very least, ask someone else to listen. Voicing fears helps to dissipate them.

❑ *Tension in shoulders.* Do stretching exercises (see pages 202–207) as soon as possible and wherever you can.

❑ *Headaches.* Before taking medication, find a dark, quiet place, breathe deeply and try to meditate the headache away. For migraines, there is new medication now—consult your doctor.

❑ *All-around bad mood.* Exercise hard to "pump" it away, then stretch out to relax.

❑ *Overeating.* Don't dwell on it. It happens. Exercise it away, then go back to your diet.

❑ *Feeling the victim.* Maybe you are, maybe you aren't. Either way, only you can transcend the feeling. It's how you *emerge* from feeling the victim that counts. It's not what happens before; it's what happens next. Your fault? Accept responsibility and get on with it. Someone else's fault? Accept that it happened and get on with it, get beyond it. Take control of what happens from now on.

In other words, stress usually comes from feeling that some other force or person has the control—and you don't. It's not the case. To manage the problem or feeling, bring it back to you. It's yours to deal with, yours to handle, yours to relinquish or accept and take care of. So, deal with it, then get rid of it. Stress management is taking responsibility, dealing with it, then letting it go.

### SETTING PRIORITIES

Fact: There is never enough time for everything. For any of us. And some things—that extra cocktail party, serving on a committee you don't have time for, organizing a dinner party the same week your big project is due—will have to go. Let go what you can, and concentrate on your priorities, for optimum health, minimum stress, maximum efficiency. My own priorities are:

**HEALTH** Mine and my family's. Even though my husband is tied into the latest medical research, I keep up with health news as vigilantly as I keep up with world news. I see that we eat right, live right. Health comes first, because it determines everything else.

**SLEEP** As anyone who is tired knows firsthand, sleep is all-important. Some lucky people don't need much. I need seven or eight hours to function at my best; if I can't get it, I feel it—every time. It's also an accepted fact that prolonged lack of sleep can weaken the immune system, even prevent the body from warding off colds and flu. If you can't get enough, *learn to catnap.* Catnaps work wonders—fifteen minutes here, half an hour there: in your office; when the baby's napping; just before dinner; during a commute or train ride; in your office during lunch or just after hours; while the washing machine is going; anytime. If you don't sleep all you need to, nothing else will go right. But if you learn to close your eyes and give in to sleep at those odd moments, it will revive you to face anything. Practice it until you learn it.

**EXERCISE** For those who don't "have time" to exercise, I say this: Exercise *gives* you time. For every half hour you exercise, you have about two extra hours

---

## IF YOU HAVE TROUBLE SLEEPING

First shut out all the light you can. (I wear sleep shades or tie a scarf over my eyes.) Then avoid exercise at least four hours before bedtime, and keep away from caffeine for twelve hours before you go to sleep. A warm, scented bath at bedtime, herbal tea or warm milk might help. Try relaxing, soothing music or tapes before bedtime, and keep away from heavy meals or snacks late at night. Develop soothing late-night rituals, keep to the same bedtime schedule night after night, even try scenting your pillow with a gentle fragrance (I use "Delicious"!). Never try to go to sleep angry—if necessary, declare a loving truce until the next day. If all this fails, try keeping your eyes *open* all night, which sometimes can put you to sleep instantly. And if the problem persists, it deserves your doctor's attention—you can't survive without sleep.

of energy. It organizes the mind. It orders the thought processes. It *empowers* you, makes you strong. Keeps your weight intact, your skin glowing—it keeps you looking good. As the ads say: Just do it. How? See pages 200–207.

**WORK** I feel so lucky that I have work to do—work that I love! No matter what the job is, it involves deadlines, responsibilities, commitments, time away from other things you love, risks. But every successful person I know does what needs to be done to keep his or her work on schedule; otherwise, tensions from everywhere set in. If it's work you love (at least most of the time), be grateful for it. If it's not, do it as diligently as you can while looking for something better. And learn that work isn't everything. As important as it is to tune into one's work, it's just as important to tune the work out. No woman is indispensable at work, but every woman is indispensable in her life. Learn to know when to let work go.

**FUN** No life is "healthy" without it. Inject it into your work, your friendships, your family life. A giggle with a friend dissipates worry and stress like nothing else in the world. Poke fun at yourself—lighten up. Fun and laughter brighten up life and make it worthwhile. If, when you stop and think about it, fun is what you're missing in your life, then life is what you're missing. And nobody can change that but you.

## LIVING FOR HEALTH

Health is never a "side dish" to the meal of life itself. It *is* the meal—it's all the sustenance there is. It involves body, soul, the ability to work, love, live. Everything starts with health, and everything comes back to it. And you're in charge. We're all, in the end, for the most part, the day-to-day keepers of our own health. We should treat our health gently, use it wisely and be grateful for it every day.

When I think of health, I always remember a quote I once heard, attributed to Stanley Marcus, the cofounder of Neiman-Marcus. His mother, he said, lived to be ninety-seven, and once he asked her how she maintained her good health. "I try," she said, "to learn something new every day."

That's life. That's health.

**B**everly Hills is so diet-, health- and body-conscious that everyone feels the pressure. Partly it's because of the twelve-months-a-year opportunity to be in a bathing suit; partly it's the movie industry, with its above-all emphasis on how you look. In my years of living there, I felt it, every single one of my Giorgio customers felt it—and the subject that came up in the dressing rooms most often was the diet/exercise dilemma: how to keep the weight down, how to keep fit.

In my role as "retail psychologist," there was one lesson I tried to teach more than any other: That—even in Hollywood—there is no one "right" way to look, and there's no "right" age to be. There is no single right weight, size, body image. If your hip bones are eighteen inches apart, you can diet and lose weight and exercise from now till forever, and you'll still never have thirty-three-inch hips. You can look fit and healthy and great with the thirty-six-inch hips you were given, but not until you accept them and get on with your life. *Self-acceptance* is the most important lesson we can teach our daughters and, if we don't know it already, learn for ourselves.

## DIET AND EXERCISE

The decision to eat right and take care of the body is a one-thing-leads-to-another decision, and it begins in the mind. You decide to project a positive attitude and live a high-energy, healthy life, and that becomes an integral part of who you are. To fuel that full, high-energy life, you have to prepare and maintain yourself—with diet, with exercise and with all the habits of good health.

The object of a high-energy life is natural weight control through knowing how to eat and eating well, not through dieting for three weeks here, two months there. *Energy leads to more energy,* and by taking care of the body and exercising, you exude more energy and you actually have more energy. How do you get there? By visualizing the person you want to be: strong, confident, weight under control. What do you eat to get that way, to make your body feel you're taking care of it? Visualize yourself over dinner—a delicious puree of spinach soup, a piece of grilled fish drizzled with lemon juice, colorful fresh vegetables steamed and flavored with fresh herbs with a light vinaigrette on the side, a scoop of delicious rice, a big green salad, even a glass of wine, perhaps, and fresh fruit poached with ginger, lemon peel, cinnamon and a little sugar for dessert. Imagine how the person who eats that meal feels about herself. Imagine how clean she feels, how light, healthy, energetic and ready to face the world. With each meal, you choose to become this woman—or not.

Same with exercise. Visualize a high-energy life. It shows with everything you do—a fabulous walk, a sense of movement that energizes your days, whether you're talking on the phone, carrying in the groceries, striding down the hall at your office, even getting in and out of your car. Look around and you'll see it: The people who have energy exude it all the time. The people who don't have it seem instead to exude fatigue and defeat, even if they feel neither tired nor defeated. *High energy is a choice,* an attitude. You can choose how straight you stand, how forcefully you walk, how animated you seem, how energetically you face the day. You can choose the high-energy life—or not.

## DIET FOR LIFE, NOT DEPRIVATION

Over the years I watched many clients, men and women alike, take up the latest diets. I heard about protein, carbohydrate and packaged diets. I heard about the latest diet pills, grapefruit diets, egg diets, Dr. Atkins, Pritikin, the Scarsdale diet, all the other best-selling diets that came and went. We had customers with wardrobes in four or five graduated sizes to accommodate these "diets." In my seventeen years at Giorgio I never learned—alas!—of a quick-fix gimmick that worked long-term or that was healthy.

Diet was a subject that came to interest me personally, however, once I moved to Beverly Hills. I had gone from a dancer's life of exercising nonstop to a new life in which, even though I was on my feet all day, my weight would have sneaked up if I let it. I began to focus on a diet for life and health, and from there, the rest came automatically. I picked up real information that worked, long-term. I edited what I read by finding what worked, and soon began passing on tips of my own to clients and friends. Today, when I hear about a headline-making study, I ask my husband's doctor friends to clarify these new reports on health, vitamins and diet. Their consensus is this: There's a lot of exaggeration by the time new information reaches you and me, and the information is often misinterpreted or taken out of context. Rarely are weight-loss or cure-everything "miracles" discovered. Before going on any way-out diet or vitamin regimen, check with your doctor or consult a licensed nutritionist (larger health-food stores often have staff nutritionists to talk to).

Too many of us have a love-hate relationship with food. Food is "sinful" and we feel "guilty" when we eat too much of it, or when we eat the wrong foods. We feel, I think, that food will control us if we let it—so we're always on guard with it, never able to relax and enjoy it, and thus never satisfied. A vicious circle.

For me, the goal has always been to eat well, to eat for taste, health and stamina and not to feel deprived. This is everyone's goal, I guess, but the only way to achieve it is to *decide* to achieve it. If you need to lose weight, try getting all your other beauty habits in order first. Take care of your skin, wear makeup, exercise, dress attractively (for yourself) all the time, project a positive attitude, watch your health. This way you're working on your self-esteem as a whole, and you will find that eating the wrong foods just feels wrong somehow, now that you're doing everything else right. If maintaining a lower weight is the goal—as it is for most of us—then your lifelong eating habits might need some rethinking.

*Fat prevention is a lifetime commitment* that pays off. These days, I eat less of some things than I used to and more of others. The better I eat, the better I feel, and I'm also less seduced by "bad" foods; with my body in good shape, a greasy cheeseburger, however tempting it might once have been, doesn't sound very appetizing, and I don't feel deprived without it. Replacing bad foods, one by one, with good foods is a trade-off for health, with the weight falling right into place. I never weigh myself anymore; my jeans

## RESPECT FOOD

Gluttony is a distorted relationship with food, and leads to obesity—a sad and pervasive problem in America today. I've noticed every time I travel to France or Italy that while I eat more, I never gain weight; my friends all notice the same thing when they travel. Why? Portions are smaller, for one thing, and the food is "real" food—no chemicals, no over-processing, no greasy hamburgers and fries wherever you turn. Even more striking, I think, is the way the Italians and French feel about food. They respect it. They eat slower, and the meals are more ceremonial, more relaxed. They enjoy eating, as a sensual, life-affirming experience. They do not snack, but instead celebrate life with three delicious meals a day, seemingly depriving themselves of nothing.

and straight skirts tell me how I'm doing. And I stopped trying to be super skinny years ago, particularly after talking to many men at Giorgio, none of whom found skin and bones attractive. There's a timeless saying that goes, "At a certain age, you have to decide between your hips and your face." Too thin takes a toll on your face, making it look haggard. A few extra (well-exercised!) pounds don't matter. Take into account your bone structure by studying yourself in the three-way mirror. Be realistic. A size 12 bone structure will look (and feel) better over the long term in a size 12 than in an 8. *Live well, eat well, aim for health, and you'll look well.*

### COUNTDOWN TO WEIGHT CONTROL

There is so much information available today about nutrition and diet that most of us have read it all and tried it all—yet far too many of us still have weight problems. Why? Because we "try" new habits, then go back to the old ways, rather than replacing old habits with new. Connect your mind to your body, and eat what your mind tells you to. Giving in to cravings will satisfy you for about a minute; giving up cravings will satisfy you for a lifetime.

Like everyone else, I used to count calories; many people still do. It was only when I stopped counting calories and began counting fat grams that my diet really began to make nutritional and weight-maintaining sense. There are nine calories for every gram of fat, and thirty-five hundred calories in every pound, but it's fat grams, not calories per se, that determine health and, ultimately, weight. Cut down on grams of fat, and you'll automatically cut down on calories without even trying—and you'll improve your health with every gram of fat you *don't* eat.

When I made the countdown switch, from counting calories to counting grams of fat, I bought *The T-Factor Fat Gram Counter,* a handbag-sized booklet as instructive as any diet book I've ever read. I began to count grams of fat, envisioning what they could do to my heart and arteries (not to mention my thighs!)—and letting them go, gram by gram. Pretty soon I needed the booklet only rarely, once the numbers became second nature. To avoid confusion over the difference between saturated and unsaturated fats (unsaturated—which is what comprises olive oil, for example—is less bad for you), check the booklet but also remember that both fats are fat, and it's best—for you and your family—to cut down on them all; if about *10 percent* of your daily calorie intake consists of fats, experts say you'll be in great nutritional shape. Check the booklet, and *read the labels* of everything you buy. As a matter of course, I pass on products that contain MSG, lard, BHA, BHT, sulfites, nitrites. Instead, I want my labels to promise me I'm eating food! Same with poultry: Why not switch to free-range chickens, grown without chemicals, antibiotics or hormones? To make label reading easy, just look at the numbers: Choose the lowest percentage of fat content, cholesterol and sodium. For fiber, vitamins, minerals and carbohydrates, strive for 100 percent. When you cut back on fat, you can eat more carbohydrates—bread, potatoes, pasta and grains such as rice.

This is actually a great era for low-fat eating, because so many products are now being made in reduced- or no-fat versions—mayonnaises, sour creams, "lite" products such as oils—great for cooking. I use them all. None of them takes very long to get used to, I never feel deprived and I feel healthier, lighter, in a way that's hard to describe—just better all around. In a great national push for health, all the magazines, too, and numerous new cookbooks have also jumped on the bandwagon. Women's magazines, cooking magazines and the home sections of most newspapers now include low-fat recipe columns, and suggest creative and tasty ways to substitute low-fat ingredients for high-fat ones. If you start to clip delicious-sounding low-fat recipes, keep them in a notebook and actually cook them day to day, you'll soon have a repertoire of meals for life—not an on-again, off-again diet. Or start with my favorite low-fat cookbook, *Great Tastes,* featuring Canyon Ranch's great spa cooking; you can order it by calling 1-800-726-8040.

Eating low fat depends not only on choosing low fat but also on *cooking low fat,* and once I got into it, I began to restock my kitchen with cookware to help.

Automatic steamers available at any kitchen store steam rice, fish, chicken—low fat and delicious. The same with Teflon nonstick pans. Pam spray rather than oil assures low-fat sautéing, and also allows the taste of the food, rather than the oil, to come through. A stand-up roasting rack enables the fat to drain off while you roast chicken, and fat separator/skimmers, also readily available, let you scoop off the fat before making sauces and gravies. Classic pressure cookers, once out of favor, are back—they cook without fat, seal in natural juices and, for busy cooks, reduce cooking time by up to 70 percent. Stove-top stir-frying, grilling and broiling are also easy to do low fat with stove-top pots and pans specially made to use almost no cooking fat, or else to drain the fat generated during cooking into draining channels. Good cooking catalogs and stores carry these, or try the Colonial Garden catalog (1-800-258-6702). Draining away cooking fat automatically drains away body fat.

The other thing I gave up in my quest for a new way of eating was adding salt to foods. It took about a month, maybe a little less, for the craving to go away entirely—but it did, and I've never craved salt since. Without adding salt—called sodium on nutritional labels—to any of our foods, we still get plenty of it; it's impossible to avoid. All processed foods have it. Without extra salt, however, food tastes better and spices come through clearer. Low-sodium diets offer the much-touted health benefits of low blood pressure and healthier hearts, reducing the risk of strokes and heart attacks. From a beauty standpoint, benefits include less all-around bloating (even premenstrually), and less chance of puffy eyes. Salt is the easiest "addiction" to break that I know.

### BREAKFAST, LUNCH AND DINNER

You don't have to look very far to find new diet programs to try, and practically anyone you meet will be happy to share their dieting tips. I know women who claim it works to skip breakfast, or lunch, or both—but long-term it generally doesn't. I know women who basically starve themselves all day, then have a midnight snack, thereby negating the entire day's deprivation (and surely not doing much for their health, either) and also eating all their daily calories late at night, when there's no chance to burn them off. (This kind of "diet" never works.) The need to lose weight is an across-the-board problem—some of the smartest women I know have the wackiest eating habits and stuggle with the same weight problems as everyone else. The jewelry designer Kenneth J. Lane tells me he now makes bracelets and necklaces in two sizes: regular and large. The problem is clearly growing, but from what I've seen it doesn't work not to eat or to eat "wacky." It works better to eat right.

I like to eat, and the only way I know to keep my weight on track is to eat three meals a day—breakfast, lunch and dinner—plus a mid-afternoon snack of fruit. We all have our personal "trigger" foods—foods that encourage us off the track; for me, it's easier to eliminate them entirely rather than ask myself each time I'm confronted with, say, an olive: Should I or shouldn't I? Personally, I've given up desserts, except for fruit or sorbet, 95 percent of the time. I've given up butter on bread (which means I seek out bread that tastes great without it); beef, for the most part; all foods fried in oil; cheeses and most dairy products except low-fat versions and 1 percent (or skim) milk.

Filling yourself up before you eat is what a lot of models (and other savvy dieters) do to keep the weight down. It takes the brain about fifteen minutes to recognize that the stomach is full, so jump-start the process by beginning the meal with a big glass of tomato juice or V-8, a bowl of hot or cold low-fat soup or even a big glass of water. Eat slowly, cut the pieces small—again, the way models train themselves to eat—and don't do anything else while you're eating (for example, reading or watching TV): You won't know how much you ate, and you'll feel you've missed experiencing the meal and the sensation of eating entirely. You've probably heard that it's a good idea when embarking on a weight-loss plan to keep a diary of everything you eat. Well, I actually tried it once, years ago, and was amazed by all the food I ate that I wasn't even aware of eating, and more shocked still when I counted up the fat grams! Learn, too, to stop eating when you're full, not when your plate is empty—and teach your children to stop when they've had enough. The earlier good eating habits are formed, the better; it's hard to change later.

*Moderation,* another dieter's password, means, to me, cutting down little by little. Most recipes today are very sugar-conscious, but if you're making something from an older cookbook, you can usually cut down the amount of sugar by one-third to one-half without sacrificing taste. Sugar raises triglycerides, insulin levels and cholesterol, and also makes you gain weight, so cutting it down makes a big difference, health-wise and weight-wise. Some people love sugar substitutes; to me, they're just more chemicals we don't need in our bodies. As with the craving for salt, the craving for sugar goes away in a few weeks.

Caffeine is another cut-back item. I know: I used to drink a lot of coffee each morning. Slowly I cut back to one cup a day; coffee acts as a natural diuretic and pick-me-up. Now I wake up slower, with tea—less caffeine, more natural, less shocking to the system. At night, herbal teas, in wonderful flavors and all caffeine-free, lull me to sleep. Like coffee, they act as diuretics—but naturally, without the jolt. (Pineapples, asparagus and red apples also act as diuretics: great to flush out the system, and much better than diuretic pills, which drain you of necessary potassium!) Japanese green tea, the kind you're served in Japanese restaurants, is another no-caffeine variation on the theme. (As an added bonus, it contains catechin, an ingredient said to lower cholesterol if you drink even only a cup a day.) I've gotten into the habit of having it as an afternoon snack most days along with fresh fruit—the hot-sweet combination is really nice.

Like low fat, *high fiber* is the other great dieting buzzword today—lucky for us. Many women I know are skeptical about eating high fiber, because eating fiber feels like eating a lot—and eating a lot can't be good, right? Wrong. In addition to keeping you full and "keeping things moving," most foods high in fiber have terrific all-around nutritional benefits, even qualities thought to prevent certain cancers. Fruits, raw and cooked vegetables (steaming preserves more nutrients than boiling), whole-grain breads and cereals, are all terrific. You can't really go wrong with vegetables. One trick is to keep canned white beans—canellini or other small white beans—on hand; rinse, drain and add them generously to practically any kind of salad—tuna, shrimp, composed chicken salads, even green salads. They're high in protein and fiber, plus they add a gourmet flourish to any meal—very Tuscan. Another trick is to keep on hand platters of your favorite prepared vegetables with low-fat dips: filling, crunchy, satisfying and delicious. Nonfat plain yogurt with cayenne pepper stirred in, to taste, is a simple dip with amazing zest.

In addition to look-good, feel-good, weight-control benefits, many food items also provide additional health bonuses by protecting our bodies against various cancers and numerous other diseases. Broccoli, for example, contains sulflorafane, which encourages our bodies to produce enzymes that fight cancer (including breast cancer). Soy products such as tofu are recommended as another breast cancer preventive by the National Cancer Institute. The subject of healing is growing fast, and is much too broad to cover comprehensively in this book. To read more about foods for health, *Earl Mindell's Food As Medicine* (Fireside/Simon & Schuster, 1994) is one of the very good books on the subject available. It offers breakdowns of the healing and preventive properties of everything from tomatoes to curry to ginger!

## DIET SAVERS, DIET ENHANCERS

When dining out, don't be embarrassed to find out *exactly* what you're ordering. The menu won't necessarily tell you. Unless you ask, you might get all kinds of butter, salt, cream, MSG—all the things you don't want. Be as discriminating about your food as you are about your perfume choice. These days, with everyone dieting, chefs expect to be flexible. Order sauces and dressings on the side, and ask for your fish or meat to be grilled, not fried or sautéed. The chef will also, on request, cook any foods without salt, MSG or whatever you don't want.

The foods in your cupboards are the foods you and your family will eat, so stocking the pantry is as important as what goes on the table. If you buy low fat of one thing and high fat of everything else, you won't get very far; for low-fat eating to work its best, it has to be an all-of-a-piece effort. The more the items in your cupboard fit into the low-fat way of eating, the better.

Our supermarkets are filled with low—and lower—fat products, which is great, but also can be a little misleading. Even cookies such as Oreos and crackers such as Triscuits now come in lower-fat versions. Check the labels. Sometimes the lower-fat versions remain high in sodium, and sometimes the percentage of fat that's lower is negligible. Reading the labels astutely is the only way to tell. Other products are entirely nonfat. Some of these taste terrible, some don't; you have to experiment a bit to find those to your taste. I happen to like Health Valley nonfat products a lot—chocolate cookies, pound cake, apricot bars, cereals. Low-fat granola bars from health-food stores are also among my favorite snacks—I always keep a couple in my hand luggage.

Variety is the spice of life, and low-fat, high-fiber eating can be as spicy as less-healthy alternatives—even spicier, since the real taste of the food comes through. Spices and fresh herbs are great flavor enhancers, and fresh juices, such as orange or pineapple, boiled down to a glaze are fabulous brushed over fish and poultry. Even a simple meal stir-fried in low-fat soy sauce can be presented in a dozen different guises—by varying the vegetables, changing chicken to shrimp, trying new spices and flavorings, experimenting with all the new "designer" grains of rice. Low-fat eating can actually expand your repertoire with taste.

### FILLING YOUR LIFE WITH FLAVOR

❑ Try brushing *low-sodium soy sauce* (regular soy sauce is loaded with salt) over poultry and fish, then garnish it with sliced ginger from a jar. A great Oriental twist, and good with stir-fried vegetables.

❑ For a light meal or snack, make a *fruit "smoothy"* (children love these): Mix three or four tablespoons of low-fat yogurt with half a cup of fruit juice and any fruit—peaches, melons, whatever. Blend until smooth.

❑ Rather than thickening soups with flour and cream, try *pureeing cooked vegetables* in the food processor together with a little 1 percent milk, then stirring the mixture into your soup. If your soup is stock-based, make it ahead of time, refrigerate, then remove the fat that has congealed on top before adding the rest of the ingredients: makes a big difference.

❑ For a great low-fat, high-fiber stuffing, try *brown rice cooked in low-sodium chicken stock* and flavored with such fresh herbs as thyme, rosemary or sage.

❑ *Lemon water,* hot or cold, soothes and invigorates at the same time—very European. Warm water with a squeeze of lemon sipped during dinner or anytime, day or night, adds to a full feeling. A pitcher of lemonade in the refrigerator—fresh lemon juice, water and fresh mint, in season—is tangy, refreshing and filling.

❑ Judiciously sprinkle a very few *unsalted chopped or slivered nuts or seeds* over simply dressed green salads. While they're high in fat (the better kind) and calories, they have no cholesterol and a lot of protein. They can balance out an otherwise low-fat meal with great taste and texture.

❑ When it comes to buying and serving *beef, lamb or pork,* it's useful to remember that *the more expensive cuts will have less fat.* Trim any visible fat before cooking. One trick, too, is to serve meat portions just a tiny bit smaller than you're used to, and to increase portions of grain and vegetables to compensate. This can save a gram or two of fat—and no one will notice or miss it.

❑ *Poultry*—as long as the skin, which holds the fat, is removed—is low-fat heaven, roasted, baked, grilled, broiled. Chicken and turkey are the leanest, while duck and goose are fattier. If you want to prepare duck, order duck breasts from the butcher and slice off all the skin and fat before serving—much, much leaner than roasting a whole duck. I'd keep away from goose (except at Christmas!).

❑ *Fish* used to be a once-in-a-while meal for most of us, and now has become a staple, with beef taking on the once-in-a-while role. Much better. Poach it, grill it, broil it. And find a fishmonger you can trust. Like vegetables, fresh fish go in and out of season, so that you can vary the fish you serve all year long.

❑ *Chicken, turkey and veggie burgers* (tuna and salmon burgers are great, too) can be delicious for family suppers. Try binding them with tomato sauce instead of bread crumbs.

❑ For sauces calling for butter and cream, try substituting a paste made of *cornstarch and a cold liquid* as a thickening agent.

❑ Keep *fresh salsa* on hand for dipping vegetables and flavoring meats and fish. Try, too, experimenting with fruit salsas for fish or chicken—papaya, orange, apricot, whatever, tossed together with onion, hot pepper and vinegar: the freshest California cuisine.

❑ To me, *open-faced or conventional sandwiches* make a much more satisfying lunch than just a scoop of cottage cheese or other "diet" fare. Use whole-grain bread, turkey, chicken breast, tuna or sardines, with lettuce and mustard or low-fat mayonnaise. Low-fat mayonnaise is also great in pasta salads with vegetables.

❑ This is a tough adjustment but worth trying: Skip the oil on tossed salads and toss only with *vinegar*—balsamic, herbed or fruit-flavored.

❑ If you're feeling bloated, try this cleansing broth I learned about from an actress friend. Drink it over a weekend, hot or cold, day or night, and you'll feel cleansed by Monday. *Boil some zucchini, string beans and celery* in a pint of water for fifteen minutes, add parsley and simmer for five minutes more. Put the whole thing in the blender (no salt, but pepper, tarragon, rosemary or dill, if you like) and drink as much as you want.

❑ Missing French fries? *Try baking them,* and serve with tomato sauce: really good.

❑ If you hate the idea of skipping butter on your morning toast (whole grain or rye), try *pureeing a banana* and spreading it on the toast instead. Or try Polaner All Fruit on toast or, for a light snack, low-fat crackers.

❑ Experiment with *low-fat, high-fiber cereals* with 1 percent or skim milk—a great breakfast! My own favorites are Post Grape-Nuts and Kellogg's All-Bran Original or Complete Bran Flakes. To vary the routine, add a dollop of low-fat plain yogurt.

❑ *Low-fat crackers* include bread sticks, matzo, oyster crackers, flat breads, graham, Finn Crisp, Bremner (low-sodium), Ry-Krisps, soda crackers, Wasa bread and zwieback toast.

❑ *Low-fat dairy products* include pot cheese, low-fat cottage cheese, skim milk, 1 percent milk, buttermilk, low-fat yogurt and no-fat sour cream.

❑ *Eggs* are the great cholesterol worry, and all nutritionists recommend eating no more than two a week, including those used in cooking. Most new recipes are very egg-conscious. If you're cooking with older recipes, try substituting two egg whites for each yolk called for—it's the yolk that contains the cholesterol. Or try cooking with egg substitutes.

❑ Bubbling waters (sodas, too) tend to bloat and distend the stomach, which, however temporary, is discouraging when you're trying to lose weight. *Flat water* is a better diuretic and also helps to eliminate toxins, giving you the same full feeling. And some things never change—six to eight full glasses per day are still recommended.

❑ As for *wine,* it has no fat at all. Enjoy a glass with dinner! (It dissipates energy and discipline if you have it with lunch, though.)

❑ With so many more of us actually preferring low fat, it's thrilling to choose among all the sophisticated new flavors of *sorbet, ice milk and low-fat frozen yogurt.* Your guests will actually appreciate it when you serve these instead of traditional heavy desserts. Angel food cake,

198

too, is another classic (low-fat) dessert enjoying a new surge in popularity. And great fresh fruits are increasingly available year-round—try papaya, mango, kiwi and anything else you can find tossed into a compote. Ginger snaps are a good accompaniment; check labels for low-fat brands.

❑ To remind yourself of your resolve, subscribe to the Fat-Free Exchange newsletter (twelve dollars a year); send to 7334 Panache Way, Boca Raton, Florida, 33433.

### VITAMINS, MINERALS, POTIONS, SUPPLEMENTS

Just as I was a guinea pig experimenting with all kinds of skin care, so, too, have I tried all kinds of vitamin regimens over the years, until I settled on the formula that makes me feel my best. More and more people are sampling what the vitamin and health-food stores have to offer, and liking what they find. Once, when I moved, I left my vitamins behind in the refrigerator, which is the best place to keep them fresh. Out of sight, out of mind. For a year I didn't take them and felt fine. Then I started again and felt better—more energy, more fit. My doctor knows what I take and approves, and you should get your doctor's approval of your vitamin intake too. Women's needs change as we get older, and your personal diet habits, special needs and stage of life might dictate a different regimen.

I take the bulk of my vitamins (except multivitamins, which I take with all three meals) every night at bedtime; vitamins on an empty stomach can make you feel nauseated and, for me, breakfast isn't filling enough to carry them. Bedtime is also an easy time to remember. Because I prefer anything natural to anything synthetic, I like Schiff and Twinlabs.

My medicine cabinet is otherwise pretty empty. I keep FiberCon, a natural laxative, for occasional bouts of irregularity; these are rare with a high-fiber diet. I gargle with Listerine to kill germs (as the ads promise). At the first sign of a cold, I add to my regular vitamins six Kyolic garlic pills and six Twinlabs vitamin C tablets (500 milligrams each), which works (almost) every time. (Garlic may reduce blood pressure, so check with your doctor if yours is low.) At the first sign of a sore throat, I gargle with salt and warm water, which sure doesn't taste good but it works. If all else fails and I have to take a course of antibiotics, I take four acidophilus pills with each antibiotic pill to prevent an upset stomach. Acidophilus is a digestive enzyme not digested in the stomach but absorbed in the intestines. These pills, available at health-food stores and pharmacies, replace the healthy flora in the intestinal and urinary tracks that antibiotics kill off, and also help to fight intestinal, yeast and urinary infections. (Doctors won't always tell you about this.)

One other remedy. If you eat more one day than you would have liked to, don't worry about it; it happens to us all. The Europeans have an age-old potion for dissolving fat after dinner, and many women take this tonic every night: Drink one tablespoon of apple cider vinegar mixed into a quarter of a glass of warm water. Then start the next day fresh, return to your good eating habits—and step up your exercise regimen.

Note: Always consult your doctor before embarking on a diet.

## VITAMINS AND MINERALS THAT WORK FOR ME:

- ❑ *Twinlabs Mega 3 multivitamin and mineral capsules*—three a day (one after each meal), to cover all the basics
- ❑ *Twinlabs Super-E Complex*, 400 I.U. natural vitamin E—one a day
- ❑ *Schiff calcium-magnesium* with natural vitamin D—three a day
- ❑ *Schiff cod liver oil* softgels—two a day (age-old preventive against arthritis)
- ❑ *Biotin*, 1,000 milligrams—two a day (for hair and nails)
- ❑ *Vitamin C* is one vitamin you can't get enough of. When I have a cold, I like to take it in powdered form, poured directly into my fruit juice, which infuses it into my system right away.

**EXERCISE** Have you ever watched a dog or a cat wake up in the morning? They stretch themselves out languidly and unself-consciously. They roll their heads and pull their shoulders up and down. They arch their backs, stretching to the limit, then sometimes they roll over onto their backs and stretch from side to side. It's a wonderful "dance" to watch, and there's a lesson in it: It's certainly a better way to use, and protect, the body than jackknifing out of bed and walking stiffly and creakily to the bathroom to brush one's teeth and meet the day. Our bodies were created to be used—all day long, every day.

Because I'm in the beauty business, I meet a lot of women, get asked a lot of questions and also hear a lot of complaints. Diet is a big worry, of course, and so is exercise—we'd all like to find a way to buy fitness on our Visa cards, and not have to earn it! Curiously, the women who complain the most about not having time to exercise are generally the least energetic. Exercising buys you time because it gives you more energy. It clears the mind, too, which enables you to think about and organize the other details of your life. Obviously, it's a big factor in weight control. And it's a bigger factor in building self-esteem. Exercise well and you're in control of your body, your mind, the very essence of who you are, how you look, and how you feel. How your body looks tells a lot about who you are.

Too many of us, I think, regard exercise as something a little bit apart from the rest of our lives, like a side dish of a meal—great if we have time for it, dispensable if we don't. Too many women forget, somewhere between childhood and adulthood, how to move through their days and through the world. Exercise is life. Every motion we make expends energy, either a little of it or a lot, depending on whether we choose a high- or low-energy way of life. For optimum fitness, we all need to exercise aerobically, for spot-reduction and to work out the heart; twenty minutes almost every day will do it. For optimum-energy living, we have to choose to move through every day at full-tilt high energy, building exercise into our lives, not trying to push it to the side.

Note: Preganant women and people with back problems should take special care before trying any new exercise. Consult your doctor first.

Karate, any kind of dance, Tai Chi Chuan, judo, hiking, jogging, tennis, squash, volleyball, swimming, biking—any of these played or practiced consistently will do it. Yoga, aerobics classes, working out with a good exercise video—any of these practiced consistently will do it, too. So will going to a gym and working up a good sweat four or five times a week. I've dabbled in as many of these programs as the best of us, but none worked long-term for me.

When Giorgio was sold I found, too, that I was traveling a lot (this was before hotels had workout rooms), and didn't have access to the classes I liked to attend. There were more gyms springing up all over, but I didn't want a program dependent on heavy machines and weights. They build up and define muscles so specifically that if you stop using them, those muscles turn immediately to flab. I admire the commitment, but it's one I could never make. What I needed was a simple, "portable" program I could build into my life, one that would become as automatic as everything else I do ritualistically, every day. I didn't need a program I had to "schedule," like a meeting, but one I didn't have to think about and could do by rote.

An actress friend sent me to see Mike Abrams, one of Hollywood's great trainers, and if I expected coddling, this was anything but! Mike develops an individual routine for each client, a portable routine that you can do anywhere. He is scheduled every twenty minutes, as numerous clients run in and out, each with his or her own routine. When I called for an appointment, I was told to bring a bikini, so that Mike could analyze what I needed and how I moved. I was scrutinized front, back and side in that bikini for several weeks, as we worked out my routine. As a result, I now do a three-minute warmup and twenty minutes on my stationary bike six days a week (well, four at least!), pedaling as hard and as fast as I can. (It's boring, so I have a reading rack and use the time to read my newspapers, with the *Today* show or CNN on in the background.) When I have time, I add a few minutes on the StairMaster and any extra exercises I happen to "collect." On weekends, with family and friends, I also try to

202

schedule some fun workouts—a hike, a "real" bike ride, a swim. But my warmups and stationary bike cover the basics, like a one-a-day vitamin for the heart and muscles.

The warmup will work for everyone, but for the aerobic workout, some might prefer running, exercise videos, an exercise class, the treadmill or NordicTrack—whatever works. The trick is to move!

### THE THREE-MINUTE STRETCH, DAILY

It's amazing how much good three minutes of concentrated stretching can do toward making you feel supple, flexible and, well, all stretched out—like the dog or cat waking up in the morning. You can stretch anywhere—at home, in a hotel room, as a houseguest, even in your office if there's a private place to retreat to. Choose a carpeted place, or get a mat. It wakes you up, makes you feel invigorated and also helps to prevent the back from shrinking, which happens as we get older, as gravity pushes the vertebrae together all day long. If you take even one good stretching class, you'll learn how important it is that the movements be controlled and definite, and also how essential proper breathing is. I actually had to "unlearn" the way I learned to breathe for dancing, where we were taught to breathe quietly, so that no one would notice. Now I make a whole lot of noise, which gathers up strength and momentum. Exercise to a one-two count—*one* as you perform the exertion, and *two* as you go back to the resting position. On the count of one, the mouth is closed, stomach distended, and you inhale as you stretch. On two, pull the stomach in, open the mouth and exhale with a "whoosh" sound.

Here are some stretching exercises:

❏ Get down on the floor on hands and knees—and imitate a cat. Stretch your head back, then down, then arch your back with your head down. You might hear little vertebrae cracks: That's good! Do it twice. Then, still on knees, extend arms and elbows straight out in front of you and execute a controlled slow slide down to the floor.

❑ Lie on your back, flat on the floor. Bring each knee up, one at a time, and, with both hands, squeeze into chest as close to the body as you can. Do each leg five times.

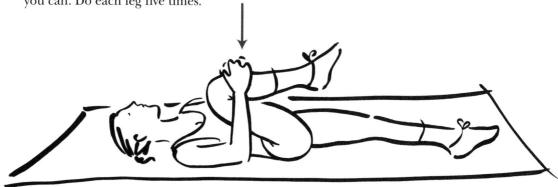

❑ Still on the floor, with knees bent at chest and ankles crossed, rock back and forth, hugging knees, three or four times.

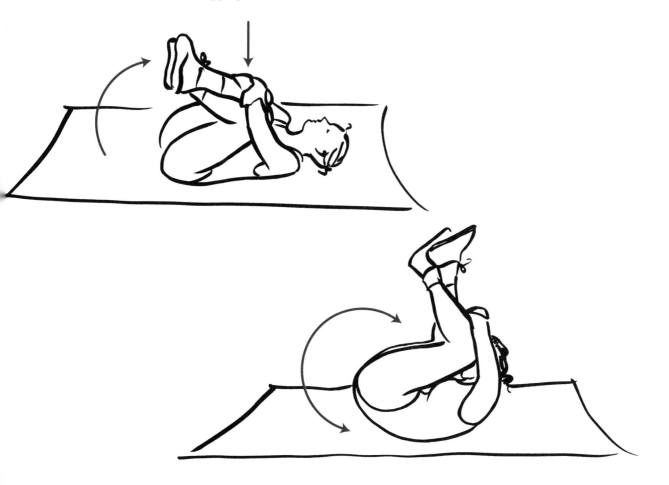

- ❏ Cross legs in seated yoga position, hands resting on calves. In careful one-two movements of a few seconds each, straighten spine, then relax it into a curve. Do this five times at a steady pace.

- ❏ The spinal twist: Sit on the floor, legs stretched out in front. Cross right leg with knee bent over left. Place left hand with elbow straight on left knee. Place right hand with elbow straight directly behind hips. Sit up straight, head up. Slowly but steadily, twist your torso to the right as far around as you can. Reverse and twist to the left. Do this three times each way.

- ❏ Lie on the floor, bringing both knees to your chest together. Stretch arms out to anchor the body. Looking at the ceiling all the while, move knees at a moderate pace all the way left, then all the way right, keeping knees together and up. Do five times each way.

- ❏ For the last stretch, lie on your stomach, putting both hands, with elbows bent, in front of your chest on the floor as you slowly raise and stretch your torso, straightening your arms. When arms are straight and you've created the silhouette of a seal, keep eyes focused straight ahead, turn your body as far as you can to the right, back to center, then to the left. Once each side is enough!

### EXTRA-CREDIT STRETCHES, FOR WHEN YOU HAVE TIME

- ❏ *Waistline.* Stand up, feet apart. Hold hands and elbows straight out in front of you and, bend at the waist to the floor. Come straight up, bringing arms straight up over head. Now turn to the left side and bend to the left, then up and turn and drop down to the right. Let the head follow the direction of the arms. Don't swing: Control the movement, keeping stomach and fanny tucked in. Do five to ten times on each side.

- ❏ *Hips.* Get down on your elbows and knees, putting a towel under your knees as protection. Keeping an absolutely straight leg and knee, head down, do leg kicks to the back as high as possible, up to twenty-five. As it gets easier, you might want to add a two-pound weight to each ankle.

❑ *Hips and thighs.* On hands and knees with head up and, again, concentrating on keeping leg and knee straight, extend leg to the side, up to twenty-five times. Add the two-pound ankle weights if you like—a double workout!

❑ *Hips and thighs.* Wearing sturdy shoes, place hands on hips, looking straight ahead for balance. (If you lose your footing easily, use a broomstick for support.) Keeping your back straight, place one foot widely in front of the other and lunge down toward the floor as far as you can without touching it. Alternate legs. Do as many as you can, starting with five times on each leg—a great trimmer.

206

❑ *Inner thighs.* Lie on your side, head resting on outstretched arm, and place your other hand in front of your chest on floor for support, raising top leg about two feet. Keep lower leg straight (wearing a two-pound ankle weight if you like), and raise it to meet the top leg. Do fifteen times fast for each leg.

❑ *Upper hips and waist.* Lie on your back, holding your stomach tightly in. Keep legs and knees straight, and raise them together, rotating hips to left, then right; control is important. For advanced level, rotate hips in 360-degree circles. To focus on outer thigh, inner thigh and upper hip, raise right leg straight up toward the ceiling. Extend leg to right side and lower as close as possible to right hand, making a circle. Return leg to original position. Keep knee straight. Do fifteen times with each leg.

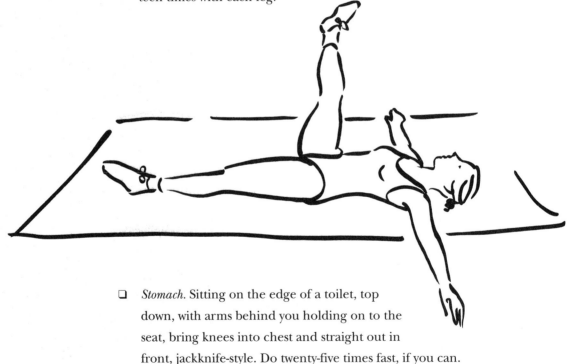

❑ *Stomach.* Sitting on the edge of a toilet, top down, with arms behind you holding on to the seat, bring knees into chest and straight out in front, jackknife-style. Do twenty-five times fast, if you can.

❑ *Hips and thighs.* On hands and knees, with or without two-pound ankle weights, bend right leg, lifting knee to shoulder height. Keep movements tight. Do twenty-five times up and down swiftly for each leg.

- *Fanny tightener.* Classic pelvic lifts. Lying on the floor with knees slightly bent, keep back flat on floor and tilt your pelvis up while tightening buttocks. Do up to fifty quick repetitions.

- *Stomach.* Two kinds of half sit-ups. One: Lie on your back, knees to chest, ankles crossed. Hug knees with arms, pulling up and letting yourself drop partway back down; shoulders and head should not touch the floor while you do up to twenty-five fast repetitions. Two: Lie on floor, knees bent, arms extended to tops of knees. Keeping feet on floor, lift your top half up, reaching toward and beyond knees with your hands, arms straight. Do twenty-five or more.

- *Isometric stomach firmer.* On your hands and knees, head straight, contract stomach muscles in and out hard. Pause on the in, exhale on the out. Do twenty-five times or more.

- *Outer thighs.* Lie on left side, left leg bent, left arm outstretched on the floor over head. Raise right arm above the head, simultaneously lifting a straight right leg to meet arm. Do twenty-five or more times fast, then switch sides.

- *Waist reducer.* Lie on floor, calves on seat of a sturdy chair, hands behind head. Raise your torso five times left, then five times right, five times left, five right.

- *To relieve sciatic-nerve pain.* Lie on the floor on your left side. Bend right knee and bring it toward your chest, crossing your arms gently around it. Now slowly twist to the right, holding the stretch for a minute or two. Reverse sides.

❑ *A preventive back remedy for life.* As a result of a taxi accident, I grew up with a curved spine. Ballet helped, but even so, I went to a doctor at nineteen for severe lower back pains. He promised me that if I did the following every day, I'd never have to see a back doctor again (he was right): Buy a chinning bar from any fitness center, put it in any doorway and slowly pick up your feet and hang from it—arms and elbows straight above your head—every day for approximately three seconds; you will actually feel how long to hang. Slowly put your feet back on the floor. It works as a mini–traction device to release pressure between vertebrae: It really works to *prevent* back trouble!

Any activity that gets the heart pumping, raises the pulse and works up a sweat is considered aerobic, and the benefits—health, beauty, weight loss, psychological—are well known. The benefits are also lifelong. Exercise when you're young, and you may never have a weight problem. Keep exercising during pregnancy, and you'll feel better throughout it, and your body will bounce back sooner; talk to your doctor, first, of course, and get her approval. Check out all the exercise tapes available for each stage of pregnancy, walk, swim, do yoga! As we get older, exercise increases bone density, especially after menopause.

How do you get started? First of all, listen to your body. You wouldn't want to jog if you have back or knee problems, for example; take into account your limitations. If you haven't been exercising, start slowly and work up—even brisk, purposeful "serious" walking is an excellent start. So is jumping (not skipping) rope for three to five minutes. Or try to create your own aerobic "step" with a sturdy box or milk crate, and step up and down, building to a fast pace. You can choose from any number of exercise videos and try them in the privacy of your own home. Or visit a gym.

If you've never gone to a gym before, it might seem daunting at first or you might feel self-conscious, but try to overcome it. Gyms aren't competitive. Each person there is working on his or her own body, no body is perfect—and nobody judges. Moreover, people there get so lost in what they're doing that half the time no one notices who's there and who isn't! Without actually joining a gym, you can usually visit one on a trial basis, paying by the day. And all gyms have trainers there to show you the machines and how to use them, and also— probably for an extra fee—to help you create your own personal workout (the way my trainer helped me with mine).

In general, machines and weights (except for two- or three-pound weights, which aren't heavy enough to build muscle) work by controlled, repetitive movement, and are used to strengthen, build, define and tone muscles. The heavier the weight, the more the muscle will build, in strength—and size.

Unless you want a real body-builder look, go easy with these; build up a muscle too much and you have to keep at it or it turns to flab. For most of us, general aerobic toning, stretching and perhaps light use of the machines is a more realistic goal. Most gyms have one version or another of the StairMaster, treadmill and stationary bikes, all of which are easy to master once a trainer shows you how to set yourself up on one; all of them, too, have easier and more difficult settings, so that you can start slow and work up. Most gyms are mirrored—not for vanity but to help you with your workout. If you watch yourself, you can see how you're standing, make sure your stomach is pulled in, see how far you're bending over—monitor your own workout. (When using the StairMaster, for example, leaning over won't build muscle, while standing up straight will; if you can see yourself, you can remind yourself.) If you have a special workout area or room at home, it helps to have it mirrored as well.

I personally don't find low-cut G-string exercise wear attractive on anyone, but exercise clothes need to reveal enough so that you can see what you're working on. If you're shy at first, a pair of boxer shorts over tights and a leotard gives a little more coverage, as does a roomy T-shirt over exercise briefs and tights. As with anything, you'll feel better if you look good, so have some fun with exercise clothes—gray, black, burgundy or navy leotards with sleek black (or ballet pink) tights: clothes for stretching!

More important are the shoes you wear while exercising—for support, comfort, protection against injury. As a rule, exercise shoes, like regular shoes, do not have a break-in period; if they don't feel right in the store, they'll never feel right. Feet expand with exercise, so select workout shoes after a workout, making sure that all toes have room to wiggle and that the shoes are roomy enough for socks. Special shoes for various activities can make a big difference. All-around exercise shoes—Reeboks and Nikes, among others—are good for most purposes, but an aerobic shoe is lighter, if you're engaged in aerobics classes. If you're doing some serious hiking, please do buy good hiking boots (Timberland makes good ones), with more traction, heft and ankle support. If you're a runner, you already know how important the right running shoes are. To make sure yours are "on track," so to speak, examine the soles of a worn pair. High arches tend to roll the foot outward, while flat feet tend inward. If your shoes are too worn as a result, ask for motion-control shoes next time, to correct the imbalance. Talk to a salesperson at a good sporting-goods store, too, if you have an unusual foot width; you may have to custom-order.

For all the equipment available, shoes are all you really need to get started (along with a positive attitude). However, if you find, as I did, that it's worthwhile to make exercise a habit, you might want to consider a home workout center to motivate you even more. Play It Again Sports is a chain of stores selling *used,* discounted exercise equipment—call 1-800-433-2540 for the store nearest you.

## HIGH-ENERGY LIVING

By standing up straight, stomach pulled in, we all automatically look five pounds thinner! *To project energy is to exude energy,* and it shows, with every movement we make all day long. Put more energy into cleaning the house and not only will the tasks go faster, but you'll also feel more energized in the end. Gardening uses up tons of energy—a really good form of exercise, especially if you pull and stretch gently as you go. Taking the stairs instead of an elevator can give you several miniworkouts during the day. Can't find a parking place? Park farther away, and enjoy the walk. Instead of driving the children to school, *walk* them to school; it's good for them, too. When talking on the phone, or whenever you can during the course of the day, pull in your muscles for an isometric stretch, and breath deeply to fill your body with oxygen. *Feel your body,* and enjoy it, as you make your way throughout the day.

Even while sitting at your desk at work, you can use and exude energy, and also prevent the aches that can come from sitting in one place for too long. Extend your legs and do foot flexes and circles to keep the blood circulating. Stand up from time to time for a quick stretch, and sit up straight, using a small pillow to support your lower back, if it helps. If you work at a computer, look away from the screen every five or ten minutes, and roll your eyes 360 degrees, fifteen times each way. To counteract leaning forward all day, lean back sometimes, flinging arms out and back.

## DO-ANYWHERE EXERCISES THAT TAKE NO TIME

- ❏ *Posture.* Stand, head up, with back and shoulder blades flat against the wall, hands at sides, knees slightly bent. Slowly rise, straightening knees and pressing the small of your back against the wall all the way. Walk away, holding the posture.

- ❏ *Shoulder tension.* Shrug shoulders as high as possible for three or four seconds, then let them drop like a rag doll. Repeat three or four times.

- ❏ *Shoulder tension.* Extend arms straight out in front of you, palms facing each other. At shoulder-blade level, swing open with elbows almost straight. Repeat four times.

- ❏ *Shoulder tension.* Bend over, leaning forehead on a table level with waistline, feet apart. With a book or two-pound weight in each hand, raise arms up to the side to shoulder height only. Do this up and down four times.

- ❏ *Isometric chest and upper-arm firmer.* A classic. Stand up, clasp hands together and push hard. Hold up to ten seconds and release. Repeat four times. Try it with hands at waist level, breast level, shoulder level, head level—four times each.

- ❏ *Arms and upper chest.* Great while waiting for the teapot to boil! With knees and back straight, do push-ups against a kitchen or bathroom counter—as many as you can.

- ❏ *Isometric fanny lift.* While standing, squeeze buttocks and release, quickly and as many times as possible. (Puts standing in line to good use!) You can also do it while sitting.

- ❏ *Hips and thighs.* Stand one foot from an open door, back straight, feet about two feet apart. Hold on to each side of the doorknob, and bend knees quickly, going into a squat—as many times as possible.

❑ *Thighs.* Hold on to the back of a sturdy chair with both hands. Starting with legs together and right foot flexed, kick right leg straight back, concentrating on straight leg and knee and good posture. Do each leg fifteen times.

❑ *Hip and lower-back stretch.* Stand, feet together, arms at side. Rise onto the ball of your right foot, which raises right hip, while keeping left foot flat. Do five times, then switch feet.

❑ *Hip and lower-back stretch.* Stand, feet together, hands on hips. Keeping shoulders back, lean upper torso to the right while raising left heel. Hold. Repeat on other side.

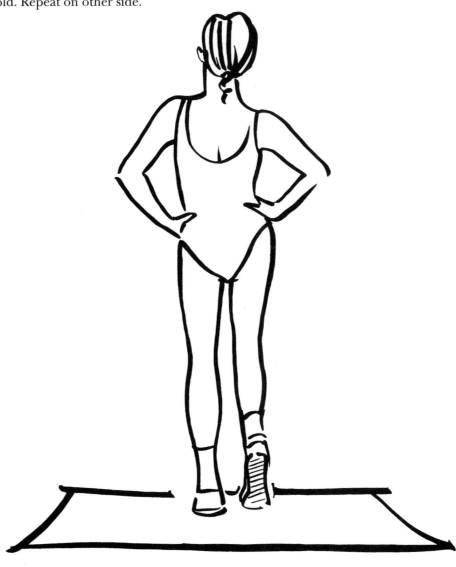

❑ *Flexibility back stretch.* Stand, feet apart, knees slightly bent. Raise arms to chest level and rotate torso from side to side with arms swinging. Head, with chin up, should follow motion of torso.

❑ *Shoulder-blade stretch.* Stand in doorway, feet together in center of doorway. Keeping your head up, place both hands on doorjamb, lean into doorway and back two or three times. Feels good!

❑ *Fanny and outer thighs.* While standing, put a book between your thighs and tighten and release your fanny. Do as many repetitions as you can.

❑ *Triceps.* When on the phone, exercise the triceps isometrically by putting your free arm behind your head and moving fist up and down as fast as you can. Switch the phone to your other ear, and repeat with your other arm.

❑ *Upper arms.* Use two unopened soup cans as hand weights. With arms out to side, make small, rapid circles in the air in both directions.

❑ *Overall stretch.* With a heavy book in each hand, arms down at sides, stretch as far as you can in each direction with back straight. Up, down, sideways—fifteen times on each side.

*Listen to your body tell you how to move:* for high energy, for stamina, for *life*!

'm known among my friends for being organized to within an inch of my life, and when one of my notoriously disorganized girlfriends recently asked me what my traveling essentials consist of, she couldn't believe my reply: "Mismatched plastic bottles and zip-top plastic bags." My bottles reduce my life to travel size, and my zip-top bags keep it visible—and dry. My luggage is perhaps more sturdy, lightweight and practical than it is "designer" chic, but I've discovered that for the traveler to be chic, travel gear and accoutrements must be, above all, functional. I'd rather *pull* a light canvas bag on wheels through an airport than *carry* a classic (heavy) leather suitcase any day.

I travel a lot, commuting from New York to Washington and back every week, plus business trips and vacations, too. The better organized you are *before* you go, I've learned, the less stress you'll experience once you get there. Is the object to travel light? Not necessarily. More important is to *travel with what you need to feel at home wherever you go.* If you leave details at home undone, you'll never arrive at your destination emotionally prepared. If the clothes you pack aren't thought out and travel-ready, you won't feel pretty once you get there. If you haven't brought enough of what you need to carry your "life" with you, you'll never feel at home no matter where your luggage is, which is when traveling becomes fun! I know this goes against those who so fear luggage loss that they carry everything on board with them, but I take the chance of checking all but my carry-on luggage, which contains jewelry and other valuables.

# TRAVEL

Setting out every day is a pared-down trip, made much more pleasant if you have with you what you need. (Try making a presentation at someone else's office, only to find yourself suddenly without your notes—very anxiety provoking!) Visualize the day every morning—where you're going, and what you'll need at each stop.

Check the weather. Just because it's cloudy in the morning doesn't mean you won't want your sunglasses later. Might the morning sun turn to showers? Or might that warm spring day turn cool after sundown, when you're going out to dinner right from the office?

Keep an ongoing list of items you've regretted not having more than once—not enough to weigh yourself down, but enough, certainly, to ensure that you'll look your best. It doesn't add a lot of extra baggage to the day, for example, to carry an emergency *safety pin*, a *Band-Aid* and a fresh *emery board*, three of the handiest "beauty" items around, as a matter of course. If you read the newspaper on the way to work, *Handy Wipes* are essential to get the newsprint off. A tiny vial carrying a couple of *aspirins* will be essential if you need them, and so will *breath mints*.

I love wonderful leather handbags, which can carry you to and from most of your day's activities, particularly if you keep a stock of beauty staples in a desk drawer at the office. Even with a handbag, however, I focus on *lighter* and *smaller*. A bag with heft to it while it's in the store, empty, will definitely be too heavy once it's filled. Dragging around a heavy handbag makes you tired. Slinging a heavy shoulder bag creates shoulder stress, which becomes facial stress (and also becomes, eventually, backache and lopsided shoulders!). A backpack is an alternative, but, again, keep it light. A fanny pack—simply a belt with a little pouch attached— holds keys, lipstick, a comb and enough money or credit cards for an outing to a museum or gallery or a nice walk; it's cute, and leaves your hands entirely free.

On days when I have to add extra supplies (umbrella, walking shoes, piles of papers, whatever), I take a tote bag—not in addition to a handbag but *instead*

## MY TRAVEL GEAR

M̲y own personal travel gear for a typical day includes the following handbag items (if I'm taking a tote, I just put all this stuff into a large plastic bag to keep it separate, then pack the other things I need into the tote around it):

❑ *Cellular phone.* A great convenience and time-saver.

❑ *No wallet, no checkbook.* Makes traveling by day much lighter. I wrap my credit cards, driver's license and medical-insurance or information card with a rubber band. The cash I might need and a couple of checks from my checkbook go into a large paper clip (use a gold one, if you like). This may not be the fanciest way, but it keeps things visibly organized, easily accessible and lightweight.

❑ *Makeup zip-top bag.* Some people carry makeup bags, but I like a zip-top bag better: It's easy to keep clean, makes everything visible and is very light. It will hold a small mirror, whatever you need for touch-ups, a small vial of perfume or cologne and a comb. (If you prefer a brush, use a small one—it takes up half the space.)

❑ *Small plastic bottles.* From the drugstore or rinsed-out sample bottles from hotels—one for hand lotion and one for sunblock.

❑ *Coin pouch.* Holds keys and change.

❑ *Slim pen, notepad.* For notes to myself, all day long. Post-its are also useful.

of one. Trying to juggle several bags (and looking in first one, then another, to find a pen or some other buried item) feels chaotic and cumbersome, and I prefer the easiness of one bag with add-an-item roominess. A light leather or canvas bag with short handles is most comfortable. If it's waterproof inside so much the better.

## PREPACKING

Some people unpack after a trip. I *repack,* refilling and replacing, in order to *prepack.* Keeping a weekend bag (and a larger bag, too, if your traveling schedule justifies it) prepacked with small-sized toiletries and ready-to-go sundries jump-starts packing every time, saving time and reducing stress. Larger-sized plastic bottles prepack a bigger suitcase for a longer trip.

EMOTIONAL PREPACKING

Waiting till the last minute to prepare, leaving things undone at home and then arriving unprepared with the wrong things will invariably make a trip, even a long-anticipated holiday, stressful. No matter what the trip—weekend, business, vacation—preparing ahead of time will make the trip relaxing and fun. Prepacking your suitcase to the extent that you can will help. So will getting yourself prepared and psyched emotionally.

## PREPACKING CHECKLIST

- ❏ Folding umbrella
- ❏ Zip-top plastic bag with Post-its, paper clips, rubber bands, pens and a self-sharpening Scripto mechanical pencil
- ❏ Hot-water heater (to make tea) and assorted teabags
- ❏ Night-table zip-top plastic bag, with travel alarm clock, night creams, sleep shades
- ❏ Spare contact lenses or glasses
- ❏ Candle stub (rubbing it over zippers that get stuck makes them ride smoothly again)
- ❏ Mini Goddard's Dry Clean spray, for spot removal
- ❏ Needle, thread and safety pins

- ❏ Extra plastic bag for laundry and miscellaneous
- ❏ Dual-voltage hair dryer
- ❏ Four Velcro rollers, with clips
- ❏ Mini hot rollers
- ❏ Ponytail holders and assorted hair items
- ❏ Birth-control and sanitary items
- ❏ Band-Aids
- ❏ Toothbrush, small-sized toothpaste and dental floss
- ❏ Plastic bottle of mouthwash
- ❏ Shampoo, conditioner, hair spray—in small bottles
- ❏ Small-sized deodorant
- ❏ Makeup remover
- ❏ Toner
- ❏ Day cream

- ❏ Moisturizer for body
- ❏ Q-Tips
- ❏ Nail-polish remover pads
- ❏ Emery boards
- ❏ Tweezers
- ❏ Fresh disposable razor
- ❏ Sunblock
- ❏ Medicine—aspirin and whatever else you tend to need while traveling
- ❏ Photocopies of credit cards, passport, driver's license, medical-insurance identification
- ❏ Identification tag on outside of *and* inside bag, in case the tag gets lost

**ATTITUDE**  So often I hear, "Oh, I *have* to go to [such and such a city] for three days on business," in a tone that sounds like a sentence at boot camp has been handed down. There isn't a city anywhere that doesn't have some wonderful attraction to it; if you're going away, why not find out all you can about wherever it is you're going and make the best of it? Even a two- or three-day business trip to anywhere allows a little free time to explore, visit an attraction or two, take a walk in the town's loveliest park, attend a performance in the evening or visit a fabulous restaurant.

What I always do as soon as I hear about a trip is to buy a guide to the place I'm going. Fodor's guides, for example, are terrific, available in bookstores or by calling 1-800-533-6478. A quick perusal always gets me excited about the trip. The same company also offers a service called Fodor's Worldview Travel Update, at 1-212-751-2600, or, by fax, at 1-800-799-9619. If you call forty-eight hours or more before the trip, they'll ask you about your special interests (exhibitions, sports, ballet, et cetera), and tell you what's happening wherever you're going.

**UNSCHEDULING**  Check your engagement book as early as possible once you know about your trip to cancel appointments that conflict. Put a big *X* through the days you'll be away to avoid scheduling blunders as the trip approaches.

**VISUALIZE THE ITINERARY**  The more you know about the trip ahead of time, the better you can *see* yourself moving serenely through your days away, begin to anticipate what you'll need to wear and think about what you might need to buy ahead of time. It's usually a mistake to think, "I can always pick up a sweater when I get there if I need it." Maybe you won't be able to, and you'll end up cold and anxious, or you might have to settle for a sweater you wouldn't otherwise have bought. Whether it's a cruise, a convention or a weekend with people you don't yet know well, there's always someone with an idea of what you'll be doing, and the sooner you get the itinerary, the better you'll be able to prepare. Call the hostess, study the brochures, ask whoever is organizing the convention, and begin to put together a list of what you'll need to take. If there's a party scheduled and you haven't worn your party dress in a while, *try it on now,* before you pack it, before you go. Never pack anything you haven't tried on recently. Hems change, fit changes, *you* change. You'll be most comfortable in your favorite clothes.

**DISTRIBUTE THE ITINERARY** Type up the itinerary and send or fax it to anyone who might need to be in touch with you while you're away. If Call Forwarding (for phone or fax) is an option, arrange to have it. (I'm an addict to Call Forwarding. Watch, too, for Remote Forwarding, a new service making its way around the country, which enables you to forward calls from any phone.)

**ARRANGE FOR COMFORT** If you want to order a special meal on the airplane, now's the time. If you want to make sure the hotel has exercise facilities, now's the time. I've discovered, too, that most hotels can arrange for a private fax in your room—a great convenience if you'll be working while you're away. Car service to and from the airport, special mattress requirements, whatever you need: Take your comfort on the road into your own hands before you go.

**PUT YOUR LIFE AT HOME TO "BED"** The familiar, often published precautions: Lock the house; set up timers to turn lights on and off; arrange to have someone water the plants and look in on the house from time to time. Good kennels fill up fast during holiday seasons, so prearrange care for your pets. Stop deliveries, and have the post office hold the mail. Pay bills before you go. Leave a key with a friend. In the summer, arrange to have the lawn watered in case of drought. To avoid coming home to ten feet of snow in the driveway in the winter, arrange in advance to have the driveway shoveled if it snows. (Much easier than closing down shop completely is having a trusted friend house-sit while you're away!)

One of the great traveling accessories to have is a folding garment rack—sold in numerous catalogs (such as Hold Everything, at 1-800-421-2264) and at home-supply shops. The best ones are on rollers and fold away when you don't need them (they also double as a coat rack when you have a large party), but any clothing rack will help you pack—even the plastic hooks available everywhere that hold four or five items and hang over a closet door. As soon as I know I have a trip coming up, even two weeks before, I begin to pack by isolating the items I know I'll want, making sure they're clean and pressed and putting them aside on my garment rack. Once I "hang my trip," I don't touch it until the day before I leave, when everything is ready to go into the suitcase.

As the trip gets closer, I begin to match what I need to the itinerary, and make a list. (Keep the lists—weekend list, two-day business-trip list, beach- or ski-vacation list, list of don't-forget items—for next time.) To be on the safe side, I call the weather report for every city in the world (1-900-976-1212), or, even better, 1-900-976-RAIN, which connects you with a real-live meteorologist. This can *really* help you plan well.

The day before, pull out the list and lay all the pieces, grouped together, on your bed. Lay a towel in the middle for shoes, handbags, accessories, then line up each outfit, side by side, all the way around the bed. A two- or three-color scheme (for example, black or navy and white, with burgundy accents—see color charts) is easiest to build upon and coordinate. Take the first outfit and start to *layer*.

A suit works for day with an unadorned T-shirt or cotton shirt, and for night with a silk or lacy blouse. A white cotton shirt and a white silk shirt go with *everything*, and a string of pearls can dress up *any* outfit. Add what you need to make the outfit work for unexpectedly warm or cold weather, and for mornings, lunches, cocktails and dinners. Opaque stockings for day, sheer for evening. A basic daytime bag, a simple clutch for evening. *Only pack clothes you feel great in*. Will a shawl do? Do you need a coat? (A raincoat sprayed with

Scotchgard water repellent will take you just about anywhere, day and night.) Layer every outfit, placing the underwear you need for each one on top, in case different outfits require different items.

I always take more shoes than average because there's nothing worse than being three thousand miles from home and having your feet hurt. Low-heel pumps, medium-heel pumps, flats and a men's style walking shoe are the basics. And I always wear them all.

What else? Exercise clothes, and ballet slippers for morning stretches right in the hotel room (they double as slippers). A bathrobe, definitely: As a house-guest, you may have to share a bathroom or pop into the kitchen for something; in a hotel, you'll need one if you're dressing and room-service coffee arrives. Hats, gloves and mufflers for winter; straw hats for summer. A big silk scarf to tie under your chin to protect your hair. A dinner dress. Khaki pants, casual shirts and a sweater for walking or sightseeing (good for curling up on the plane, too).

## PACKING

Reinventing the wheel by putting it on suitcases is no less than a traveler's breakthrough. One of my favorite discoveries is my two-zipper expandable bag on wheels—only $12.99 (Hanover House, three-in-one travel bag, 1-717-633-3377). It starts out small and has two zippers, so that you can expand it twice. Wheels, pull strap, canvas—a great carry-on bag for essentials! Conserving energy is essential for any traveler, and wheeled luggage is key. If your luggage doesn't have wheels, you can buy ones that attach with Velcro at a luggage store and have them put on. Other sources for travelers' equipment:

- ❑ Eximious catalog (1-800-221-9464) sells large red and blue tags with your name printed on them to help you identify your bags quickly.
- ❑ Orvis catalog (1-800-541-3541) sells great safari clothes.
- ❑ Bags on Wheels catalog (1-800-756-1444, extension 390) sells a wide assortment of wheeled bags.

- Hammacher Schlemmer (1-212-421-9000, or 1-800-543-3366) sells a great "Uni-Pack Style"—a small, wheeled hanging bag and suitcase all in one.

- Tutto Luggage (1-800-949-1288) offers a compact office case, with built-in files and slots for pens and pencils, and a computer "cruiser" that fits under an airplane seat.

- Safety Zone catalog (1-800-999-3030) sells travel items such as converters, portable lamps and self-defense sprays.

- Early Winters catalog (1-800-458-4438) sells travel clothes, sun clothes and camping gear.

- Travel Smith (1-800-950-1600) sells the ultimate warm polo sweater!

- If you're traveling abroad and confused about electricity, the Franzus Company (1-203-723-6664) will send you their free brochure, called "Foreign Electricity Is No Deep Dark Secret."

Whether you travel with a suitcase or a garment bag is a matter of personal preference; either way, pack clothes in plastic dry-cleaner bags or with tissue paper between each item to keep them from wrinkling. Socks go into shoes, underwear goes into plastic bags and miscellaneous items get tucked around the edge. If packing lasagna-style into a suitcase, toiletries go on the bottom, then heaviest articles of clothing, followed by the lightest ones. Extra plastic bags for dirty laundry and miscellaneous go in corners and sides. To pack a felt hat, gently fold in half and roll loosely into a cylindrical shape, anchored with a rubber band, if necessary. Tuck into the side of your suitcase, and unfold as soon as you can after arrival. To pack a straw hat, place it upside down in a flat suitcase over one or two garments to cushion the top. Fill the crown with scarves, underwear, miscellaneous. Stack sweaters, T-shirts and so on under the wings of the hat for support. In other words, create a brace for the hat with your clothes.

## CARRY ON

All valuables, any irreplaceable items, belong in your carry-on (preferably roll-on) luggage. A checklist:

- ❏ Passport and vaccination cards (with a photocopy at home and a second photocopy in your checked suitcase), if going abroad
- ❏ Jewelry and earrings in one plastic bag, necklaces in another, and all small bags put into a bigger one
- ❏ Prescription medicine, plus emergency aspirin and Alka-Seltzer

- ❏ Sleep eye shades (essential for the plane)
- ❏ Kleenex
- ❏ Flat full-face mirror
- ❏ Makeup for touch-ups
- ❏ Wash'n Dris
- ❏ Breath mints
- ❏ Pens, a Scripto mechanical pencil, a highlighter pen and pads of paper, plus Post-its
- ❏ Shoe horn (feet swell on a plane, and sometimes when changing climates dramatically)

- ❏ Power granola bars (quick energy!)
- ❏ Small container of eye cream
- ❏ Hand cream
- ❏ Dollar bills for tipping
- ❏ Daily calendar
- ❏ Address book (with a copy left at home)
- ❏ Work and plenty of reading material— preferably paperbacks over hardcovers

### EN ROUTE

Use traveling time to *relax and conserve energy*. You're private, away from phones, with time to catch up on reading, work, letter writing—to catch up with *yourself*. I always meditate for the first fifteen or twenty minutes, which opens up my mind to the trip ahead. After that, my carry-on bag offers plenty of reading material to take me through the flight, even accounting for inevitable delays.

Savvy travelers always drink a lot of water during the flight to prevent dehydration. I'm always careful, too, not to wreck my diet first thing by eating food on an airplane that I'd never eat at home. Stretching, flexing your feet, doing isometrics, walking the aisles occasionally—all will keep you from getting uncomfortable. If the flight is a long one, sleep is essential. Eye shades help a lot. So will a Dramamine or a glass of red wine: whatever works.

On a long flight, you can also use the time to *prevent jet lag.* The book *How to Beat Jet Lag,* by Dr. Dan Oren and several other physicians (published by Henry Holt), comes with dark glasses and an eye mask and explains in detail how, by resetting your body's clock by using light or darkness (depending on whether you're traveling east, when jet lag is generally worse, or west), you can overcome jet lag, or at least reduce it a lot. Our sleeping/waking cycles are governed by light, these researchers are discovering. The pineal gland secretes the hormone melatonin at night, which tells us it's bedtime. At the first sign of sunlight, melatonin production stops, telling us it's daytime. By exposing ourselves to light or inducing darkness, we can "trick" the body into assuming the sleeping/waking patterns of the time zone to which we're going, thus reducing jet lag by helping the body to reset its rhythms. As a general rule, if you're flying east—New York to Paris—you can induce Parisian nighttime while still in New York (using dark glasses, an eye mask or shades), and trick yourself into sleeping; to wake the body up on a Paris schedule, expose it to light for an hour or two—even the sunlight out the window of the plane on the way to Paris, or, better still, by walking in the daylight when you get there, no matter how tired you feel. A word about melatonin, the drug (hormone) that you can get at health food stores. Yes, experts agree it does regulate your body clock and therefore eliminates jet lag in most people. However, experts also agree that it can produce such side effects as nightmares, grogginess the next morning, depression and headaches. The main concern in the scientific community is that it may be harmful in ways we don't know, as clinical trials will not be completed for ten years.

## UPON ARRIVAL

The first thing I do when I get to the hotel is to rearrange my room as I unpack. An ashtray or saucer becomes my jewelry dish. I set my travel clock on the night table. I move hotel paraphernalia out of the way so that I can take over surface space myself. If I'm to be away for any length of time, I bring comfort items—scented candles, family pictures, bubble bath, my (prepacked) teas, all kinds of books and magazines—and set these out, too. On a working trip, I set out my work right away and make an "office" in some convenient corner. I don't hang up my shawl, if I brought one; that gets laid over a chair or on the bed—a familiar reminder of home that I can curl up with to read.

I like my suitcases out of sight, so I unpack everything. If you've packed (or hung) clothes in dry-cleaner bags, wrinkling probably won't be too much of a problem. If it is, the valet can have important clothes pressed, but that's expensive. Another method (assuming there's abundant water in the place you're visiting) is to hang the clothes in the bathroom, turn on the hot water in the shower full blast with the curtain closed and close the bathroom door. Fifteen minutes later, run in, shut the water off, run out and quickly close the door behind you. (A scarf around your head will save your hair.) A couple of hours later, your clothes will be wrinkle-free. A third way to remove wrinkles upon arrival is to pack a travel iron or steamer, and iron what you need to on a towel on the floor (handy for touch-ups, like collars).

If jet lag threatens, and you've arrived in the morning, this is a good time to expose yourself to the light—by taking a brisk walk, or even sitting at the window of your room for an hour or more with your eyes toward the light.

Last, I explore. Every hotel has a directory that's usually on the desk and worth browsing through. The hotel's manager or concierge will be happy to help with any arrangements you haven't prearranged. Passing through the lobby sometimes yields more brochures and ideas of things worth doing. From there, I do my best to keep up with my beauty, health, diet and exercise regimens (otherwise I feel sluggish)—and have fun!

### AFTER THE TRIP

It's amazing how much useful information we all collect on trips and then forget! Keep a little file on each city you've been to, listing places you liked seeing, people you met in passing, restaurants that were terrific, that pretty hotel you walked by and wish you'd stayed in. You might be back!

# PART 4

# HOW DO I FEEL?

I met her many times in the dressing rooms of Giorgio; we've all met her: the victim. Blames everyone else for all the things that go wrong—her marriage or the fact that she doesn't have a boyfriend, her children's problems. A bit of a martyr, she can also be a real complainer: She doesn't have a minute for herself, never has time to exercise, can't lose weight no matter how hard she tries, doesn't have the right clothes. She's usually exhausted. Give her a problem and she'll give you a negative excuse, never a positive solution. Probably she's smart, maybe she's well educated, she might even be successful at her work in spite of herself. But she's definitely not beautiful—no matter what she looks like.

I'm in the beauty business, not a therapist, but the two are not without their parallels. For years, I observed women lamenting tediously over how they didn't dress right for this occasion or that, how they said the wrong thing here or there, *using up all their energy on the negative.* There is no outfit, however expensive, that will show to advantage if the woman wearing it isn't comfortable in or with her body. No makeup or skin cream is going to bring a glow to an unhappy face. No one will ever be eager to meet someone who slumps into a room expecting to have a bad time. Outer beauty can only light up what's inside, can only radiate inner beauty. You can heighten what you were born with

# ATTITUDE

on the outside by practicing good skin care, wearing carefully chosen clothing, makeup and so on. So, too, can you heighten what's on the inside by mastering the *emotional discipline* to enable you to express, and be, your best self.

At Giorgio, I used to see more than body language—I call it body attitude. Some of the most beautiful women with the best bodies and faces were the most self-critical, self-conscious and uncomfortable, while many women with much less to start with were perfectly comfortable with what they had, and it *showed*. They took their flaws in stride and presented themselves to the world with an aura of confidence that drew other people to them wherever they went. The way we think about ourselves is all in the mind. The lesson I learned from all these women is that *attitude is a choice—a choice we all make every minute of every single day.*

*Self-esteem* is the great media buzzword these days and for good reason: *Lack of self-esteem is the number-one "beauty problem" in this country today.* This may sound overly simplistic or dramatic, but I don't think it is. Some years ago, we began to see the connection between health and beauty, which launched a movement toward eating better and exercising, which naturally makes all of us who follow healthy guidelines look better as well. Health and beauty now seem like an obvious pairing.

The next obvious and essential connection is between inner and outer beauty. Feel good, look good. Look good, feel good. It's that simple. I've seen it (and mastered it!) myself: *You'll never be beautiful until you teach yourself and allow yourself to feel beautiful.*

Self-esteem is basically an estimate of how each of us feels about ourself at any given moment. Some days we'll wake up feeling great; other days we'll wake up full of self-doubt and feeling anxious or inadequate. Self-esteem can also go up and down many times even in the course of a single day. A good self-esteem day always promises to be a good day all around, but low self-esteem, particularly if it's one's predominating sense of self, saps vitality, confidence, beauty, courage, sexiness—unless we learn to "roll with it," deal with it and get out of our lives what we desire.

How? By adopting a positive attitude. By learning to manage stress. By finding the glass half full, not half empty. By *managing your thinking*, the key to destiny, and replacing negative thoughts with positive ones. Expressing an attitude—positive or negative—is taking action. Expressing a positive "up" attitude will raise your spirits, your mood and ultimately even your self-esteem.

The power of positive thinking is hardly a new idea, but it works. Self-esteem is the emotional "raw material" of any given day, but the attitude we bring to it empowers us to brighten a low self-esteem day, and also to live a high self-esteem day to the fullest.

I was an only child. My father died when I was just a year old, and from then on, my mother and I were pretty much on our own, with no larger family structure to keep us afloat. I can still remember leaving New York with my mother as a teenager, and also leaving my five years of studying ballet behind, to take the train all the way to Los Angeles—and the unknown. I cried the entire way. When we arrived, I stopped crying. My choice was to make the best of it or not, so I made the best of it.

My life evolved from there, and I remembered much later that when I was eight, nine, ten years old, I would imagine, every night before going to sleep, having my own retail store—a dream that had nothing at all to do with my real life, which had no connection with retail. I would see myself going up a ladder in the stock room and picking out small items to put into a basket. I remember that it was my own store because I had a key and went in whenever I wanted to (like the key I later had to Giorgio Beverly Hills).

Coincidence? Maybe, maybe not. Today the technique is called visualization—when you imagine something so strongly, vividly, actively, that you can actually *make* it happen. Visualization is one way to channel and organize the mind; meditation is another. There are others still, and it doesn't matter which ones appeal to you. The important thing instead is believing that *you can manage, control and organize your mind in the same way you manage, control and organize every other aspect of your life.* There are tools, techniques and exercises to help. As with skin care, diet and exercise, consistency is the key. And it's surely worth devoting as much time each day to how you feel on the inside as how you look on the outside.

Beauty resonates on ever-deeper levels, and *inner beauty shows as much on the outside as the looks you were born with and the way you take care of them.* Health is part of it, and learning to manage all the pressures and stress that are so much a part of our modern lives (see pages 179–181). So are diet and exercise (see pages 184–214)—taking care of our bodies so that they take care of us. So is the radiance that accompanies a life well lived, in which love, friendship, family—the relationships that connect us to others (see next chapter)—are of primary importance to us. Skin care, makeup, fashion and so on are beauty's outer packaging, and they matter: Look good, feel good. The beauty that's *inside* is a gift, the beauty you share with the world. Feel good, look good. You will.

## TAKING YOUR EMOTIONAL TEMPERATURE

I've always loved people, and loved observing human nature and behavior at work. I noticed early on how some people always seem happy, and some always down. The curious thing is that the way so many people present themselves to the world, happy *or* sad, often has no connection at all to what's really happening in their lives. Rich, poor, beautiful and successful or not, life is a continuous flow of ups and downs, obstacles and challenges, for *everyone.*

We all make our lives happen; we create our lives. And it's up to us whether we use positive or negative energy in the construction. We all wake up sometimes with low feel-like-crawling-under-the-bed self-esteem. *All* of us. And we're also constantly distracted and influenced by negativity: negative world news, negative personal news, negative comments from others. Then what? Every minute we have the choice to accept or reject the negative. To reject it is to create an invisible armor to protect us against more of it.

Everyone gets depressed from time to time, and many times depression is a choice. Sometimes we choose it because we're not getting the approval we want from others. Sometimes it's from being too hard on ourselves. (Sometimes, of course, it's clinical, which is paralyzing. If that's the case, there's only one choice to make, which is to seek help from a doctor or therapist.) But in many cases the choice is to stay depressed or get over it: forget it, make yourself start moving, get busy, force yourself to smile, and often the smile soon becomes real. (It takes many more muscles to frown than to smile.)

My interest in the mind and mental attitudes has been a serious study. I'd always wanted to get the most out of life, and it took me years to understand fully that how much I got out of life was up to me. In ballet, we were taught that every physical movement, control and procedure, including facial and hand expressions, started with *thought.* In life, we think before we act, and if we *learn* to think positive, then we act and live positive, and positive comes back to us. I know a CEO who instructed his phone staff to smile before answering the phone: Attitude shows in your voice. Karl Lagerfeld says that when he chooses his models, their attitude is more important than their looks.

If you had a high fever, you'd do what you had to to take care of yourself. Same thing with an "emotional fever." If you're not feeling up to emotional par, *you have to take the steps to change it.* It's a choice to look your best by taking care of your skin, body, clothes and makeup, and it's a choice that will build up your self-esteem every day. A strong, healthy self-esteem is a gift from you to you, and only you can confer it upon yourself. If you wait for it to come to you, you'll never find it. *Affirm yourself.* Imagine yourself doing all the things you want to do with confidence. See yourself with your family and friends, happy, outgoing. Refine the vision, hone it, turn to it throughout the day.

A positive attitude means getting *into* yourself, and also getting *out* of yourself. It's attractive, it's sexy and it spells and creates confidence. It's worth it to choose it.

We have this idea in America that it's bad to be selfish: It's not. Taking care of yourself, loving yourself first of all, is the only way to earn love from others, build self-esteem, lead a successful life and enjoy the success that you'll build from that kernel of self-love. In Europe, women go to spas as a matter of course, whereas we consider it a privilege we have to *earn*. Taking care of ourselves is not a privilege, it's not selfish (in a bad sense)—it's *essential*.

After Giorgio was sold, my three stepchildren were grown and my former husband and I divorced. It was the biggest reevaluation of my life, scary, challenging. I knew I would continue my career, but I didn't have to be in Beverly Hills any longer. I put every lesson I'd ever learned from life to the test, took care of my life, refocused my career. I concentrated on achieving my highest good, even if I wasn't quite sure where that would lead. I didn't want to limit myself by asking for specifics—I just lived the best I could each day. And then I met my husband, a Harvard professor. Who would have dreamed I'd move back to New York, where I was born and raised, and commute to Cambridge, Massachusetts, and the world of academia?

It wouldn't have happened if I hadn't worked on my self-esteem every day of my life. How we live matters. You can't like or love others if you don't love yourself—love is something that's *shared,* and to share it, you have to have some to start with. And you get it by knowing and accepting and loving who you are.

Working on a positive attitude is *preventive problem solving*. Talk to yourself. Ask yourself: "What's the worst that can happen?" Play it out, then ask: "What's the best that can happen?" Play that out, too, then *choose* to focus on the solution, not the problem. Whenever you feel anger, ask yourself: "Is this really worth what it's doing to me emotionally?" Review what you have, not what you don't have. Run through your friends in your mind, and take pleasure in their successes; *surround yourself with their successes* and join in the energy. Focus on the goal, not on the fear of it. Take action instead of worrying. Force out anger and negative thoughts—just say "Cancel" over and over until they're dispelled. It's a

## GETTING INTO YOURSELF

First, sit upright (if you're reclining, you might fall asleep), with your hands, palms up, relaxed on your knees. Or, if it's more comfortable, sit on the floor with legs crossed into yoga position, hands resting on knees, thumb and third finger touching each other.

Next, breathe slowly and deeply with your eyes closed, focusing on what's called the third eye—the area between your eyebrows. Even the most experienced at meditation have wandering, cluttered minds, and the object is to clear them. Starting at one hundred, count backward, mentally saying each number with each deep breath.

Or try repeating a yoga mantra with each breath—two of the standard ones are *Sut-nam* and *Om-nama-shivya*. Or just try repeating any word (even *Kleenex* will do) over and over as you breathe, until your mind begins to clear.

Don't get frustrated if your mind starts to fill up with thoughts, worries, all kinds of things. Ignore the clutter and *gently* draw your mind back to your mantra. Even a wandering mind will reap the benefits. You'll feel relaxed and invigorated at the same time, clearheaded, ready to pursue the rest of the day—and you will get out of yourself.

mental diet, and it works. Consciously force your facial muscles to relax when you're tense and nervous, then let your shoulders drop and your entire body relax. See the humor in life. Gain control. It doesn't matter what happens. What matters is how you react to it. *Being positive before the problem arises is an advantage.*

Spend some time with yourself every day—a minivacation to review and restore the self. When making an important decision, slow the world down. Take an hour or a weekend to meditate quietly on the answer and the guidance you need. Quiet your mind and *allow* the answer to come.

I hope you will try meditation, a wonderful tool that has taught millions of people, including me, to search within ourselves for answers, for peace, for strength and energy. For me, it's not tied to any religious belief, but is simply a way to clear my mind when it gets cluttered—like resetting an adding machine to zero. To me, meditation is restorative.

We are constantly influenced and distracted by negativity: negative world news, negative personal news, negative, cynical comments from others around us. Every negative message presents us with a choice: to accept it, agree with it and sink into it, or to reject it, disagree with it and rise above it. To reject it is to create a protective armor against it. If several people are gossiping in a mean-spirited way about someone, why not be the one to say something *positive* and stop the negative flow? If several more people are bemoaning the state of the world, why not be the one to interject some *good* news?

The more wrapped up in ourselves we are, the less wrapped up we are in the world. Know yourself, love yourself, take care of yourself—and then get *out* of yourself. How? By turning your attention to the world around you. When you meet someone new, put yourself in that person's shoes. What would you like to have happen to you? Then do it. Give everyone a chance. I learned this in retail. I genuinely liked people, and had a positive attitude to start with, but I learned how much I enjoyed helping people to feel good about themselves by dressing them up, pointing out their attributes, trying to instill in them the confidence they deserved to have. I perfected the attitude partly because it was my business, but more so because I enjoyed getting out of myself.

The more open we all can be, the better. A genuine smile from the eyes and a wave go a long way. So many people never hear a kind word or any form of acclaim. Why not be the one to give it? People like to hear and receive good things; we all do: thanks for efficient service, holding open the door, an invitation for tea. Being a good friend is the best "therapy" of all.

I keep ongoing lists of people to call, fax and write to just to stay in touch. A quick "Hi, how are you?" means you care. Clip articles for friends. The way to feel good about yourself is to do something good for someone else.

A friend of mine stops by a nursing home after work and reads to a patient for half an hour twice a week. Take time for others. Talk to the lonely, listen to the ignored, volunteer for *something*. Feeling blue? Take some old clothes to a clothing drop or buy a few cans of food for a homeless shelter. Getting away from yourself in this way not only helps others but also gets your mind off yourself. And perhaps it's semi-insurance for the time you may need help yourself.

## LADIES' CHOICES

There are two types of poise: inner and outer. Inner poise comes from feeling peaceful about yourself and your life. Outer poise reflects good posture, head held high, a calm facial expression, a good walk (no dragging feet, swinging hips). It's sitting up straight in a chair, legs crossed or knees together, hands held softly together, not twitching, clenched or nervous, even—*especially*—if you are inside. Poise is listening during a conversation instead of thinking about what *you're* going to say next, and it's looking directly at the person you're speaking to at a cocktail party rather than over her shoulder to see who else is there. Poise is eye contact, a voice with a smile, a firm handshake. All these actions reflect choice.

This is a great time to be a woman, now that we've finally made our way into business, courtrooms, government, the cockpits of air force planes. Doors have been opened. A three-piece man-tailored suit is no longer necessary to compete with men. A good deal of the storm has passed. We no longer have to be self-conscious as women holding our jobs: We're ourselves in our jobs first, and the fact that we're women is only that—one fact about us. The new direction that feminism is taking us in is the realm in which we can really be ourselves, personally and professionally.

From what I've seen, age does nothing to change attitude; a positive attitude is neither young nor old—it's just *positive.* I've seen women *decide* to give in to what the media tell them they should feel about their bodies; it's not automatic, for example, that PMS or menopause can make your life miserable. It's interesting how some women have a terrible time with these, and some have little or no trouble. Surely some of it is the attitude we bring to these natural passages, and buying into the myth will only make you feel worse. Taking two

Bufferin for PMS and estrogen therapy (if you and your doctor decide it's right) for menopause and *forgetting about it* is a more positive choice to make. If we accept ourselves and our bodies for what they are, and do the best we can to nurture ourselves, we'll also accept the changes that come with time. A positive attitude is ageless and has no gender.

And a positive attitude is beautiful. Being a beautiful woman is also being a lady. That's part of the fun—the sexiness, the pleasure, the *grace.* Grace is listening, and it's sharing your strength with others. Grace is not complaining, and it's "wearing" a smile when you don't feel like it. It's virtue, it's kindness, it's the aura of a life well lived.

### GETTING AHEAD

The best way to meet the future is to prepare for it as much as you can. You can't control it, but you can help to shape it by the way you choose to live now. Be willing to learn all you can to work hard to achieve your goals. Do your best. Do *more* than you're supposed to do. Teach yourself to be curious. Choose to be enthusiastic.

Always prepare. Think in advance how you want to look. Don't get frantic at the last minute. If you have to make a speech, write out what you want to say three or four times, then highlight the main thoughts on a four-by-five index card. Practice talking to yourself—about *anything*—in the mirror, eye-to-eye.

Writing thoughts out in longhand always clarifies the future. Make a long list of all the things you like to do, the subjects that interest you—big things, little things. Then make another list of things you don't like to do. Then a third list of what you'd like to see yourself doing and where you'd like to live in ten years, five years, four, three, two, one. Put these papers away, then take them out and reassess them after one week. You'll start crossing out things and changing the lists. Put them away for another three weeks and then look at them again, making more changes as you see fit. This will become your personal plan. I find this helpful whenever I feel the need for a change. I did it when I was going through my divorce, and by doing so I recognized when I met my new husband that our new life would work because it encompassed a lot of things on my wish list.

And because I visualized it into happening.

Whatever the occasion (party, job interview, first day at work), the way to dress for it is to pick an image and *wear* the part. But *it's just as important to think the part as it is to dress the part*. Think the part, visualize the part, see yourself at the event, see yourself *succeeding* at the event—living the future ahead of time through visualization is a powerful way to carve out the future the way you want it to be.

You can visualize while sitting up, lying down, walking, meditating, just about anytime except when driving; you can do it with eyes open, eyes closed, it doesn't matter. Try it several ways until you find your own way.

Picture your goals through all the senses: see them, hear them, smell them, touch them, taste them. As a practice exercise, picture yourself walking through your favorite park, feeling the sun touch your body (not your unprotected face, though!), hear the birds chirping, smell the foliage. Envision the calm of looking at the ocean, feel, smell and taste the freshness of the salt water, hear the waves.

Then switch to the goal you have in mind.

I remember falling in love once with a house that wasn't on the market. I *wanted* this particular house. I looked at everything else, but kept *visualizing* this special Santa Fe–style house with me in it—I saw a fire in the fireplace, my furniture in the rooms, my pictures on the walls. Then one day I got a message in Europe from my realtor. "Remember the house you wanted? Well, the couple is separating, and it's now going on the market." Three weeks later it was mine.

Luck? Maybe in part. But seeing your dreams through to the end, stretching the vision and taking action whenever possible to make it real, *can* make it real. Ask yourself: Is it right for me to want this dream to come true? Will it harm anyone? Then let go. Go about your business accepting that the goal is yours. Whatever the dream, see yourself in its surroundings. If it's a new job you have in mind, visualize answering the phone, speaking with your colleagues. Overweight? See yourself slim. Imagine the way you'd feel wearing the clothes you can't wear now. Feel yourself happier being slimmer. Confirm the vision with an I-already-have-it attitude. Refine the vision and turn to it as many times as you can during the day. And if it doesn't happen, it wasn't meant to be.

If you stay up to date with your beauty regimen, exercise, meditation, diet, proper sleep and positive thinking, everything becomes less scary because you'll feel your best, which will empower you to do your best, which is all anyone can do. Before stepping into any new situation, take three deep breaths and *smile*.

At Giorgio there were three types of women: those who dressed only for the men in their lives; those who dressed only for themselves; and those who dressed for both—who tried to please both themselves *and* the men in their lives. Without a doubt, this last type of woman had the most fun and the best relationships.

At Giorgio, too, it was interesting to observe how many stunning women came in complaining that they couldn't find a man. And also to observe many plumper, less striking women (of *all* ages) who never had relationship complaints at all! Clearly, the beauty that invites other people in and makes them want to stay is far deeper than skin level.

I'm not a psychologist, but over the years I've observed hundreds of relationships closely and have had a few of my own. It has always been interesting to see the ones that worked and those that didn't, and to try to analyze the reasons why. I'm not exaggerating when I say that you can tell a *lot* about any woman's relationships by how she behaves when she's in a dressing room—all by herself. Why? Because that's, in effect, where self-esteem begins. Put a woman and a mirror together and you can see how *she* sees herself, accurate or not, and how well she likes what she sees. How a woman feels about herself ultimately determines

# RELATIONSHIPS

how she expects to be treated, which itself determines how she *will* be treated. The cycles of all her relationships begin with a woman's self-esteem.

Just as we make choices about how we take care of ourselves, the image we present to the world day to day and the energy we exude, so, too, do we choose relationships: either relationships that are supportive, loving and fun, or relationships that make us feel we don't deserve to have fun, or to be supported and loved. And just as we choose the attitude we want to project to the world, so, too, do we choose how to behave in our relationships. Working on the relationship often boils down to working on *who we choose to be* in the relationship and coming to terms with what we expect from it. The better we feel about ourselves, the better our choices and the better our relationships will be.

## A PARTY OF ONE

You can't like others if you first don't like yourself, and others can't like you, either. Self-esteem informs every relationship you have. It's not only the "real" you who lives in your relationships—it's also the self-esteem within you. A good, strong self-esteem shows off the best of you; a low self-esteem underscores the worst. *Nurturing your relationship with yourself is the first essential step in nurturing your relations with others.*

One of the great joys of being in the beauty business has been helping other women improve their self-images and self-esteem. At Giorgio, I would tell someone, "Maybe this skirt should be an inch or two shorter to show off your great legs," and now I might offer someone a shade of eye shadow to bring out her beautiful hazel eyes. These have never been sales pitches—they're true; but I've been amazed over and over at how many women aren't even aware of their great legs or beautiful eyes! Their "self-estimate"—self-esteem—is simply too low.

Even if we're lucky enough to have grown up in families that make us feel worthy, many of us still emerge into adulthood with self-doubts—about how pretty, smart or capable we are. This is when the choice factor comes in: You can either let those self-doubts tell you who you are, or you can work through them, by improving the things you can change and accepting those you can't. You can choose good beauty and health habits. You can change a negative attitude to positive. And you can begin liking, loving, supporting and having fun with the person you're becoming and working on the most important relationship you'll ever have: your relationship with yourself. Only then, in my experience, will the relationships you hope for with others follow.

*Inner strength is like any other kind of "muscle," and has to be exercised in the same way.* If you like yourself, it shows. You contribute—to your work, social engagements, friends and family—in a strong, healthy way. You don't depend on others, but learn to depend on yourself. At the same time, you encourage others to be independent as well, and not to depend on you. You can say yes. You can say no. You live up to your own demands, not the demands of others. You're in control.

Choose joy, choose curiosity, enhance your life with new interests and experiences—and new relationships will follow. It's your life, and no one can fill it but you.

After graduating from high school, I took a secretarial position at a life-insurance company, and at night taught dance at an Arthur Murray dance studio. When I stopped teaching, I took shorthand and French at Los Angeles City College at night, and later took psychology, art and physical-education courses at Beverly Hills High night school—all before Giorgio.

I didn't have much money, but you don't need money to be curious. No matter where you live, there's art, theater, lectures, opera, movies, ballet, libraries, night classes, parks, political campaigns to join or volunteer work to help other people: all kinds of life! I remember the first car I owned, a hundred-dollar Hillman, when I was still finding my way. I hated being at home on beautiful Los Angeles days when I had studying to do or letters to write, so I'd drive to Will Rogers Park, Griffith Park or the beach (in my big shirt, sunglasses and hat, of course), and do my work there—in the sun, by myself but also out in the world among other people. There's never a need to sit home alone. I liked to travel, too, and once saved enough money for a Eurailpass and traveled around

Europe for three months with a girlfriend. Looking back, I can see that I didn't know where I was going, but I sure didn't want to miss anything while I was getting there. And while I couldn't have articulated it then, I was also learning to be with *me,* and building self-esteem in the process.

There's plenty of self-help information available for building self-esteem, and professional help if you feel you need it. Make the choice to do good things for yourself. Make the choice to push self-doubts aside and walk into a room looking your absolute best and confident about who you are. Deserve good relationships; *expect good relationships.* Become a person you can believe in, and then believe in yourself.

## ROOM IN YOUR HEART, ROOM IN YOUR LIFE

Generosity of spirit is a quality that can't be taught—but it can be *learned.* Acts of generosity, even the simplest ones, are *choices:* You choose to make a call to a sick or lonely friend, choose to invite someone newly separated to dinner, choose to drop a note (or a funny cartoon, or a magazine clipping of interest) to someone you enjoyed meeting, choose to help out if someone needs it, choose to be kind. Acts of generosity are almost always returned (and if they're not, *you're* never the loser, because acting generously is rewarding in itself).

The busiest, most successful, most attractive women I've ever met are always those with the fullest lives: healthy intimate relationships, a few really close friends, full social lives, a varied circle of acquaintances. This isn't something that just happens: It's something we *achieve.*

One of the keys to sustaining an intimate relationship is being able *not* to have it. A well-balanced life is not unlike a well-balanced diet. It's balanced among work, friends, family, interests and an intimate life. If one of the elements falls out of place—a job loss, for example, or an intimate relationship that ends—then the rest of the elements remain intact to help you support the loss and get back on your feet. The more expansive the life to begin with, the less there is to lose. One of the questions women often ask me is what to do when they're in between relationships. With a full life, you're never in between relationships; you're simply between men. To put it another way, in all my years of working with women, I've seen far too many put all their energies and hopes into one man, only to see the relationship fail, leaving them with nothing. It's far wiser, and far more exciting, to put those energies into building a full life of work, friends, activities—a life for yourself that's rich and satisfying; and such a life, I've seen (and learned myself), is far likelier to draw the "right" man.

Back to my dressing rooms at Giorgio: a training ground for human nature. Occasionally there were women who were terrifically supportive to the girlfriends they shopped with, and downright rude to the sales help—never a glance, a smile, a please or a thank-you. Occasionally there were men who were brusque with *everyone,* even telling their wives as they were trying on new clothes, "Take it off. It looks terrible!" Some people, men and women alike, would leave the dressing rooms a mess. But mostly not, which is why the few people with bad manners stand out in my memory.

Good manners should not be turned on for some situations (or people), like a light switch, then turned off for others. They reflect respect for yourself and for everyone around you; they show good character. Bad manners, on the other hand, reflect an unhappy, selfish, uncaring person: People remember and despise rudeness, just as they remember being treated with consideration. Good manners evolve naturally out of the decision to convey a sunny attitude, but there are also tips you can learn, practice and make your own.

**AN ETIQUETTE BOOK** Manners should be essential lessons you teach your children—they can be intimidating and embarrassing to learn later on. How do you teach manners? By example. By practicing good table manners at dinner, every night. By forcing the habit of writing thank-you notes. And by keeping on hand any standard etiquette book; refer to it yourself once in a while in your children's presence, and sooner or later they'll refer to it, too. There's a terrific video you can send for: "Table Manners for Everyday Use," by Landy Vision, 11 Hill 99,

Woodstock, New York 12498 (phone 1-914-679-7046, fax 1-914-679-4674). Teenagers may scoff, but they'll watch it. Everyone wants to do things right.

**EYE CONTACT** It's extraordinary how often people fail to look directly at other people—during initial introductions, during simple exchanges at stores, when saying good morning at the office, at cocktail parties (where half the people are looking over one another's shoulders), even husbands and wives dining together at restaurants! Making eye contact is a great quality—polite, direct— that shows interest, attentiveness and confidence. It's easy to tell if your eye contact is good: Just pay attention to it the next time you're at a cocktail party or large gathering; if your eyes wander, consciously bring them back to the person you're talking to each time it's necessary.

**VOICE** A tape recorder can be used to check your voice the same way a mirror monitors your appearance. Listen to yourself: Too nasal? Too high pitched? Keep listening until you have it the way you want it.

**ON THE PHONE** "Is this a good time to talk?" and "Have I reached you at a good time?" are very thoughtful ways to begin a phone conversation—much better than plunging in when someone is on her way out the door. I've actually taught myself to do this; to slow down and check my bad habit when distracted or very busy or too eager to "go" too abruptly over the phone.

**"PLEASE"** Another habit. It's easy to forget (when talking to an operator, ordering from a waiter, getting into or leaving a taxi), but just as easy to remember if you practice. Curiously, this nicety is often skipped in intimate relationships, where it's needed most. "Please" says as much to those you love as saying "I love you."

**"THANK YOU"** As important as "please" throughout the day—to helpful people who perform services, to colleagues at work, to your husband, to your children. Thank-yous in the form of a call or a note (or a small gift)—to thank your host or hostess after a dinner, party or weekend visit. Thank-you notes for gifts you receive yourself, or kindnesses you appreciated. It takes much less time to write the note or make the call than it does to feel guilty about having neglected to do so.

**"PARTY" TALK** I can't imagine that there's anyone who doesn't feel a little shy about walking into a new situation or a roomful of strangers, and the best way I've found to get around it is to go *through* it: Be the one to take the lead. Take a deep breath, relax your shoulders, approach someone standing alone or a small cluster of people, smile and say: "How do you do? I'm Jane Smith." That's all. Most people will introduce themselves in turn. From there, easy starters include: "It's a lovely party. What brings you here?" "How do you know the hosts?" Make a comment about the *reason* for the party. And the dialogue goes from there. What's the worst that can happen? Nothing. Then you move on, smiling still: "Excuse me, I see someone I'd like to say hello to. I've enjoyed meeting you." What's the best that can happen? The conversation takes off naturally—to what's happening in the news, to a little about each of you, to surprising topics you couldn't have planned—and you've met a new friend. Party talk is a dance, and these first few opening "moves" will draw you gracefully onto the dance floor. *Being friendly is more important than what you say.*

**EMPATHY** Holding doors open for others, giving up your seat to an older person, remembering to say "Excuse me" and "Pardon me," meticulous attention to table manners—all these graceful acts are easily overlooked when we're harried, distracted, caught up in our own lives, worries and needs. Manners can be taught and learned, sure, but achieving a kind of grace makes them more natural. Common courtesy is putting yourself in another person's shoes. If I'm the one who has had a door slammed carelessly in my face, I might take greater care the next time I open a door first. How can you know for sure whether you behave well? By putting yourself in the other person's shoes.

**PRIVACY** As important as it is to connect with the world at every level you can, it's also wise, I've discovered, to withhold a little bit, keep a sense of privacy, even mystery, around yourself, too, like a shawl. Allowing other people the privacy they need makes them comfortable, which is good manners; ensuring the privacy you need yourself is simply good policy. Not everyone you meet needs to know everything about you, and "Why do you ask?" is a good all-around response to intrusive questions you don't want to answer. A measure of privacy or reserve can serve you well at the office, where you definitely want to keep your doubts about your boss and your troubles at home off the gossip circuit. (Some companies today condone dating among colleagues, but tread carefully. Company policy notwithstanding, an office romance that fails usually has a miserable aftermath.) Privacy needs in an intimate relationship must not only be intuited but also discussed. We all have different needs when it comes to the time and space we need for ourselves, and negotiating these well is a huge step toward a successful relationship. Parents and stepparents need a zone of privacy as well, into which children must not intrude. They'll respect it.

None of us can ever know how it feels to be another person, and to build a successful life in which you can love others and others turn to you with love requires immense care and kindness. All it takes to have a friend is to *be* a friend.

## THE TWO OF YOU

At Giorgio and elsewhere throughout the years, I've seen women who actively searched for egocentric men because they lacked an ego themselves. Some search for strength and identity for the same reason. Some women are always with a new man, never managing to make a relationship last, and some keep holding on to the wrong man. I've seen people (in Los Angeles, New York and D.C.) whose fortunes go up and down; some truly have relationships that can withstand the bad times, and some people, together for the wrong reasons, invariably split up at the first signs of trouble.

What makes some relationships work and others fail? If I knew for sure or had an easy answer, I'd have cracked the mystery of human nature and the human heart—which even science can't figure out! But from what I've seen, successful relationships are those in which you can see the man clearly and the woman clearly: Their identities don't blur or get subsumed by each other. Successful relationships are "modern" in the sense that each person has goals that he or she is working toward, and the relationship is strong and expansive enough to embrace and encourage both sets of goals without either partner becoming threatened or feeling left out or left behind. In successful relationships, each person wants what's best for the *other* as well as what's best for him- or herself—and also what's best for the relationship.

In every good relationship, the woman is beautiful and worthy, because the man makes her want to be beautiful and worthy, and also makes her *feel* beautiful and worthy.

If you show real interest in all the people you meet, you might be surprised; Mr. Uninteresting-at-first-glance may turn out to be Mr. Wonderful. Often we're so busy thinking about what *we're* going to say next, we don't really hear what the other person is saying, which is too bad, because only by *really listening* can we discern the true character of a person. Just as it pays to be friendly to everyone and not judgmental in casual social situations, it pays even more to be *very judgmental* in intimate situations. And very judgmental *before* getting involved. No one is perfect. My motto for happiness is "75 percent right." In a relationship, if 75 percent of the relationship works, its a good relationship. You're not going to find 100 percent. Given human nature (on *both* sides), it's the formula for happiness that works for me.

It's hard to do when passions are running high, but being clearheaded and practical at the outset is an investment in the long term; if real compatibility doesn't kick in after the romance settles, there won't be much to build on later. Make two lists—of what each of you like (and don't like) to do; of your values and his, of your goals and his. How well do they match up? Are you totally,

*totally,* relaxed with this person, or guarded? If the shoes aren't comfortable in the store, they won't be later. If the guy in your life is not supportive and loving now, he won't be later, either.

The very first *suggestion* of physical abuse *must* send you to the nearest exit, but there are also subtler means that some men use—to build themselves up or for whatever reason—to put women down. The partner who subtly criticizes you all the time, tells you you don't know anything, tells you he's just trying to "help" you with your "problems." The partner who tells you you were nothing before him and would be nothing without him. The partner who never gives you credit for what you do and, in fact, takes the credit for things you've done. The partner who smiles to the world when with you, only to berate you later, when you're alone. The partner who thinks only of himself and never you unless it coincides with his desires. The partner who tries to make you think *he's* special but you're not, so you had better "behave." Do any of these ring true? Then you're in an abusive relationship. You don't have to be. Victim Services in New York (1-212-577-3807) recognizes how destructive such situations can be, and will direct you to support groups in all parts of the country.

## IN DEFENSE OF NOT COMMUNICATING

The importance of communicating has been drummed into our heads so much in recent years that I see plenty of couples who *communicate* all right, but at the expense of conversation, laughter and spontaneity. Sometimes you can communicate a relationship right into the ground. I've noticed too many people who misinterpret the message to mean they should feel free to complain whenever they want to, or to use "communication skills" as a means to control the relationship or change their partners—a futile exercise, since we can't change other people. Positive works better than negative. When things are going well, remember to say so. When your boyfriend or husband does something you like, say so. When something *isn't* going well, why not try to enter the discussion *from the beginning* with the intent to compromise, rather than to win?

Communication that descends into psychobabble or beats a dead horse is boring, destructive and tedious.

Also, *communicating is not the same as talking.* None of us is a mind reader, and we can't expect others to know what we don't tell them. I have a friend who once called me, upset that her husband didn't respond to her call telling him she had been in a car accident. She said he didn't care about her, he was disappointing like all the other men in her past, et cetera. When I asked her what exactly she had told him, she said, " 'I've been in an accident. Everything is fine. I'll be home a little late.' " Her husband had no idea she was on her way to the emergency room with shattered glass all over her, and how could he if she didn't tell him? Don't test him with a "code" he has no reason to understand. If you're upset, say so. If you're frightened, say so. If you're feeling ill, say so.

## PUTTING THE RELATIONSHIP FIRST

I have seen arguments last weeks because neither partner was willing to apologize or take the blame. The longer the anger lasts, the more damage there will be. Most times both parties are at least a little bit to blame, so to me, whoever says "I'm sorry" first begins to alleviate the damage, clear the air, address the issue and *let go.* But who "wins"? The relationship wins. When you're in a relationship you care about, and what's at stake is only pride, the most important thing is preserving and protecting the relationship.

*I think we should all give in on the small issues and not on the big issues.* What does it matter if he doesn't like you in a certain dress? It's not important—it's a dress. Don't wear it around him. What does it matter who puts the toothpaste cap on, or leaves the top off the cookie jar, or picks up an occasional towel off the floor, or uses the Itty Bitty book light to read while the other is sleeping? Express your anger, certainly, and by all means stand up for what's fair and what you need from the relationship. But the more you can forget the trivial and focus on what's important, the more *harmonious* the relationship will be.

What makes a relationship last? I can't answer that for sure, and there aren't any guarantees, but to me, the most pleasurable "work" there is is working on a happy relationship. A daily "sound bite" in the form of a quick call or fax, just to check in and see how everything's going. Experiencing every day that frisson of excitement just before he gets home, when you freshen up for the evening ahead. Looking for new things to do together as well as the comfortable ones, and anticipating how pleased he'll be at trying something new. Surprising him sometimes by getting tickets to something that *he* likes, and enjoying it yourself for that reason alone. Thinking back to the things you did when you were courting, and *doing* them again, *saying* them again, *feeling* them again. Experiencing the true intimacy that comes from loving someone unconditionally. Learning that newness isn't sexy in the long term, but that energy is sexy, humor is sexy, laughter is sexy and love is sexy. Work toward happiness, and expect it. Above all, accept it when it comes.

# INDEX

## ABOUT THE AUTHOR

———

GALE HAYMAN is the co-founder of Giorgio, Beverly Hills, the creator of the fragrance Giorgio, and the founder of her own line of cosmetics, Gale Hayman, Beverly Hills, Inc. Hayman transformed her childhood dreams of stardom into the retail success story of a lifetime when she turned a run-down Beverly Hills store into one of the most glamorous and influential clothing stores and pefumeries in the world. She lives in New York.

## ABOUT THE TYPE

———

This book was set in New Baskerville, a version of a typeface which was designed by John Baskerville, an amateur printer and typefounder, and cut for him by John Handy in 1750. The type became popular again when The Lanston Monotype Corporation of London revived the classic Roman face in 1923. The Mergenthaler Linotype Company in England and the United States cut a version of Baskerville in 1931, making it one of the most widely used typefaces today.